ENAMEL BUTTONS

KAREN L. COHEN
Edited by Barbara Barrans

STACKPOLE
BOOKS

Essex, Connecticut
Blue Ridge Summit, Pennsylvania

STACKPOLE BOOKS

An imprint of The Globe Pequot Publishing Group, Inc.
64 South Main Street
Essex, CT 06426
www.globepequot.com

Distributed by NATIONAL BOOK NETWORK
800-462-6420

Copyright © 2024 by Karen L. Cohen

Barbara Barrans, Button Classification Editor
Barbara Barrans, Copy Editor
Tom Ellis, Enamel Technical Editor

All rights reserved. No part of this book may be reproduced in any form or by any electronic or mechanical means, including information storage and retrieval systems, without written permission from the publisher, except by a reviewer who may quote passages in a review.

British Library Cataloguing in Publication Information available

Library of Congress Cataloging-in-Publication Data

Names: Cohen, Karen L., author.
Title: Enamel buttons / Karen L. Cohen.
Description: Essex, Connecticut : Stackpole Books, [2024] | Includes bibliographical references and index. | Summary: "An in-depth research and illustrated collector's guide on the various techniques and history of enamel buttons"— Provided by publisher.
Identifiers: LCCN 2024015421 (print) | LCCN 2024015422 (ebook) | ISBN 9780811776523 (cloth) | ISBN 9780811776530 (epub)
Subjects: LCSH: Enamel buttons—Handbooks, manuals, etc.
Classification: LCC NK8459.B88 C64 2024 (print) | LCC NK8459.B88 (ebook) | DDC 737/.24—dc23/eng/20240505
LC record available at https://lccn.loc.gov/2024015421
LC ebook record available at https://lccn.loc.gov/2024015422

First Edition

I dedicate this book to all enamelists, past, present, and future, for the beauty they add to the world with their wondrous creations. Enameling takes knowledge, patience, experimentation, and creativity, which is why we all love this medium. I hope that this book inspires button collectors to better appreciate and understand the enamel qualities we work with in our preferred art form.

Contents

Foreword vii
Preface viii

1: History — 1

Pre-Sixteenth Century 3
Sixteenth Century and Painting *with* Enamels 4
Seventeenth Century and Painting *on* Enamels ... 7
Eighteenth Century and Transfers 8
Nineteenth Century and Early Twentieth
    Century 12
Modern Era—Twentieth and Twenty-First
    Centuries 19

2: The Material: Enamel — 27

Firing Temperatures and Stages 28
Forms of Enamel 30
Types of Colors 33
Chemistry of Enamel 36
Metal Substrates 38

3: Buttons as Enamelware — 40

Techniques 42
    Basse Taille 42
    Champlevé 45
    Cloisonné 49
    Crackle Enamel 52
    Émaux Peints 53
    Enamel Buildup 58
    Eutectic Effect 60
    Gin-bari 60
    Graphite Pencil 61
    High-Fire Techniques 61
    Plique-à-jour 62
    Pull-through 64
    Reticulated Foils 64
    Ronde Bosse 64
    Separation Enamel 65
    Sgraffito 65
    Stenciling 66
    Transfers/Decals 66
Enamel Topcoats 68
    Glossy 68
    Matte 69
    Sugar Fire 69
Embellishments 70
    Embellishments Not on the Enamel 70
    Dichroic Extract Powders 70
    Gemstones 70
    Glass 71
    Glow-in-the-Dark Materials 76
    Metal 76
    Mica 81
Other Characteristics of Enamel Buttons 81
    Borders 81
    Combined Techniques 83
    Commemorative Buttons 83
    Enamel Background Buttons 83
    Mounted in or on Metal 84
    Mechanical/Movable 84
    Openwork 84
    Pictorials 84
    Sew-through 85
    Shapes 85
    Verbal 85

4: Enamel Button Artists, Producers, and Purveyors — 86

Diane Echnoz Almeyda, Georgia 87
Helene Carter, Canada 87
Chinese Cloisonné and Champlevé, Modern 88
Chinese Plique-à-jour, Modern 88
Karen L. Cohen, Pennsylvania 89
Marie Demicco, Maine 90
Sandy Dingman, California 90
Nancy DuBois, New Jersey 91
Marie Elwyn, Massachusetts 92
Émaux Ardéchois, France 92
Peter Carl Fabergé, Russia 92
William Hair Haseler, England 93
August Wilhelm Holmström, Russia 93
Charles Horner, England 93
Inaba Cloisonné Company, Japan 94
André Keim, France 94
Dorothy Kendall, Pennsylvania 94
Jessie Marion King, England 95
Archibald Knox, England 95
Kokuto Co. Ltd., Japan 95
Mona Ledwin, Tennessee 96
Heinrich Levinger, Germany 96
Liberty & Co., England 97
Linda Lingren, California 98
Phil Linley, Connecticut 98
Herman Lowenstein, Florida 99
Motiwala Brothers, India 100
Simon Mower, England 101
Sachiko Nishida (西田 幸子), Japan 101
Carolyn Noga, Illinois 102
Glenda L. Ott, California 102
E. J. Peeler, Kansas 102
Michele Raney, Washington 103
Linda K. Reynolds, Kansas 103
Ada Snow Smith, Unknown 104
Joseph H. Spencer, Florida 104
Janet White, California 105
Diana Wieler, Canada 106
Yanaka Red House Button Gallery, Japan 106

Appendix A: Buttons with Enamel DF or OME — 108

Metal Buttons with Enamel DF or OME 108
Other Base Material Buttons (Not Enamels) That Have Enamel OME 109
Decorative Enamel Borders 109

Appendix B: Enamel Look-alikes — 110

Cold Plastic Enamel (CPE) 110
Flame Painting on Copper 111
Foil or Metal under Glass 111
Niello 112
Pertapghar Enamels 112
Porcelain 112

Appendix C: Enamel Restoration — 114

Appendix D: Button versus Enamel Terminology — 115

Appendix E: Japanese Enamel Terminology — 116

Appendix F: Checklist for Collecting — 118

References and Bibliography 123
Notes 128
Acknowledgments 132
About the Author 134
About the Editor 135
Index 136

Foreword

I was first introduced to Karen L. Cohen when she contacted me while researching Birmingham buttons for her book on enameled buttons. Erika Speel, our English modern enamel historian, had previously interviewed my mother, Toni Frith (the original "Button Queen"), for one of her books. It was through research with Erika that Karen made the connection with me. Ms. Cohen's initial inquiry was regarding Matthew Boulton and his possible connection with enamel buttons that are owned by the Birmingham Museums Trust in England. She previously had been in touch with that museum and the Victoria and Albert Museum, which currently display these buttons. I remarked that, as far as I knew, the connection between Boulton and early enamels has not been studied in depth. Thus, our discussions moved to other aspects of enamel buttons.

I was pleased and honored to be invited by Ms. Cohen to write a foreword to this new book on enameled buttons. I have, myself, been in business for more than 40 years, trading as "The Button Queen," a title that I inherited from my mother. I recognized the lack of available detailed information about enamel buttons. This book offers valuable information about the various techniques and how they are achieved, different characteristics and styles of enamels that can be articulated and illustrated in buttons, and charting the history and makers of many of the buttons we collect today. I am certain that the reader will be enriched with knowledge about all kinds of enamel buttons, from the coveted eighteenth-century ones to the current creative examples made by contemporary studio artists.

Although the book has hundreds of button illustrations, it is much more than a coffee-table book with a lot of pretty pictures. The captions and the accompanying text provide solid educational information that the reader can apply to new buttons they may encounter in their future collecting. From our initial contact and subsequent discussions, I could tell that Ms. Cohen spent quite a while researching the subject thoroughly. She has been a teacher for all of her adult life and an enamelist for many years, having previously written books on enameling for enamelists. In this, her latest effort, she explains all aspects of enameling to people who specifically collect enamel buttons. I am confident that this book will become a valuable tool in the armory of the button collector. It ranks along *The Big Book of Buttons*, *Fairbairn's Book of Crests of the Families of Great Britain and Ireland*, and *Buttons* by Diana Epstein and Millicent Safro.

Martyn Frith
Managing Director,
The Button Queen Ltd.

---

1. Antique Émaux Peints with cut steel border.
2. Antique openwork Champlevé / Émaux Peints viola with outer enamel border.

Preface

3

Enamel—correctly called vitreous enamel—is glass fused to metal at high temperatures. The process of enameling is a specialized art form that has existed for thousands of years. The earliest known enamels are six Cloisonné gold rings that date back to 1300 BCE during the Mycenaean period! Enamel, though it is glass and thus can crack and scratch, is a very sturdy material that can last for lifetimes and still remain beautiful, even if buried for centuries.

As an enamelist and educator for more than 40 years, author of two enameling books, and a Studio Button artist for more than a decade, I am interested in sharing my experience with collectors. Thus, this book is not the typical button material book, as its focus is explaining enamel and how that relates to enamel buttons. Although it explains the various aspects of enamel buttons mentioned in the *National Button Society* [NBS] *Blue Book, Official Classification Competition Guidelines*, this book does not follow its structure, as this presentation of material follows my perspective. This book is a teaching tool to educate the collector to better understand the button in front of them (in all chapters, button photos are shown to illustrate what I am discussing; see the sidebar "Button Photo Tips"). This approach necessitates that I relate technical information not just on the various types of enamels but also on how the enameling techniques are accomplished. My job is to explain this technical information in a way that button collectors will understand. Ideally I have accomplished this task.

I realize that my perspective is that of an enamelist, not a collector (although I do collect enamel buttons!), and I know that these two perspectives are not the same. For example, look at button 3 and describe it to yourself before continuing to read. You might have said: Central Émaux Peints flowers with a border of Encrustations and six gold Paillons set in metal. When I looked at this piece, I immediately knew that the Encrustations were something special—no known enamel fires that color. Although they look like opals, they could not be, as opals could not take the heat of the kiln. Much to my amazement, in my research I found a formula for enameling these opal-like elements (see section "Faux Opals," page 72).

The art of enameling has changed over the centuries, with improved enamel materials and new techniques and usage being developed. Thus, I provide an abridged history of enamels and how that subject relates to changes in buttons in chapter 1, "History."

In order to understand enamel, chapter 2, "The Material: Enamel," is a discussion of what enamel and

---

3. Antique Émaux Peints enamel set in metal frame border with gold Paillons and an inner border of Encrustations imitating opals.

the general enameling process is all about. This overview allows the reader to better appreciate the work and materials used by enamelists around the world and will define terms that I use later in the book.

Of course, the most important information about enamel buttons is describing their attributes. This is done in chapter 3, "Buttons as Enamelware." I provide some technical information in specialty sidebars called Enamel Tech Talk (ETT). The ETT sidebars include more details than a reader might absorb on first reading and thus can be read when one is ready to gain this extra information.

The final chapter, "Enamel Button Artists, Producers, and Purveyors," describes companies and individuals that made or commissioned enamel buttons, showing their marks when available.

A few appendixes provide related information. Appendix A shows buttons that include enamel but are not classified as NBS enamel buttons—these are shown outside the main text so that there is no confusion with those considered NBS enamel buttons; appendix B is about enamel look-alikes, including the difference between Cold Plastic Enamel (CPE) and real (vitreous) enamel; appendix C is an explanation of restoring enamels; appendix D is a chart to help with the translation between button and enamel terminology; appendix E is an overview of Japanese enamel terminology; and appendix F is a checklist to aid in collecting. Finally, my list of references is included for your further research.

So, welcome to the wonderful world of enamel buttons, which "have always been the aristocrats among buttons."[1]

BUTTON PHOTO TIPS

This sidebar provides information on how to view buttons in this book. More than 500 button photos are presented:
- Most have been enlarged for clarity, and thus sizing is not accurate.
- Buttons shown are mostly illustrative of the points being made. Unless explicitly dated, do not consider that the button shown is from the time period discussed—only that it is illustrative of what is being said.
- Dating buttons is an art in itself and requires a lot of study. Some of the button descriptions might have dates or say "antique." The term "antique" (also referred to as Division I in the *NBS Blue Book*) means that the button was made prior to 1918. Dating buttons is a topic for further study and could be the theme of another book.
- In the captions, if two or more techniques describe the button, they are separated by a "/" (as in Champlevé / Émaux Peints). I have tried to list all techniques for a button in the caption except for the "Framed Champlevé" discussed on page 46.
- To shorten the captions of the buttons, note the following terms used in Émaux Peints buttons: Some painted enamels will say "Émaux Peints" (the NBS term for these pieces). However, some will say only Monochrome, Polychrome, Pâte, or Limoges-style (all forms of Émaux Peints). Using these other terms implies Émaux Peints.
- All button captions are listed at the bottom of their respective pages.
- Button callouts are in blue so they are easily found.

---

4. Eighteenth-century Émaux Peints with Paillons and Pierreries.
5. Antique Champlevé owl on branch with counter enameled back. This is not considered a "realistic," as the shape is not just that of the owl.
6. Eighteenth-century cobalt enamel with elaborate Paillons mounted in metal with paste border.

1 History

According to the National Button Society's *National Button Bulletin* (*NBB*) December 1999 article "18th-Century Enamel Buttons," buttons were not mentioned in literature until the early sixteenth century when the French king, François I, commissioned his jeweler to create a set of enameled gold buttons.[1] The history of buttons, though, can be found in the records of costumes and clothing styles of the day and also in the many articles of the *NBB* and *Just Buttons* magazine, as well as related books on the subject. Although objects such as wall pieces, boxes, jewelry, and chalices are mentioned in many of the enameling books and web articles, buttons are mentioned rarely. Throughout the centuries, though, Émaux Peints (painted) and Champlevé (buttons 7 and 8) buttons dominated the button market.

Why is the history of buttons important? For one, it's just plain interesting. In addition, this background information will help collectors date buttons and put some of their collection into context. Knowledge is gained by studying not only enamel buttons but also other objects made during these periods. One needs to learn about the metal fabrication, possible color choices, design styles of the day, and how other items were incorporated to give clues about the period in which a button was created. To gain insight into this topic, I suggest further reading of the books *Buttons* by Diana Epstein and *Buttons* by Diana Epstein and Millicent Safro.[2] These books show buttons by century and describe the environment in which they were created. If your interest is in Émaux Peints buttons in particular, I suggest you read the book *Painted Enamels: An Illustrated Survey 1500–1920* by Erika Speel,[3] which is most interesting. In 1905, renowned English enamelist Alexander Fisher said, "One advantage that the quality of enamel possesses over all other pigments or materials used in art: it reigns supreme over them in luminosity, in transparency, and translucency."[4]

The history of enameled buttons is influenced by the migration of craftsmen from centralized art centers to other countries, changing fashions, the development of new techniques in both enameling and metal work, innovation in manufacturing, and more. The information that follows provides some insight into this history. In general, this chapter is organized by century.

7. Antique Polychrome couple with outer gold Paillon border.
8. Antique Stamped Champlevé openwork Art Nouveau design with inner wide brass / cut steel border and outer enamel border.

VARIATIONS ON A THEME

Artists have always used similar studies for their work. Sometimes it might be a learning exercise—that is, to see whether they can reproduce a master. Sometimes it might be because a certain study has inspired them. One thing is clear: the time it takes to create a piece of work includes the time to design the piece. Thus, sometimes artists will use elements of another's work as a starting point to save time. Whatever the reason, the concept of using common design elements in different ways was done in buttons, even from two different companies (buttons 9 and 10; buttons 11 and 12). Unfortunately, none of this practice seems to be documented.

WASHING

Ever think about how all these gorgeous buttons held up to washing while attached to clothes? A clothing historian told me that, in earlier times, clothing was not washed but was brushed, shaken out, or patted with a damp cloth! This practice continued until today's modern dry-cleaning method. Although enamel buttons can usually withstand water for hand washing (without a scrub board), it is advisable to remove them before cleaning your garment with any kind of machine or solvent.

KOUMPOUNOPHOBIA

An interesting fact: Koumpounophobia is the fear of buttons!

FASHION MUSEUM

When traveling, if you are in an area with a textile and fashion museum, go! These locales are fabulous for viewing old buttons.

---

9 and 10. Two variations of Antique Émaux Peints / Basse Taille enamel with glass balls (button 10 with a Paillons outer border).
11. Antique enamel with painted Liquid Gold bird and cut steel border.
12. Antique Monochrome bird with cut steel border.

PRE-SIXTEENTH CENTURY

Buttons, on the one hand, had a sparse history before the sixteenth century. Made of shell, the earliest known button was found in the Mohenjo-daro region in the Indus Valley (present-day Pakistan) and is thought to be 5,000 years old. This button, as with other early examples, was thought to be used for decoration, not fastening. Not until the fourteenth century was the word "button" first used; this term probably came from a French word for either bud ("*bouton*") or push ("*bouter*"). The first fastener for buttons was a loop through which the button was pushed. The buttonhole is said to have first been used in 900 CE, which impacted the fashion of the day. The word "buttonhole," however, was not in use until 1534. In the early thirteenth century, the first guilds were established in Paris, and the first button makers' guild was established in 1250.

On the other hand, enameling has a rich history before the sixteenth century. The first three forms of enameling, all done in this period, included metal around the enamel sections. These were Cloisonné, Champlevé, and Plique-à-jour. Ancient cultures that knew enameling include the Phoenicians, Egyptians, Greeks, Romans, Assyrians, and Etruscans. The Byzantine Empire (about 395 BCE–1450 CE) produced mostly Cloisonné enamels, which were an important decorative art. Their peak enameling was done in the tenth and eleventh centuries, and they continued to influence future enameling throughout the world.

It was originally thought that the metal between the sections of enamel, used in the first three techniques, was needed to hold the glass in place. This belief, however, was eventually disproved in sixteenth-century Limoges, France (more about this subject later). Vitreous enamels in the early periods were inferior to what came later. Not only did they not have as many colors, but the quality was also lacking. In later centuries, chemists were employed to improve the enamels and thus helped develop what we have today. These changes occurred at multiple times through the next few centuries.

Metal and enamel work continued to evolve. For example, Greek jewelers of the sixth century BCE soldered Filigree work onto bases and filled the resulting spaces with enamel, as a type of Cloisonné. "Filigree" comes from the Latin word "*filum*," which means "wire."[5] This development eventually led to using Filigree work in Plique-à-jour.

The earliest known enamelware made in China—a Cloisonné-backed mirror[6]—is thought to be from the Tang dynasty (618–907). The earliest known marks were during the reign of the last emperor of the Yuan period (1333–1368). The most productive period of Cloisonné fabrication was during the Ming dynasty (1368–1644), with the most frequent mark being from the Jingtai reign (1449–1457), and the Qing dynasty (1644–1912). The pitting in the enamels during this period could be from impurities in the enamel, a byproduct of the type of fuel used for their furnaces, or the enamel not being packed properly into place.[7] These pits are called "sand eye" (砂眼) or "chipping blue" (崩蓝) and are not considered errors (buttons 13 and 14).

In the late eleventh or early twelfth centuries, copper Champlevé became very fashionable, especially in the city of Limoges, France. In this period, with the increasing prosperity in Western Europe, churches were constructed—thus the need for liturgical objects, many of which were adorned with enamel.[8] Although Limoges is best known for its painting enamels, the artists of Limoges were unique throughout Europe in that they sustained the art of enameling during the Middle Ages (476–1520) and the Renaissance (1400–1650).[9] Their Champlevé for liturgical and domestic items was highly prized and continued to be made well into the fourteenth century. The end of the fourteenth century saw the beginning of a style called En Ronde Bosse,[10] which was done on three-dimensional sculpted metal (page 64).

In the early twelfth century, a monk by the name of Theophilus wrote the book *On Divers Arts*.[11] Today this book is considered the foremost medieval treatise on painting, glassmaking, and metalwork, being consolidated from three separate writings (note: contention exists regarding the actual author of the original three texts). Theophilus describes working in copper, silver, gold, brass, lead, iron, steel, and tin. He also discussed simple machines and specialized tools like dies and

---

13. Antique Chinese twisted wire Cloisonné ginger jar on screen back showing "sand eye" pits.
14. Antique Chinese Cloisonné double koi design showing "sand eye" pits.

stamps for metalsmiths, as well as the techniques of casting, repoussé, openwork, punching, raising, sinking, engraving, wire drawing, filing, and chasing. In addition, he wrote about enameling and Niello (appendix B). These materials and processes were well known by this time, and many have been used to construct buttons throughout history. It is interesting that Theophilus's thesis does not describe any mechanical power to replace human muscle.[12]

From the twelfth to the fourteenth centuries, the art of enameling was perfected in southwestern Europe.[13] Champlevé, influenced by Byzantine enamels, became an important decorative art and was practiced in both Limoges and Conques in France, as well as in Spain and England.[14]

Early on, enameling was used by jewelers in lieu of expensive gemstones, as enamel showed similar brilliance and gave color to their work. In 1905, Alexander Fisher wrote, "It is not till we come to the twelfth century that the fine craft of enameling begins to assert its independence as an art and its full capacity for change and progress. From that time onward we meet with enamel done per se."[15] That is, from that time onward we see enameling valued for its own sake and not just as an embellishment for other artwork. Fisher, however, felt that enameling did not come into its own as an art form until the advent of painted enamels in the sixteenth century.

By the early fifteenth century, enameling techniques had been refined. Much was done by goldsmiths who were supported by the patronage of the kings of France and dukes of Burgundy. Plique-à-jour was now made. The earliest known piece was the Mérode Cup from France. Goldsmiths around Venice worked in Filigree enamel, as was also done in Hungary. The artists in the Burgundian and Habsburg Netherlands during the fifteenth and sixteenth centuries were called the Netherlanish; they created primitive paintings with enamel (the most famous was the "Monkey Cup"), as did the artisans in northern Italy. These were precursors to the Limoges School painting style.[16] The Netherlanish also were working in a primitive style of Grisaille, also a precursor to painting.[17]

During the late Middle Ages (1300–1500), transparent enamels were developed,[18] which effected a new style of enameling. This style, called Basse Taille, had its roots in Champlevé, was done primarily on gold or silver, and it was another precursor style of Limoges School painting. Early Champlevé was done with engraving, leaving metal strips between opaque enameled areas. With the use of transparent enamel, the engraving could be done lower and covered in enamel and still be seen. The low-relief engraved Basse Taille could be "painted" with enamels by placing the colors next to each other over each engraved component of the design. Button 15 and button 455 (page 100) are modern versions of what this approach could look like. The lower engraved areas would produce a deeper color (the more layers of a transparent, the deeper its color [buttons 16 and 17]). Many gold and silver pieces have not survived, as these were melted down for the precious metal in them. By the close of the fifteenth century, there were basically five styles of enameling: Cloisonné, Champlevé, Plique-à-jour, Ronde Bosse, and Basse Taille, with a new method of painting with enamels just beginning.

SIXTEENTH CENTURY AND PAINTING *WITH* ENAMELS

By the mid-sixteenth century, enamel buttons were made all around Paris. These items were made by specialist workshops for goldsmithing and metalworking guilds. Thus, these buttons, mainly for men's clothing, were made with jewelry techniques. Included in the early work of this century were Pierreries (page 59)—simulated gemstones of enamel over gold Paillons. However, the term "*Pierreries*" didn't come into use

---

15. Silver Basse Taille Deccan button with engraved areas colorized with transparent enamel over each object, as they did when Basse Taille was originally created.

16. Basse Taille on silver, by Michele Raney. It shows how one color can be used for shading. In this case, the ibex is the same color as the field around it, which has more layers of the same transparent enamel.

17. Antique Basse Taille with outer metal border, by Marius Hammer. Notice that the purple center has light and dark areas—this is caused by more layers of the color in some areas.

LIMOGES TERMINOLOGY

The word "Limoges" is used in various ways, and one should be clear on what is meant when using it. Here are some uses:

- Of course, foremost, "Limoges" is a city in southeastern France (formerly in the province of Limousin). The other usages that follow were named because the technique was developed in this city.
- **Limoges School enamels:** The name used when painting with enamels was first developed in Limoges. This category included Grisaille.
- **Enameling world:** "Limoges" is the technique of painting with enamel—that is, Émaux Peints of any style. This is supported in two ways. First, Speel says that, in the nineteenth century, the term "Limoges" became generic for a description of the technique (painting) rather than a description of where the piece was created. Second, Herman Bangeman Jr. says, "Were we students learning the art of enameling, we would be taught that when the enamel is painted, or shaded . . . it is Limoges enameling."[19]
- **Button world:** "Limoges-style" is a specialized form of Émaux Peints (page 53) using transparent enamels over foil. *Note:* Some in the button world might just call this style "Limoges." But this terminology gets totally confusing with the enamel world meaning of the word "Limoges." It would be better for button collectors to use the term "Limoges-style" to eliminate this confusion. After all, it is a style of painting, called this only by the button world. See more information on Limoges-style on page 56.
- **Porcelain:** "Limoges" porcelain is a hard-paste porcelain manufactured at various factories around Limoges, France, since the late eighteenth century and is just called "Limoges."
- **Limoges School Revival:** See page 16.

until the early twentieth century.[20] It was in the sixteenth century that foils under transparent enamels became popular. In addition, Liquid Gold (called gilded by button collectors) (button 18) was used for details at the end of the enameling process. Today, Liquid Gold (page 78) and gold powder mixed with a medium are also used in enameling.

The sixteenth century saw a huge advancement in enameling in Limoges, France, which has affected the art form ever since. See more about the term "Limoges" in the sidebar "Limoges Terminology." At the close of the fifteenth century or the beginning of the sixteenth century, in Venice, Italy, painting glass on glass was discovered. This was only opaque white glass on glass vessels, but eventually painting was done with transparent enamels on Basse Taille engravings. The Italian glass painters migrated to France, where the art of painting with vitreous enamels was developed in various stages into a new art form. Also at this time, someone figured out that if a thin sheet of metal were enameled on both sides, that enamel would not pop off after cooling. This new discovery, called counter enamel (page 36), had a profound effect on this art form, as thinner pieces of metal could now be used. As many objects were made with gold and silver substrates, this development allowed enamelists to reduce their costs. Most of the work done in Limoges was counter enameled.

In Limoges, the technique of painting with enamel (Émaux Peints in button language) was perfected. This was one of the first times that enamel was applied without the use of metal between colors, as is done in Cloisonné, Champlevé, and Plique-à-jour. Thus, a new technique of enameling was born and a different type of artist would now be able to create with enamels. In fact, this development also led to enamel work being considered a fine art instead of just an embellishment.[21] This technique dominated in Western cultures until the twentieth century.[22] Enamel painting reached perfection in the 1580s but then lost its appeal until the nineteenth-century Limoges School Revival (page 16). The painting of enamels was originally limited to a small group of families (Pénicaud, Limosin/Limousin, Reymond/Raymond, Court, Courtois, de Court, Laudni, and Nouailher) in Limoges, France.

18. Antique Polychrome plaquette with Liquid Gold DF in saw-tooth mounting and stamped wide outer frame border of white metal.

Contemporary enamel historian Erika Speel says[23] that there were four painting developments in Limoges. Three phases were in the sixteenth century and one in the seventeenth century. An overview of these follows.

The "Early Style" (1475–1530) was characterized by white under-painting and colorized by transparent enamel colors. Most of the images used were from published printing plates. These images were traced and then their outlines pricked. They were then laid onto a prefired enamel field, and a fine dust of soot or enamel powder was "pounced" over it, which, when the tracing was removed, left small pin dots to show the outline (figure 1.1). These were then drawn over to produce a basis for the full image. Some layering of transparent enamels with layers of white was then done. At this time, they had no good flesh tones, so body parts were left white (button 19), with perhaps some purple (the closest color they had to red) or dark blue shading. One enamel historian and enamelist, Henry H. Cunynghame, called these pieces "corpse like."[24] Further research has found that the church may have wanted certain figures to look this way to represent death. Liquid Gold (gilded) and Pierreries were used to highlight the design. Léonard (Nardon) Pénicaud was the greatest artist of the day. For generations, Pénicaud's family enameled in this technique and was part of its development.

Figure 1.1 Outline of dots of soot or enamel powder used to transfer a design onto enamel. Courtesy of the Carpenter Enamel Center.

The "Fine Style" (1530–1580) was the zenith of Limoges art. This period was the beginning of true Grisaille enameling, which reached its peak between 1545 and 1580. Instead of just under-painting, the artists worked multiple layers of white to show depth and shadows. They used a specially formulated white (called Blanc de Limoges or Grisaille White) with a technique called "enlevage à l'aiguille,"[25] or possibly "travail à l'aiguille," which is using a fine needle to draw outlines (similar to Sgraffito, page 65) and to sculpt the white into place before firing. Coloring was still done by transparent enamels and could be layered between layers of white. They now had a flesh tone (red iron oxide), which sometimes they would paint as a flesh tone (button 20) or mix with water to give a thin wash of color (perhaps like button 21). During this period, artists started drawing their own images rather than using prepublished prints. Liquid Gold was still employed, and by mid-century foil was used to embolden the polychrome effect.[26] Léonard Limosin was the most famous and innovative enamelist of this period, and Pierre Reymond was probably the most active Grisaille artist.

The "Minute Style" (1580–1630) involved the use of more colored Grisaille and bright transparent colors over gold and silver foils. Still, though, the colorizing was done with transparent enamels—painting *with* enamel. This type of work went out of style,[27] and after 1630 a new style emerged called Onglaze enamel painting (see the next section on the seventeenth century for more information about this development).

19. "Early Style" of painting with enamel—antique Limoges-style of woman's head mounted in ornately decorated frame. Notice the corpse-like (white) face and neck.
20. "Fine Style" of painting with enamel—antique Limoges-style over Guilloché with Liquid Gold accents man with fancy headdress mounted in ornate openwork frame border. Notice the skin tone.
21. Antique Limoges-style showing a wash of red for the skin tone.

SEVENTEENTH CENTURY AND PAINTING *ON* ENAMELS

After 1630 in Limoges, France, a new style of painting emerged, which was the fourth stage of painting development—now it was painting *on* enamel and was known as Onglaze painting. Instead of colorizing the image with transparent enamels, as in the past, Painting Materials (page 31) were used (buttons 22, 23, and 24). Due to an increase in Onglaze enamel painting, Basse Taille lost favor in this century.

Because there was a shift in the materials used, and thus in the look of painted enamels, in the button world today there are two major types of Émaux Peints buttons. Those colorized like the first three stages of painting development with transparent enamels and foil are called "Limoges-style" (page 56), whereas those colorized as in the fourth stage of painting development with Painting Materials are called just Émaux Peints buttons. These types of buttons can easily be distinguished from each other—those colorized by transparent enamels and foil are brighter and show more depth, but the ones colorized by Painting Materials show more detail but are not bright and luminous.

Onglaze enamel painting was an innovation of a French goldsmith named Jean I. Toutin, whose sons, Jean II and Henri, perfected painting enamels in miniature. One of their students, Jean Petitot (1607–1691), became the most famous miniature enamel painter of his time. Jean Petitot innovated an excellent skin tone, a red-brown tint that was made from crocus martis, which is the same as rouge de Mars or iron red. Perfected by Toutin the elder and continued for many years, the painting style was in the manner of Pointillism painting called pointillé or stippling (it's not clear any buttons were made this way, but it's fun to look for them). Pointillé was a controlled set of dots (stipples) or short stroke (hatches). Where the light background showed between them, the color was lighter; where the color was closer together, you got a darker or shaded area. The pointillé method worked better in very small images (around one inch). When larger pieces became popular by the middle of the eighteenth century, a new method had to be employed, particularly because of the firing procedures needed for larger enamelwork. This approach was innovated by English enamelist Charles Boit (1663–1727), who used brushstrokes. Painting miniatures was done in other countries as well, like Sweden and Germany. Today the art form of miniature painting continues with famous enamelists like Gillie Hoyte Byrom in England and Evgeny Baranov in Russia. Of course, other styles of painting also continue, using both transparent enamels and Painting Materials (and a mixture of the two).

Enamels have always been known for being luxury items, and it was no different in seventeenth-century France, which was the recognized center for these items. This trend continued until the revocation of the Edict of Nates by Louis XIV in October 1685, which resulted in the Calvinist Protestants of France, the Huguenots, no longer being allowed to practice their religion freely. Thus, they migrated to many other countries, including England, Switzerland, and Russia. Many of these Huguenots, from the wealthy middle class, were the craftsmen of the day. The migrating Huguenots carried their knowledge and craftsmanship to many other countries, thus introducing enameling art in other areas of the world. The most famous descendant of these people was Peter Carl Fabergé, who lived in Russia but died in Switzerland. Jean Petitot, mentioned earlier, was born into a family of French Huguenots living in Geneva, but he eventually moved to France and worked for the French king. He was there for decades until he was forced to return to Geneva after the king revoked the Edict of Nantes. Geneva soon became the center for enamel painting. In England, some of the migrating Huguenots settled in Birmingham, which eventually became an important button production center along with Bilston and

---

22. Antique Polychrome with foil inclusions mounted in brass with cut steel.
23. Émaux Peints colorized by Painting Materials.
24. Antique oval Polychrome figural with outer paste border.

South Staffordshire. The consequence of all these transitions was that the art of enameling declined in France, and enamel became used for making snuff boxes and coat buttons rather than important work, according to Cunynghame.

Since the seventeenth century, special box-like buttons (button 25; button 490 in appendix A) were used for smuggling items such as drugs. Other buttons were made to look like these but did not open to hold anything (button 26).

Enamel painting was introduced into China in the seventeenth century,[28] most likely by missionaries. This enamelware was called Canton enamels (page 54) because they were primarily manufactured in Guangzhou (what we call Canton) (button 27). The best pieces using this technique were from the eighteenth century, and many were made for export, as this technique was considered alien to the Chinese culture.

EIGHTEENTH CENTURY AND TRANSFERS

At the turn of the eighteenth century, jewelers made more than just jewelry to supplement their lines. Objets d'art were common, but they were mainly produced for the elite of the upper classes, such as royalty, nobility, and wealthy merchants. That situation changed after the French Revolution in 1789, when not many jewelers were active, and inferior pieces were produced in France.[29] Before the revolution, ornate buttons were mainly for men's clothing; women's were much more subdued. Toward the end of the revolution, women's clothing started getting fancier, and ornate buttons were made for women as well.[30]

Up until this century, enamels were hand painted. In England in the 1740s, those Onglaze painting enamels were called English Painted Enamels. These were labor intensive and thus time consuming and costly—that is, until a huge innovation came with the invention of transfer printing.

The origin of transfer printing is disputed by historians, as the process was used not just on enamel but also on pottery and other substrates, and a few people have claimed to be the inventor. Given that, it is best known in the enameling and button worlds to have become prominent at the Battersea Enamel Factory. One version, and perhaps the most logical as to how Battersea came by this technique, is the following: An eighteenth-century artist, Simon François Ravenet, first studied engraving and etching in Paris but, in 1750, was contacted by William Hogarth, a famous English engraver and artist, to help him with his "Marriage a la Mode" set of engravings. After this work was completed, Ravenet remained in England, as his services were much in demand. Eventually, he was employed by Stephen Theodore Jansen, who had established the Battersea Enamel Factory. This factory was located on the premises of the York House outside of London by the river Thames. John Brooks, another engraver, was

BATTERSEA TERMINOLOGY

The word "Battersea" has multiple meanings. Any one of these uses may be described as just "Battersea," but the full expression is better to use.

1. **"Battersea Enamel Factory"**: A business, established by Stephen Theodore Jansen, and in production for three years (1753–1756). It produced some of the finest enamels of this period.
2. **"Battersea-style enamels"**: Enamels of the style from the Battersea Enamel Factory, which were also done after the factory closed and its equipment was sold to other English firms, particularly in Bilston and Liverpool.
3. **"Battersea-type enamels"**: Same as Battersea-style.
4. **"Battersea/Bilston enamels"**: Same as Battersea-style but may be used more readily by modern antique dealers and auction houses.
5. **"Battersea Pewter Company"**: A modern company, located in Wisconsin, that produces pewter buttons and other items.

---

25. Seventeenth-century smuggler's button (frequently called Austro-Hungarian or court jewels).
26. Seventeenth-century button made to look like a smuggler's button, but it does not open (frequently called Austro-Hungarian or court jewels).
27. Chinese Émaux Peints button (frequently called Canton enamel).

also employed by Jansen at Battersea. Besides Ravenet, who called this process "décalquer," Brooks is sometimes said to be the inventor of this process. In fact, Brooks had applied for patents on transfer printing to enamels, but one was never granted. Not all buttons from this period include transfers—some buttons were hand painted (button 28) and some were transfers, either just outlines (button 29) or outlines plus hand painting (button 30). For more information about transfers/decals, see page 66 and the sidebar "Development of Transfers/Decals." For more information about Birmingham and transfers, refer to the book *English Painted Enamels*.[31]

At this time, transfer printing relied on engraved plates. Because these plates were reusable, this method became an inexpensive way to get a design onto enamel. Because the plates were at their best when used only 200–250 times, new designs had to be worked up. Signed pieces from the Battersea Enamel Factory itself are very rare, and it's not clear whether any buttons can be attributed to the factory at all. But later buttons were sometimes back marked.[32]

The Battersea Enamel Factory closed after three years (1753–1756), and their stock of metal, engraved plates, and more was bought at public auction by other English factories. The workshops in Bilston, in central England, became the leaders of this style of wares, working with both hand painting (button 31) and transfer techniques. The Sadler and Green firm in Liverpool became another center for this style of enamelware. The style of the Battersea Enamel Factory, whether by those at the factory or those who had bought their equipment or even others, is called Battersea-style in the button world. It's not clear who made buttons with this style, as it's not documented.

DEVELOPMENT OF TRANSFERS/DECALS

The initial transfers were printed on hand-made tissue paper, which made this method laborious to use. This approach changed nearly 70 years later, in 1820, with a new invention: paper-making machines. However, earlier in 1796 the invention of lithography by Alois Senefelder of Austria also made transfers easier to use and thus less expensive. Multiple transfers could be used to provide more than one color, but the innovation of multicolor printing by the Pratt Brothers in 1840 gave the ability to print more than one color onto the paper. This development allowed transfers to grow from one-color images to an unlimited palette.

Transfers have always been multilayered, but the invention of the water-mount or water-slide decal, around 1930, was a big step forward. These decals included a top or cover coat that, when immersed in water, allowed the design to stay together but be removed from the paper backing. In the 1960s, this type of transfer became dominant and is what we use today—although how the images are printed has changed with the advent of computers. For more information on transfer printing, see page 66.

EIGHTEENTH-CENTURY PINK

The pink color in enameling was so popular it was known as "roze." When found in buttons (button 31), it might be associated with eighteenth-century buttons. In the next century, this color had two names, both after mistresses of Louis XV: "Rose Pompadour" in Bilston[33] and "Rose du Barry."

---

28. Eighteenth-century Battersea-style Guilloché / Émaux Peints with Liquid Gold detail and counter enameling.
29. Battersea-style Monochrome / Transfer button (note the "engraving" influence in style and the detailed design).
30. Antique Battersea-style Transfer / Émaux Peints.
31. Eighteenth-century Battersea-style Émaux Peints with Liquid Gold border (frequently called Battersea Cows).

From about 1740 to 1880, another style of art came into favor. This was called Chinoiserie (button 32), which Wikipedia defines as "the European interpretation and imitation of Chinese and other East Asian artistic traditions, especially in the decorative arts."[34] Although done in the century before, it gained favor in the eighteenth century because of the increased trade between Western and Asian cultures. The allusion to China in the name was because, in Europeans' minds, China represented all the countries in that area.

The period circa 1760 to 1840 was called the (first) Industrial Revolution in England. This term was used previously by the French but was popularized by Arnold Toynbee (1852–1883), an English economic historian, although today the term is used more broadly. During this period, power-driven looms and spinning wheels led the way for new factory employment, moving people from agricultural areas to the cities. This change allowed for an increase in productivity and efficiency, which reduced the cost of manufactured items and thus increased the buying power of the lower class.

Three more innovations at this time allowed faster production and thus less expensive enamelware. One was the use of thinner metal (about 24 gauge). With the advent of the steam engine in the early 1700s, mechanical methods of producing stamped metal had a profound effect on enamel buttons. Now mechanically stamped thin metal allowed for less expensive Champlevé buttons because the metal no longer needed to be hand crafted. These can be seen in the numerous stamped brass Champlevé buttons (buttons 33, 34, and 35). The second innovation was the covering of the base metal in white enamel by a dipping method to quickly coat the metal rather than sifting layers onto it.[35] The dipping could be done by inexperienced people, so there was cost savings in both the dipping process and workers' wages. The third innovation was the firing process, which now could be done in bulk by using coal-fired furnaces with two-part containers of clay that could completely cover items and be stacked for many pieces to be fired at once.

The English were influenced by the fashions in France, including the love of precious enameled items. In eighteenth-century England, Birmingham was the center of the world button trade and the center of the Industrial Revolution. Matthew Boulton was one of the driving forces and was known for his steel buttons and mountings. Buttons 36 and 37 are from this period and from Birmingham; these have been on display at the Victoria and Albert Museum since 2001.

STAMPING VERSUS CASTING CHAMPLEVÉ BUTTONS

Just because there is a pattern on the front and on the back of a Champlevé button, do not assume it is stamped. Consider button 38. Both sides have a pattern. But if you look closely, you will see they are not the same. Therefore, this piece cannot be stamped and must have been cast.

---

32. Antique Chinoiserie Polychrome mounted in peek-a-boo brass frame.
33. Antique Stamped Champlevé head with edge border of cut steels.
34. Antique Stamped Champlevé with both inner and outer metal borders.
35. Antique openwork Champlevé with integrated border.
36. Eighteenth-century copper-gilt button with chased edge set with an enameled disc decorated in a chequerboard pattern in blue, black, and gold. Courtesy of Birmingham Museums Trust on behalf of Birmingham City Council; accession #1953F432. Luckcock Collection.
37. Eighteenth-century copper button, silvered, the edge machine-chased set with an enameled green medallion, decorated with a raised flower (Encrustation) design. Courtesy of Birmingham Museums Trust on behalf of Birmingham City Council; accession #1953F432. Luckcock Collection.
38. Cast Champlevé verbal button with different patterns on the front and the back, thus telling you it was not stamped.

The enamel buttons of the eighteenth century were worn by the nobility and used as a form of jewelry. For example, Louis XIV (known as the Sun King) desired such beautiful and precious buttons that he employed his own boutonnier. Sometimes these precious enamel buttons were even used as a secondary currency, as a single luxury button could be used to pay off a large debt. As fashion changed, so did the button designs.

Although already used for soft materials such as ivory and wood, in the eighteenth century the engine-turning machines that produce intricate patterns for Guilloché enameling were first employed on metals such as gold and silver. Thus, many buttons were produced using this beautiful technique (buttons 39, 40, 41, and 42). It eventually fell out of favor but was revived in the late 1800s and is popular again in modern times.

More is known about buttons of France, England, and America. However, buttons were made around the world, including in Germany, Italy, Holland, Spain, Sweden, Japan, China, and Hungary. Throughout the eighteenth century, buttons were frequently made in sets of 5–35 and sold in beautiful leather jewelry boxes lined in satin. These sets, meant to be used on one outfit, might be designed for telling a story (button set 43) or centered around a theme.

In 1724, Georges Frédéric Strass, a French jewelry designer, is said to have invented paste jewels, which were made of leaded glass that he cut and polished to resemble gemstones (buttons 44 and 45). *Note:* Archaeological diggings have found imitation glass jewels thought to have been used in ancient Greece. In addition, Joseph Strasser, a Viennese goldsmith, claimed in 1758 that he invented Strass Paste. Paste was readily used in eighteenth-century buttons.

39. Antique Guilloché / Polychrome on silver, looped floral wreath design.
40. Eighteenth-century Guilloché with fine gold Paillon central star pattern and border of C-Scrolls, mounted in metal.
41. Antique Guilloché with Paillons border, by David-Anderson.
42. Guilloché / Émaux Peints from about the 1940s or 1950s, by Ole Petter Raasch Olsen.
43. Eighteenth-century Polychrome / Guilloché set of six buttons, with Liquid Gold rococo borders, that probably depict a story.
44. Eighteenth-century enamel with Pierreries in silver mounting and Strass Paste border.
45. Antique openwork enamel of birds on branch with interior paste and outer border.

There are a few distinguishing characteristics of eighteenth-century enamel buttons (button 46). The December 1999 *NBB* article "18th-Century Enamel Buttons" provides a way to remember these attributes: the acronym of PPPP+CE—Paillons, Pierreries, Paste, Painted, and Counter Enamel. Please keep in mind that just because a button includes these elements does not automatically indicate that it comes from the eighteenth century (button 47). The color *bleu-de-roi* (also called blue royal) was prominent (button 48) during this era.

NINETEENTH CENTURY AND EARLY TWENTIETH CENTURY

More is known about this period because it is well documented in historical records. Innovations and advances were made all over the world, and new art movements were started. A chronology would be difficult to write because of the interweaving of time and place. Thus, this section is organized first by specific geographical locales and then by movements. It is not always easy to divide historical information into distinct centuries because of the overlap and how a discussion of one topic might reflect on something that occurs in a future century. This section does relate information into the twentieth century, which overlaps with the next section on modern enameling. Please bear this point in mind.

Countries
England
By the early 1840s, English Painted Enamel production virtually stopped, with imitated copies of older pieces appearing after that. Sometimes these are difficult to differentiate from the originals, and only experience helps in this endeavor. The year 1870 started a revival of the enamel industry in England, with new pieces being clearly marked to distinguish them from older versions.

In the 1860s, photographic transfers became popular after the invention of photography. This nineteenth-century technology was a new way of transferring a design onto enamel, usually with copper bases, by recreating photographic images with Painting Materials. Several methods were patented. Most of these images on enamel were coated with flux (i.e., clear enamel). Usually Monochromes, which could be hand painted, were done, but some of the patented methods allowed for multiple colors of transfer (button 49). Lafon de Camarsac (1821–1905) of Paris was the most well-known producer of this type of work.[36] In the button world, this process was used by the Motiwala Brothers of India (page 100) in the mid-twentieth century.

The Victorian era (1837–1901) was named for the time when Queen Victoria of England ruled. This period saw the British Empire grow into the first global industrial power, shaping the world today. During this era, new machines were invented that made manufacturing easier, and thus more buttons were produced. There were many beautiful buttons in a variety of materials made at this time, but none more beautiful than the enamel buttons (button 50).

A favorite of the queen was marcasite jewelry, which grew in popularity during her reign, although pieces had been made in previous eras by Inca and ancient Greek jewelers. Marcasite stones, made from pyrite (fool's gold), are usually set in silver. They were sometimes used instead of diamonds because of the difference in cost. An interesting fact is that when diamonds were banned from being displayed in public in Switzerland, marcasite and cut

46. Eighteenth-century Guilloché enamel with Paillons and mirrored glass in silver mounting and wide Strass Paste border.
47. Antique Oval enamel button with Paillons and Pierreries with central jewel; not eighteenth century, as the button shape and the fabrication of the mount are characteristic of nineteenth-century styles.
48. Eighteenth-century Champlevé / Guilloché enamel with *bleu-de-roi* field, Paillons focal design, inner crescent border, and white enamel outer border.
49. Nineteenth-century four-color transfer with a metal outer border.
50. Eighteenth-century enamel mounted in copper frame.

steel were used as substitutes.[37] Marcasite was also used in Art Nouveau and Art Deco pieces. Both cut steel and sometimes marcasite made beautiful additions to enamel buttons (button 51).

In the later part of the nineteenth century, the workshops in Birmingham started enameling on coins, frequently silver coins. These were also enameled in Geneva. Mostly done for jewelry and watch fobs, buttons were also made. Coins from various periods were enameled, and foreign coins were used as well. These coins were enameled by engraving away areas where the enamel would be fused in, thus producing Champlevé or Basse Taille buttons.[38] Interest was lost by the end of the first decade of the twentieth century, and after 1920 it became illegal to alter (enamel, for example) gold, silver, or base metal coins of England. Today a few modern enamelists have made buttons by enameling coins, but often only as the substrate, which is covered in opaque enamel. These individuals include Diane Echnoz Almeyda and Herman Lowenstein, among others.

Just as boxed sets of buttons were popular in the eighteenth century, the Edwardian period (1900–1910) was a heyday of boxed sets of buttons (called "Case Sets" in England) for men's waistcoats. These were presented in leather-, fabric-, or paper-covered boxes, which usually held sets of six buttons (button set 52).

MARCASITE HEALING PROPERTIES

The pyrite form of marcasite is believed to have healing properties. Some of these include being a defense against negative energy and inspiring relaxation, reflection, spiritual development, focus, and clarity. The ancient Egyptians used marcasite to calm anxiety.

These buttons were not sewn on but passed through two buttonholes and clipped from behind with one of two types of fasteners (figure 1.2). At the end of a day's wear, they were unclipped and returned to their cases for safe storage. The ability to take them off allowed the wearer to switch out designs. Frequently these buttons included enamel. At the same time, cased sets for women's clothing usually came in sets of three and sometimes included a matching brooch or occasionally a hatpin (button set 53). Of course, other sets were also available. The best-known makers of these buttons were Liberty & Co. of London (page 97), particularly Archibald Knox and Charles Horner. Boxes were frequently stamped with a company name, but these were usually the retailer and not the maker.

Alexander Fisher, an English enamelist, author, and educator, trained many enamelists specializing in miniatures. In the early 1900s, Fisher wrote a book[39] in which he talked about Pâte enamel (button 54), the second reference (for the first, see "Geneva" section, page 14) I found about this material. Fisher referred to Onglaze painting not as an enameling technique but, instead, as a painting technique *on* enamel. This attitude was not his alone.

Figure 1.2 Button fasteners—cotter pin and split ring.

51. Antique Guilloché with marcasites and central ruby.
52. Antique men's vest button set—realistic Tudor rose flowers on silver, clips shown.
53. Antique vest button set, Basse Taille woman's enamel clothing buttons with matching brooch and fasteners; square enamel on silver pinwheel design.
54. Antique Pâte enamel (with mellow yellow field) Polychrome mounted in metal.

France

In the mid-1800s, Henri Brouilhet invented a machine to produce solid and Ronde Bosse wares inexpensively, thus allowing for metalsmiths to produce these more economically. In the early 1890s, two Paris salons (La Société des Artistes Français and La Société Nationale des Beaux-Arts) extended their membership from only painters and sculptors to allow jewelers to join. This development gave the newcomers access to new collectors, the press, and thus the general public. At the 1900 Exposition Universelle in Paris, many of these jewelers, with expanded artistic self-expression, still showed their enameled objets d'art in the jewelry section of the show, Lalique being one of them. Many were of unconventional mixed materials like the Cross of Lelièvre, which was of an oak frame within an enamel and metal mount.[40]

The company of Samson et Cie in Paris was known for many reproductions of Battersea-style enamels. Its pieces were marked with an S. The company stopped production in 1975.[41] At this time, there was a big market for authentic older enamels, and many convincing imitations were produced and made to look like antique enamels with added chips and such. Dealers were easily fooled because it was thought that older techniques could not be reproduced, but, as we now know, that is not the case.[42] Others working at this time were Eugene Marquis from Paris and AP & Cie from Paris (button 55).

Geneva

From the mid-seventeenth century onward, Geneva was the center for enamel painting.[43] Two processes dominated until the late 1800s. These were painting over Guilloché (buttons 56 and 57) and the Genevan method of crowning or fluxing (adding clear enamel over a painting—page 68). They also specialized in the technique of En Camaïeu (page 56).[44]

In 1835, Charles-Louis Dufaux (1802–1884) founded an enamel-manufacturing company that supplied high-quality enamels to all of Europe. His great-grandson was Louis-Eliè Millenet (1874–1973), who took over the manufacturing company and was an enamel painter in his own right. The Millenet-Dufaux factory closed in 1958. It is not known whether they made any buttons. However, they manufactured the Pâte enamel (page 57) used as a field for some Émaux Peints buttons. Although their formulas were sold to a German company, Pâte enamels cannot be found to have been manufactured after the original factory closed.

The son of the founder, Marc-Louis Dufaux, was credited with starting the revival of Limoges School painting in Geneva, and the city became *the* major center for this type of enamelware until the twentieth century. Louis-Eliè Millenet worked in Paris for 15 years and was a professor of enameling in Switzerland. Most of his work was in the Limoges School Revival on copper in both painting and Grisaille.

In 1911, Millenet wrote a how-to enameling book.[45] This volume was especially informative on older-style enameling. Like Alexander Fisher, Millenet referred to Onglaze painting as a painting technique *on* enamel rather than an enameling technique. He devoted a page to describing the Pâte (button 58) enamel we find on buttons. That was the first reference to Pâte that I had found anywhere, including the internet. In addition, he described the Geneva-innovated technique of fusing a layer of flux (clear enamel) over a painting. This method was called crowning and helped protect the thin Painting Materials and harmonize the colors. Additionally, it was first developed to give extra brilliance of a painting over Guilloché. This method is still used today by enamel painters, which may or may not be over Guilloché.

---

55. Nineteenth-century Émaux Peints, young man with foil-enhanced garments with a rococo outer border, by AP & Cie, Paris.
56. Antique Guilloché on silver with Polychrome stylized bell flower.
57. Guilloché / Émaux Peints flower, by Douglas Clock & Co. (shield on the back). Notice the black outline on the flower—this is not the same as Levinger flowers (page 96).
58. Antique Pâte Polychrome head with outer plain brass border.

Millenet's book was one of the few enamel texts that refers to buttons. It says, "Nickel can also be enameled, as well as certain base metals derived from copper, such as tombac, gilding metal, bronze, etc., but their employment is always attended with risk as to the adherence of the enamel [hence why they roughened up the surface to form a mechanical bond], and in any case they are only employed in the manufacture of cheap commercial articles, such as buttons, badges."[46] What I don't understand is why, with such beautiful enamel buttons from before this period, buttons were not considered fine work by the enameling community.

India

In India, enameling is known as minakari (button 59). It was introduced into India by Persian craftsmen during the Mongol period (1206–1368). By 1880, enameling was done all over India, with the center being in Jaipur, whose craftspeople were considered the best. The major style was a form of Champlevé work with gold repoussé and chasing over a mold.[47] See page 47 for more information on Indian buttons.

Japan

Japanese enameling expanded in the early part of the nineteenth century when Kaji Tsunekichi (1803–1883), considered the founder of modern Japanese Cloisonné, made many innovations and started teaching the enamelists of the future. One of his developments was enameling on three-dimensional surfaces. He also discovered that, instead of soldering Cloisonné wires to the substrate, he could fuse them into an initial layer of flux. His enamels were speckled with impurities and included background wires, which were called diaper designs and used to stabilize the enamel in place. A diaper design is a repeating uniform motif (button 60), which the button world calls "all-over" patterns. In the 1850s, trade opened up with Japan. In 1862, Japan showed items at the International Exhibition in London. This display set a course for Japan's art style to influence the West, especially the Art Nouveau style (button 61).

The Meiji period, from 1868 to 1912, saw the modernization and westernization of Japan. During this time, the Japanese were making strides in various areas of enameling. Gottfried Wagener, a German chemist, is known for introducing Western enameling techniques to Japan. With his aid, many innovations were made. For example, enamels now had more intense colors. By 1893, the innovation of making enamels with fewer impurities meant many of the diaper designs of previous Cloisonné enamels were no longer needed, thus allowing for more natural designs. In addition, before this time, pitting in Japanese enameling was common, but now these pits were eliminated by removing the impurities. The 1880–1910 period was considered the Golden Age of Japanese enamels. Namikawa Sōsuke (1847–1910) was considered the greatest Shippō artist (enamelist) of this era.[48] During this period, Gin-bari was developed as a less expensive way to give the look of Basse Taille (page 42). See appendix E for more information on Japanese enameling terminology.

In the early 1880s, the Namikawa Yasuyuki family developed a type of enamel called Tea Goldstone (*Chakin-seki* in Japanese). This material often was a brown transparent enamel with metal flecks in it (usually copper), which gave a glittering appearance (button 62 and appendix E for a box using Tea Goldstone). However, the origin of goldstone enamel is disputed. Today this enamel is still available. However, today crushed goldstone glass (page 72) can be mixed with enamel, and this embellishment is more flexible to work with.

During the Golden Age, the Inaba Cloisonné Company was established; the company closed in the 1990s. I was fortunate enough to go to Japan in 1979 and visited them. The Inaba Cloisonné Company did manufacture buttons (button 63). The only surviving company from the Golden Age is the Andō Cloisonné Co., established by Andō Jūbei.

59. Champlevé from Deccan, India.
60. Cloisonné buckle with diaper design, which represents clouds.
61. Antique silver Champlevé (frequently called Japanese Enamel on Silver).
62. Antique Tea Goldstone Cloisonné enamel mounted in metal.
63. Champlevé peacock button from Inaba Cloisonné Company.

Today they still produce high-quality enamelware. The Andō Cloisonné Co. developed many innovations. An important one, thought to be developed by Hattori Tadasaburō and Kawade Shibatarō, was the technique of Moriage (page 59), which means "piling up" and allowed sculptural relief on enamels.

Korea

Not much is known about Korean enameling.[49] Some enamel buttons were made as shown on a vest at the Sookmyung Women's University Museum and at the National Palace Museum of Korea. However, not many examples exist today.

Russia

Russia was introduced to Cloisonné enameling by Byzantine craftsmen around 978–1015 CE. In the seventeenth century, though, enamel painting was introduced. Interestingly, the Russian painters frequently also painted their counter enamel. Peter the Great was a big promoter of painted enamel miniatures and tried to get French enamelists to come to St. Petersburg. However, because of the distance and the harsh weather in Russia, the French didn't want to make the journey. Thus, more Russians themselves started painting (button 64). The European style was studied, and in 1723, the technique of Onglaze painting with the pointillé method was started. The designs were oftentimes Russian Folk Art images or icons, which the devout considered bridges between heaven and earth.[50]

By the 1850s, Russians were enameling in the following techniques: Champlevé, Guilloché, Plique-à-jour, and Émaux Peints miniatures. The House of Fabergé (page 92) produced the most renowned Russian enamels of this century. Fabergé's use of Guilloché was innovative and made his eggs and frames world famous. Lastly, Émaux Peints remains a prominent technique today with some of the best enamel painters in the world. Today, the Kremlin has the greatest Russian treasures in its enamel collection. The brand of enamel used by Fabergé was Soyer, from France, which Soyer proudly documents on their website.

Art Movements

In the nineteenth century, there were three main art movements that affected enamelware. They occurred in various countries at the same time. These are discussed below. Note that Art Deco (page 20) could fall into this category but is listed in the next section on the "Modern Era."

Limoges School Revival

The Limoges School painting with Grisaille and transparent enamels declined toward the end of the sixteenth century. As previously mentioned, in about 1630 the painting style turned to Onglaze painting rather than transparent enamels. But the older style of painting was quite beautiful, and an increased interest grew into the Limoges School Revival in the nineteenth century, with special interest by the 1860s. Much of this revival used Grisaille while still using foil and transparent enamels.

The aim of the Limoges School Revival was to emulate antique pieces.[51] Maurice Ardant studied the old Limoges methods and materials through the use of the formulas that were preserved by the Nousailher family of Limoges.[52] With this knowledge, he was one of the primary artist-scientists to start the Limoges School Revival.

By 1840, many chemists and artists were actively working to bring back the old methods, especially at the porcelain factory in Sèvres, France. One of their chemists helped redevelop Grisaille White. In the 1860s at the Dufaux workshop in Geneva, many enamelists were being taught small-scale enamel painting in this style. Louis Dalpayrat in 1881 published a detailed guide for art enamelists and encouraged the use of the technique of enlevage à l'aiguille for sculpting the Grisaille White under-paintings. This technique used a fine needle to push, pull, and lift the Grisaille White into place to form the shape the artist wanted.

It's possible that some of the Limoges-style buttons (button 65) we have today were made during this revival, but it's not documented.

Arts & Crafts Movement (1880–1920)

Mass production in the industrialized Victorian era led to a decline in design. This development was exemplified at the Great Exhibition of 1851, which show-

64. Russian Émaux Peints of an angel, set in German Silver and back marked.
65. Antique Limoges-style woman's head with Liquid Gold accents.

cased mass-produced items. The Arts & Crafts Movement was a reaction to the perceived decline in the decorative and fine arts. Both Englishman writer/critic John Ruskin and designer/activist William Morris influenced the Arts & Crafts Movement. Their anti–Industrial Revolution philosophy was for items to be handmade and for the forms to be simplified. Their concept was that how something looked was no more important than how something was made. The movement was named by T. J. Cobden-Sanderson in 1887 at a meeting of the [British] Arts & Crafts Exhibition Society. It initially started in the British Isles but spread throughout the rest of the British Empire, Europe, and America. Each country had its own name for this movement, except for England and the United States, which used the same term.

Massachusetts saw the first Society of Arts & Crafts of Boston (SACB) in 1897. Other societies were then established in hundreds of US cities. In the late 1890s, Elbert Hubbard, along with Gustav Stickley, started the community of "Roycroft" outside of Buffalo, New York. Hubbard had a printing company/book binding business; his printing methods were influenced by William Morris of England. Soon the Roycroft Campus drew in artisans working as metalsmiths, leatherworkers, and furniture makers. These artisans were known as Roycrofters, and they had a strong influence on designs in the early twentieth century. Americans utilized styles from many countries.

Roycrofters realized that art and non-mechanization didn't mix very well, as products were too expensive for the masses. Standards, though, were established, and as craftspeople had to make a living, many objects created were only for the wealthy. In the United States, there was an emphasis on beauty from nature, skilled craftsmanship, usability, and ornamentation as an end in itself. Buttons fit this theme perfectly: they were ordinary objects that were functional and beautiful.

Rosalie Berberian notes, "The Arts & Crafts Movement revolutionized the decorative arts here and in the rest of the industrialized world. It established a new way of thinking about the crafts and integral part of 'the arts' that laid a foundation on which artistic craftsmanship now stands."[53] Common during this time was enameling with the following techniques: Basse Taille (button 66), Champlevé (button 67), Cloisonné (button 68), En Ronde Bosse, Émaux Peints, and Plique-à-jour. Jewelry now became a visual expression of this era as per Charles Robert Ashbee, who started the Guild and School of Handicraft (button 69) in 1888 in London, England.

We know some of the artists and companies making enameled buttons from this period. Some of these are listed in chapter 4, "Enamel Button Artists, Producers, and Purveyors." Enamel buttons were made by such companies as W. H. Haseler & Co. (page 93), James Fenton & Co. (button 70), and William Hutton and Sons (button 71), all in England (button 72), and by button designers such as Beatrice Cameron, Karl Karlson, and Jessie M. King (page 95). Liberty & Co. (page 97) buttons are also considered Arts & Crafts buttons.

For more information on the Arts & Crafts Movement, read the excellent December 2008 *NBB* article by Elaine Cossman, "Collecting Buttons of the Arts & Crafts Movement."[54]

66. Arts & Crafts Basse Taille / Champlevé design suggestive of Art Deco on silver.
67. Arts & Crafts Champlevé / Émaux Peints on silver with bezel-set blue moonstone and integrated border.
68. Arts & Crafts Cloisonné design suggestive of plant life with pearl center.
69. Arts & Crafts button from the Guild and School of Handicraft.
70. Arts & Crafts Champlevé with heavy silver focus, by James Fenton & Co.
71. Arts & Crafts Champlevé-shaped stylized plant life design, by William Hutton and Sons.
72. Arts & Crafts Basse Taille / Champlevé of the Tudor Rose, by Pearce & Sons, Birmingham, 1904.

Art Nouveau (1890–1910)

The Art Nouveau style was characterized by long, flowing, organic lines. In England, it was called the Modern Style; in Germany, Jugendstil; in Austria and Hungary, Secession Style; in Italy, Stile Liberty; in Spain, Modernismo; and in the United States, Tiffany Style. Alphonse Mucha, a Czech artist, was considered the father of the Art Nouveau style. The dates shown reflect when Art Nouveau flourished.

During this period, designs frequently reflected the times. For example, during this era people wanted to show how cultured they were by wearing buttons depicting what was happening in the world. In 1894, Sarah Bernhardt gained prominence by starring in the play *Gismonda* (button 73). The poster for the play was designed by Alphonse Mucha, and it made him famous. Mucha probably didn't design any buttons, but it's thought that he designed jewelry for master Art Nouveau and Art Deco jeweler Georges Fouquet. However, buttons were made using his style, which were mostly images from his posters (buttons 74 and 75). Another important theme at the time was love, represented by a white bird (button 76).

Enamels played an important role during this time frame, especially Plique-à-jour enameling, which frequently used the flowing lines of the Art Nouveau style. These pieces in particular separated themselves from the mass-produced pieces of the time. The philosophy was that all household objects should be aesthetic, including buttons. Cabochons in natural gemstones, such as turquoise, were employed more than faceted stones, and enamels in blue and green were popular (button 77). Another influence in design was that of Japan, as previously mentioned. The work of the day is shown in the Liberty & Co. enamel buttons (button set 78), particularly Archibald Knox's designs for the Cymric line[55] (page 97). At the turn of the twentieth century, enameling itself defined modernism as the Japanese-style designs embraced nature as part of the Art Nouveau period, with use of transparent enamels. Lalique was considered the supreme artist with his lifelike use of enamels, although other artists were also recognized. In addition, during this period, items could be done in less expensive metals, as electroplating (button 330, page 81), especially with silver, was popular around 1900.[56]

Women were not allowed to work in the decorative arts except as low-level workers without much skill. One American woman, Clara Driscoll (1861–1944),

73. Antique Émaux Peints of Sarah Bernhardt as Gismonda, on silver, in the style of Alphonse Mucha. Enhanced with Liquid Gold and back marked sterling.
74. Antique Émaux Peints Mucha-style woman's head painted on tooled bronze, including one of his signature design elements of a circle in the headdress.
75. Antique Polychrome Mucha-style woman's head.
76. Antique Émaux Peints bird, a Victorian symbol of love.
77. Antique Art Nouveau Champlevé stylized plant life in typical colors of the time.
78. Set of Liberty & Co. silver Champlevé buttons in original box.

managed Louis C. Tiffany's women's leaded glass department. She is credited with designing the first Tiffany lamps with leaded glass shades, like Dragonfly and Wisteria. Although these did not include enamel, she championed women working in the decorative arts, including enamelwork. Driscoll organized a protest in 1903 to stop a men's strike against women doing leaded glass work. Tiffany was very supportive of women (called Tiffany Girls—all worked in a women's department) for their use of color and delicate work, although he required that they leave if they got married. Tiffany enamels did use the encrusted/beaded enamel effect[57] (page 58). In the mid- to late nineteenth century, some art schools that allowed women opened, schools such as Central School of Arts & Crafts and the Royal College of Arts in London, and others in Liverpool and other areas of England. Some women did make a name for themselves, such as Scottish designer, enamelist, and button maker Jessie M. King (page 95).

MODERN ERA—TWENTIETH AND TWENTY-FIRST CENTURIES

In modern times, there have been many advances in both enameling and the button world. Most important in the button world is that the National Button Society was founded. This section discusses its founding and then describes changes in the art and enameling worlds. After that, I present three artful expressions of contemporary life that include enamel buttons. This then brings us to the present and the end of this chapter on history.

The National Button Society (NBS)
Gertrude Howell Patterson was featured on a 1937 radio show about her passion for collecting buttons. This appearance contributed to the founding of the National Button Society (NBS) the next year, in 1938, thus establishing button collecting as a national hobby. The first NBS show was in 1939 in Chicago, which featured a hand-painted wood favor button.

The NBS published the first issue of the *National Button Bulletin* (*NBB*) in January 1942. This began a tradition that continues today, publishing bulletins several times a year for their membership. The initial *Official Classifications of the National Button Society* was included in the *NBB* each year from the beginning, which always included enamel buttons. Eventually, in the early 1980s, the NBS published its first separate version of the classifications as the *Blue Book* (BB), with, of course, a blue cover! This book was totally reorganized in 2005 by Joan Lindsay and Barbara Barrans. Their organization emphasized consistency between material classes and terminology and remains very close to today's version. Barrans describes the BB:

> *"The organization of any subject matter, in this case buttons, is key to understanding it. Many button collectors (and competitors) rely on the terminology/definitions put forth in the National Button Society's official guide called the Blue Book [BB]. This publication is updated and issued periodically to the NBS membership and is divided into four main parts. At the front of the book is a list of 'basic rules and guidelines governing button competitions.' The central (main) part of the BB, however, is the Classification Listing, an organizational outline that has evolved over time, with input from within the hobby, to help collectors understand and thus properly classify the buttons they love. The Classification Listing groups all buttons into major classes or subclasses depending on their various attributes. All buttons can be segregated according to their Age, Usage, Material, and Face design. This is an outline only; it cannot cover the entire scope of information available about each button. Following the Classification Listing is an Appendix and a Glossary, which define and elaborate the button terminology used in the outline. Of course, not all button terminology coincides with the non-button world."*[58]

The NBS Classification's "material section" about enamel buttons has changed dramatically over the years. The May 1957 issue of *NBB* had an article titled "Proposed Classification for Enamel Buttons" by Jane Ford Adams.[59] In general, this article provided a list of some enamel button attributes. Her specific outline, as presented, was not adopted. Many of her concepts, however, have been reorganized into the current enamel classification.

One major change in the enamel and all "material" sections was made in the 1999 classification. Prior to that time, the terms "Ornamentation assorted" and "Trim" had been used interchangeably to include some Decorative Finishes (DF) as well as Other Material Embellishments (OME), thus creating confusion. In

1999, "Embellishment" and "Finishes" were renamed OME and DF, respectively, and new definitions were included that separated the two concepts.

By around 1951, the term "Studio Button"[60] was being used. In addition, by 1987 the *Blue Book* had a class for these handmade buttons, sold primarily to collectors. It's not clear how the term changed meaning at any point, but today a Studio Button is essentially one created by an artist, primarily for collectors, which is handmade and not mass produced. Artists who made enamel buttons are listed in chapter 4, "Enamel Button Artists, Producers, and Purveyors." In that chapter, some individuals are considered Studio Button artists, and some are not. This term has caused confusion over the years, so the chapter doesn't distinguish between Studio Button and non–Studio Button artists.

The most current BB is always the best information available at the time of publishing, with updates shown in gray text, making it easy to find out what has changed. Any references in this book to the BB will be for version titled *NBS 2023 Blue Book, Official Classification & Competition Guidelines*.

Art Deco (1920s–1930s)

The Art Deco–style (buttons 79 and 80) was also called "Art Moderne." This style, which began in the 1920s, reached its high point in the 1930s and continues to inspire artists in the twenty-first century (button 81). The Art Deco style is characterized by simple, clean lines, frequently with repetitive geometric shapes and stylized representational forms. Used not only for decorative art items but also in architecture, it was meant to symbolize wealth and sophistication with its antitraditional, sleek elegance. René Lalique (1860–1945) was one famous artist who worked in both Art Nouveau and Art Deco. Unfortunately, although Lalique made glass buttons, he did not make enamel buttons, even though he was an enamelist. One of the most famous enamelists working in

BACK MARKS

There are websites that provide company/individual/metal marks put on buttons, jewelry, and other objects. Here are two that have separate listings for various countries:
- 925-1000 (https://www.925-1000.com)
- Silver Makers Marks (https://www.silvermakersmarks.co.uk/MakersMarks.html)

Art Deco was Camille Fauré (1874–1956), who started a unique style of building up enamels for a sculptural look. Although Fauré didn't make buttons, today his method of enameling is taught and called the Fauré method (page 59).

Enameling in the Twentieth Century to Present

The twentieth century saw a revival of interest in the art of enameling. The Arts & Crafts Movement had an impact on contemporary enameling in the United States. It was centered in Boston, which helped that city become a center for the decorative arts. In the 1930s, European-born craftsmen immigrated to the Boston area to escape Nazi Germany and brought their craft traditions with them. At one point, many from Boston moved to Cleveland, then the largest city in the United States. Cleveland, in the 1930s and 1940s, became a significant center for enameling education and exhibitions. The mid-twentieth century also saw an increase in enamel interest in California, which continues today. This trend started in southern California and then grew to the Bay Area later in the century. Thus, California became the second state, after Ohio, with significant enameling production. Museums gained interest in enameled items and held exhibitions throughout the United States, which caused more people to collect enamels and more artists to work with the media. The press reviewed the exhibitions, and interest continued to increase.

Interest in enameling was especially keen in the 1950s for a few reasons. For one, enamel was now easier to work with because of the development of the

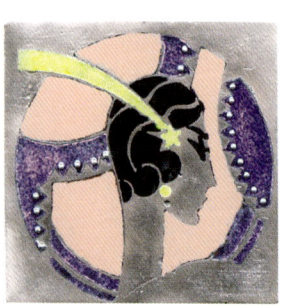

---

79. Antique Champlevé Art Deco geometric design with cut steel OME.
80. Antique Champlevé Turn-over pattern.
81. Etched Art Deco woman's head on copper using vitreous leaded enamels with gold mica luster and fine silver balls on top, by Karen L. Cohen.

electric kiln. Earlier kilns were fired by coke, gas, or petro. These were all large and expensive (and dirty). The new electric kilns were small, perhaps still expensive early on, but they had better temperature control. When the price came down and kits were sold with very small kilns, anyone could buy one and use it in small home studios.

The second reason for enamel revival was that craft schools and colleges started programs for noncredit and for-credit enamel education. Cloisonné (button 82) was frequently taught as an initial enameling technique. At the turn of the century, Alexander Fisher of London trained Laurin H. Martin, who also studied at the Birmingham School of Arts & Crafts in England. Martin then became a leading teacher of enameling in the United States. His most famous student was Kenneth F. Bates (1904–1994), who is well known, loved, and influential to contemporary enamelists. Bates graduated from the Massachusetts School of Art before becoming a teacher at the Cleveland Institute of Art in 1924. Another early enamelist and teacher was Edward Winter, who graduated from the Cleveland Institute of Art in 1931. Both of these teachers published multiple books on this art form.

Another of the best-known enamelists of this period was Doris Hall (1907–2000), who had originally studied as a painter and printmaker. She graduated from the Cleveland Institute of Art in 1928 but didn't start enameling until the 1940s. Because of her painting/printmaking background and the influence of European modernist artists like Pablo Picasso and Marc Chagall, she developed a style of enameling that her husband, printmaker Kalman Kubinyi, called "painting with fire." Although not traditionally thought of as enamel painting, her enameling techniques produced colorful pictorials in the form of wall pieces, jewelry, and at least one button (button 83).

In New York City (NYC), the Kulicke Academy of Jewelry Arts began in the 1960s and evolved into a school run today by the daughter, Fredricka Kulicke. The school is now called the Kulicke Jewelry School (https://kulickejewelryschool.com), located in New Jersey; many Roman and Greek jewelry techniques, including enameling, are taught. Another NYC center was the School of Visual Arts. One of their staff members, also a teaching assistant at the Kulicke Academy of Jewelry Arts, was Lori Hollander, who created enamel reproductions for the museum store for the 1978–1979 King Tut exhibition at the Metropolitan Museum of Art in NYC. I was fortunate to be trained in Cloisonné (button 84) by Hollander.

Another famous enamelist and teacher was Latvian-born Valeri Timofeev, who moved to the United States in 1993. Timofeev actually lived near me in Pennsylvania, and I knew him personally. Although trained as an engineer in Russia, he studied metalsmithing and enameling, being especially interested in the older Russian Plique-à-jour technique. Given access to museums and other historical information in Russia, he revived the Plique-à-jour technique that is used today. In 1992, Russia held an exhibition at the Kremlin commemorating the House of Fabergé, and Timofeev was one of three artists showing his Plique-à-jour work. His work is known worldwide, which includes some jewelry but mainly objets d'art like stemmed glasses and eggs. He taught for many years. Studio Button artist Diane Echnoz Almeyda (button 85) was one of his students who made Plique-à-jour her main focus.

Studio Button artist Diana Wieler studied enamel portrait painting (button 86, page 22) with Gillie Byrom, who had studied with enamelists in a lineage from the Limoges period, illustrating how education in this art form has been passed down for generations.

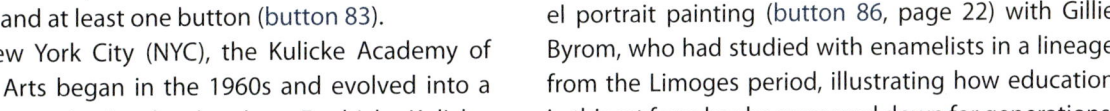

82. Cloisonné with gold wires over silver foil, by Rose Marie Diem.
83. Innovated enameling of a face with seed bead outer border by Doris Hall. Image courtesy of Lion & Unicorn Auctions.
84. Cloisonné / Guilloché (moiré pattern) dragon with both fine gold and silver wires with fine silver foil and fine silver balls on top, set in roll-printed sterling silver, by Karen L. Cohen.
85. Paisley Filigree Plique-à-jour on silver, by Diane Echnoz Almeyda.

With increased teaching came innovation, especially in the 1970s and 1980s. Some current craft centers that teach enameling include Penland School of Craft in North Carolina, Arrowmont School of Arts & Crafts in Tennessee, Peters Valley in New Jersey, and John C. Campbell Folk School in North Carolina. Diane Echnoz Almeyda has taught at Arrowmont, and I teach at John C. Campbell Folk School. In addition, many colleges and universities today teach enameling in their metals departments.

A third reason for the renewed interest in enameling in these centuries was the availability of the materials in small enough quantities to work in small, independent studios. Many companies found on the internet sell copper cutouts or silver and copper forms, like dishes and candlesticks, to be enameled. Fused glass suppliers are readily available with products that are compatible with enameling. And companies manufacturing enamels can be found in the United States and internationally.

In the late 1970s, Woodrow (Woody) Carpenter, a ceramic engineer, developed a new line of lead-free enamels for metal with the brand name of Vitrearc. Up until this time, all enamels used by art enamelists were leaded. He eventually bought the Thomas C. Thompson Company, combined his two companies, and rebranded to be named Thompson Enamel. Thompson Enamel, currently located in Bellevue, Kentucky, is now the only "jewelry enamel" manufacturer in the Western Hemisphere. In 1985, Carpenter decided to expand the lead-free color palette. Two of his employees are well known in the enamel world. Bill Helwig became Thompson's technical support, developer of product, educator, and resident enamel artist, functioning in that capacity until his death in 2012. Tom Ellis still works for the company as technical support, educator, and enamel artist, and he has served as the technical enamel editor of all three of my books. Both of these men and Carpenter have had a huge impact on the enameling world, and I am privileged to have known all three of them. Today, Carpenter's grandchildren, Guido and his wife Joanna Maehren and Mark Maehren, own the company, which is the world leader in lead-free enamels for metal and other substrates.[61]

Many of the newer American enamelists use the Thompson Enamel lead-free line. But those who enameled in the middle of the twentieth century might have used the vintage leaded line. I use the leaded enamels on my silver work and unleaded on the copper pieces. The Japanese enamels are leaded, quite beautiful, and compatible with the vintage Thompson Enamels, which I also use.

Other enamel manufacturers exist in other countries: Milton Bridge in the United Kingdom (which makes enamel lines called Milton Bridge; Schauer, formerly from Austria; and Blythe, formerly from Johnson Matthey), Hirosawa Enamel Institute in Japan, Ninomiya Enamel in Japan, Nihon Shippo Enamel in Japan, Soyer Enamel in France, and W. G. Ball in the United Kingdom.

Not only were individual artists now working in enamel, but commercial companies were also using this enduring material to make badges, lapel pins, liturgical medallions, trophies, road signs, and more. And some enameled larger items like washing machines and tubs. These were supported by the Porcelain Enamel Institute (https://www.porcelainenamel.com), founded in 1930, which continues today.

About 1976, the Guild of Enamellers (https://guildofenamellers.org) in England was founded. This group supports everyone from beginners to professionals. In 1985, the British Society of Enamellers (https://www.enamellers.org) was formed for professional enamelists as an offshoot from the Guild of Enamellers, although today any level of artist may join. Many enamelists in England belong to both organizations. The equivalent in the United States is The Enamelist Society (https://www.enamelistsociety.org), which was founded in 1987. Although The Enamelist Society was started as a US organization, it includes many members from all over the world. Various websites and social media groups are also available for enamelists to network and learn new techniques. In addition, various areas of the country have local guilds to join, the largest of which is the Enamel Guild/Northeast, which covers Vermont to Florida.

In the twenty-first century, because of increased communication ability, enamelists and button collectors can network even better than in the past. When the COVID-19 pandemic started in 2020, The Enamelist Society began holding weekly Zoom meetings, which gave us the ability to gather together "in person" each week and discuss various topics, see each other's work, and sometimes enamel together in "jam"

86. Émaux Peints portrait, by Diana Wieler.

sessions. When I gave a Zoom talk on antique enamel buttons, many enamelists were surprised, as they had not seen this kind of beautiful art in miniature before. Button clubs across the country frequently had Zoom meetings that not only brought collectors together but also provided a wealth of information, some of which has found its way into this book! Lastly, during the pandemic, many online enamel classes began, which helped train new people and teach new techniques to experienced enamelists.

Contemporary enamelists were also enlightened by the articles in the industry magazine, *Glass on Metal* (*GOM*). *GOM* was started by Thompson Enamel in 1982 but is now out of print. However, the first five issues provided information on the chemistry of enamel, and the magazine, in general, was a major source of innovative ideas and new products.

Quite a few independent enamelists in the twentieth and twenty-first centuries have made buttons. These are documented in chapter 4, "Enamel Button Artists, Producers, and Purveyors." Their wares vary from craft-style buttons to some true pieces of art. All are loved by button collectors. In the twentieth century, there were still a few companies making enamel buttons, like the Inaba Cloisonné Company (button 87) in Japan and the Motiwala Brothers in India (button 88). So far in the twenty-first century, only individual enamelists are making them.

A wide range of techniques have been used in buttons, such as the old favorites of Champlevé, Cloisonné, and Plique-à-jour. Modern techniques have also been used, and I expect newer ones in the future will be as well. The techniques used in buttons are described in chapter 3, "Buttons as Enamelware."

Artistic Expression of the Times as Shown with Buttons

Just as in earlier eras, in contemporary times artists are either inspired or commissioned to express their emotions in art by telling a story. Here are three that use enamel buttons as part of that expression.

COVID-19: Jean Mandeberg

Jean Mandeberg is an artist, metalsmith, and community arts advocate in Olympia, Washington, where she taught interdisciplinary art at Evergreen State College before retiring as a faculty emerita.

Jean's current work combines vitreous enamel on copper with found textiles. Enamel buttons, like dice and money in her earlier work, are a focus: small, humble, essential, easily hidden, personal, and beautiful. During the COVID-19 pandemic, these buttons became markers of a time filled with uncertainty, with a button representing each day in the pattern of a monthly calendar. Sometimes the buttons echoed the black and blue of bruising days (COVID Calendar #3), or feeling broken (COVID Calendar #5), or being lost (COVID Calendar #1, shown in figure 1.3, and Calendar #2). Often the days felt tangled (COVID Calendar #6) or simply a blur (COVID Calendar #4).

Over the two years of the pandemic, Jean's studio was full of materials, forms, and juxtapositions that allowed her to ask questions and make art that was responsive to our collective fear and loss. Hankies and buttons are objects with both cultural and aesthetic purposes. The layering of worn-out hankies and newly enameled buttons provides a unique combination of impermanence and permanence during a search for visual metaphors for grief.

Figure 1.3 COVID Calendar #1 with buttons representing being lost (May 2020, 16" x 16" x 1", enamel on copper, steel, cotton); wall piece by enamelist Jean Mandeberg. Photo credit: Tom Collicott.

---

87. Champlevé button, by Inaba Cloisonné Company.
88. Basse Taille on silver, by Motiwala Brothers (frequently called Liquid Enamel).

HISTORY

Figure 1.4 *Sorrow*, Eastern Europe, Émaux Peints wall piece by Ora Kuller. Notice that there are buttons attached to the piece and some painted onto the piece.

Remembering the Holocaust: Ora Kuller

Ora Kuller is an Israeli enamelist who sometimes resides in the United States. She specializes in Émaux Peints enameling and has projects in both of my books on enameling. However, Ora also works in other enameling techniques like Cloisonné and Grisaille and does beautiful wood carving and painting in other media.

Ora writes, "In 2002, I journeyed with my family to the death camps of Auschwitz and Birkenau, seeking traces of our families' fate. There is a corner in Birkenau that was a sorting station of looted possessions, named Kanada, because whoever worked there could hope to survive and reach that magical free land, Canada.

"After the war, the pile of belongings was left in place, caged by chicken-wire. We walked around the cage after a heavy rainstorm, and something sparkled in the mud. I knelt to pick it up and my heart stopped beating! It was an old-fashioned glass button, blue and white and silver. I looked around and saw that the whole earth around the cage was covered with a multitude of buttons, all taken from those who died there. We gathered them up and let them fall back into the cage, but the weight and feel and image of that first button remained as if etched into the palm of my hand. This blue and white button changed my life.

"That night I wrote a poem about the unique button, trying to imagine who it was that wore something so precious and beautifully adorned on that most horrible of days. I already envisioned recreating the beautiful glass button [button 89] as the core of an artwork mourning the richness of Jewish life destroyed by the brutality of hate and ignorance. But even after completing that piece [figure 1.4] that button I held in Birkenau still called to me—and so I continued to create buttons, some functional and decorative, and most of them depicting my beloved, lost family. It took fifteen years to paint all their faces and set them lovingly in settings of silver and gold. These images [figure 1.5] are now displayed in a custom-built cabinet, keeping the memory of my family alive."[62]

89

Figure 1.5 Émaux Peints enamel buttons and jewelry pieces of some family members, by Ora Kuller.

89. Cloisonné button representing the first button Ora Kuller saw at Birkenau.

Abolition: Dianne Chmidling

Dianne Chmidling is a button collector who was inspired to commission Studio Button artist Diana Wieler to produce this introspective set of buttons.

Dianne says, "While on vacation with my family at a private condo, my curiosity was piqued by the book *Amazing Grace*, with the subtitle, *William Wilberforce and the Heroic Campaign to End Slavery*, by Eric Metaxas. I enjoyed this seldom-found time to read about the history of the abolition movement, as I'm usually absorbed with button world activities.

"William Wilberforce was born in 1758 in England and became a member of the Parliament at age 21. In 1785, after a sudden change to Christianity, he approached politics from a position of morality. He carried, through the House of Commons, bills for amending criminal law, suppressing vice (immoral criminal activities), and reforming public manners. Then in 1787 he became the parliamentary leader of the abolition movement. Several of his friends were also involved in the abolition movement, and that included Josiah Wedgwood, the designer and creator of eighteenth-century buttons we all know and love. This was when the lightbulb went on for me, linking button enthusiasts from a knowledge of beautiful jasperware buttons by Josiah Wedgwood to a critical issue of morality that doesn't come up in many current conversations.

"This realization that Wedgwood was involved in the abolition of the slave trade energized me to further study the lives of other people who were either abolitionists or were beneficial to the cause. Working through this history, it was often hard to hold the tears back. How could masses of people have such immoral thoughts and actions against other wholesome human beings! I hope in some small way, these buttons will remind all of us to be introspective in our thoughts and actions, especially at this time in our history.

"After about a year of study, I commissioned my friend, Diana Wieler, to create a set of Émaux Peints technique enamel oval buttons, about two inches tall, of 10 historical figures who deserve credit for their many years of fighting against slavery. It was a challenge to keep the number of those figures down to 10 for a matching set, complete with their names at the bottom of each button. I also asked Diana to create a three-inch oval button, in black and white enamel, of the icon designed by Josiah Wedgwood for his medallions. It shows an African slave, shackled, including Wedgwood's heart-wrenching words, 'Am I Not a Man and a Brother?' I am so grateful to Diana for all her own research, ideas, and the many hours she worked to create these pieces of art [button set 90] representing a very important part of our history that we need to remember."[63]

90. Commissioned set of abolitionists Émaux Peints verbal buttons, by Diana Wieler.

2 The Material: Enamel

The word "enamel" comes from the French word "*émail*," which itself comes from the Old High German word "*smelzen*," or the smelt, which is part of the process of making it. The word "enamel" is used in three different ways: it refers to the *material* used, to a *finished piece* (also called enamelware or, in Japanese, Shippō [appendix E]), or to the *process* (i.e., as a verb). In the words of the late contemporary enamelist Lilyan Bachrach, "You enamel enamel with enamel."

The definition of enamel is glass fused to metal at high temperatures. This material is correctly called *vitreous enamel*—derived from or containing glass. Many materials are sold as "enamel," such as paints, nail polish, and resins (in the button world, resin is called CPE—Cold Plastic Enamel). None of these are actually enamel but try to take advantage of the preciousness of vitreous enamel by labeling their products as such. One way to differentiate is to ask whether the piece was fired at a high temperature—if not, it's not vitreous enamel.

Enameling is an ancient art form used around the world for centuries. In ancient times, it was frequently used in the depiction of religious or symbolic themes. However, enamel buttons, antique and modern, show a wide variety of subject matter from everyday life, such as people, animals, and plants (button 91), as well as nonpictorial designs. Enamel is a very sturdy material, although it can crack and chip (button 92)—it *is* made with glass.

Some refer to enamel fusing as enamel "melting." This term is a misnomer, as only solids melt to become liquids, and glass is not truly a solid—it's an amorphous solid (something between the state of being a solid and a liquid). In correct terms, enamel softens as it gets hot and eventually flows, at which point it can be molded or formed into a shape. When enamel softens, it pulls together into a mass and, with gravity and fusion flow, will puddle into a shape that is domed on top and flat on the bottom, such as an Encrustation that represents a cabochon (button 93). This is true whether the enamel that is softening is an initial "lump" of enamel or a mound of grain enamel that has been made by a process called wet-packing.

91. Antique Cloisonné enamel, with pitting.
92. Antique Champlevé / Émaux Peints with two cut steel inner borders and enamel outer border, with chipping.
93. Antique Polychrome with Encrustations.

No matter how much an enamelist knows and no matter how much care they put into their piece, enameling is a medium in which things can "just go wrong"—like a chemical reaction or the piece falling when coming out of the kiln. When this happens, a piece may not turn out the way one expected. However, it might be a wonderous surprise and become an "oops, perfect" result.

In various chapters are a few sidebars called Enamel Tech Talks (ETTs), which provide more technical information about the enameling process. This information is listed separately, as some readers may not want this detail on first reading.

The following pages offer some information on the materials and processes of enameling that may provide greater understanding of this art form and your buttons. This information is applicable to any enamelware, such as buttons, jewelry, boxes, and wall pieces. Within this section are some terms that will be used later in the book. Chapter 3, "Buttons as Enamelware," has more on how some of this information relates to buttons and other enamelware. Anyone desiring more information about enamel or the enameling process can find it in my book, *The Art of Fine Enameling* (2nd ed., 2019).

FIRING TEMPERATURES AND STAGES

If enamel is glass fused to metal at high temperatures, what are high temperatures? Each enamelist finds what works best for them, but in general I fire between 1350°F and 1650°F. As examples: when I fire an enamel painting with the use of China Paints (page 32), I fire at the lower end (button 94); when firing normal copper enameling, I fire around 1450°F (button 95);

when firing a transparent lead-bearing enamel in a silver Cloisonné, I fire around 1500°F (button 96); and when firing for the high-fire techniques, like Scrolling or Webbing Design (page 62), I fire over 1600°F (button 97). Some designs may require the temperature to be adjusted multiple times for various properties of the design (button 98).

In earlier times, those working with enamel did not have temperature gauges and had to use the color of the heat in the kiln as their guide. Today some enamelists still do that. See the sidebar "Heat Color versus Temperature." All enamelists work differently, and all procedures are valid as long as they accomplish what they set out to do.

Firing enamel can occur in a furnace/kiln or by use of a torch. Studio Button artist Joseph H. Spencer (page 104) specialized in torch firing and, in fact, developed a method for using two torches for larger pieces. For more information, see the sidebar "Difference between a Furnace and a Kiln."

Keep in mind that firing an enamel is a fairly quick process, typically one to four minutes. The timing depends on the thickness of the metal, the thickness of the enamel, how quickly the kiln recovers to set temperature after the door is opened, and more. Most enamelists do not go strictly by time, but this topic is too complex to discuss here. I usually know about the time it takes to fire completely, so I go for the minimum and then keep checking. Note that there are times when you may want to underfire the piece, so that also has to be considered with certain techniques.

94. Émaux Peints using unleaded enamel and China Paints with a Sugar Fire topcoat—fired at 1350°F, by Karen L. Cohen.
95. Basse Taille on copper with Paillons and Pierreries fired at around 1450°F, by Karen L. Cohen.
96. Cloisonné / Basse Taille on silver fired at 1500°F, by Karen L. Cohen.
97. High-Fire Webbing Design realistic moon button with gold Paillon stars, fired at 1650°F, by Karen L. Cohen.
98. "Green Glitter" Goldstone field with Faux Opal center and twisted wires and balls, by Karen L. Cohen. This design required three changes of temperature—one for normal copper enameling (1450°F) and two for the Faux Opal (1475°F and then 1435°F).

HEAT COLOR VERSUS TEMPERATURE

If an enamelist does not have a pyrometer to show the heat setting of their furnace, and their furnace has exposed elements of an electric kiln, they can go by the color of the heat. The color is viewable by either slightly opening the door or looking through a possible small door eye-window. This was done in earlier times by viewing the color of the fire heating the kiln. Here are the equivalents.

COLOR DESCRIPTION	TEMPERATURE
Dark red	1300°F
Cherry red	1400°F–1500°F
Light orange/red	1550°F–1600°F
Yellow orange	Over 1600°F

DIFFERENCE BETWEEN A FURNACE AND A KILN

A kiln and a furnace can actually be the same piece of equipment, but they are used differently. In a kiln, the piece is inserted at room temperature, heated to required temperature, fired for as long as needed, and then cooled down before the piece is removed (like for pottery). However, a furnace is more like a preheated oven—in a furnace, the piece is inserted at firing temperature, fired for the required length of time, and then removed while still hot. Although technically enamelists use a furnace, typically the meaning of "kiln" or "furnace" as it relates to enameling is understood to be the same. In this book, I use the term "kiln."

If fired too high or for too long, an enamel can burn. However, sometimes the burnt enamel looks great, and modern enamelists use this as a technique (button 99 and button set 100). Burnt flux also looks good and turns a greenish color, as does white.

Enamel fuses in stages. Normally we see the final stage—smooth glossy surface. However, the other stages have their uses. One in particular is a Sugar Fire topcoat (page 69). Figures 2.1a–d show a textural view of the four stages of fusing (ignore color).

99

100

Figure 2.1a Stage 1—Sugar Fire.

Figure 2.1b Stage 2—more flow (this stage is a continuum between stages 1 and 3).

Figure 2.1c Stage 3—Orange Peel (almost done).

Figure 2.1d Stage 4—Smooth and glossy.

99. Overfired white enamel with a black decal of Medusa (notice the greenish/turquoise color, which is the burnt white area), by Karen L. Cohen.
100. Overfired white enamel on a set of buttons, maker unknown.

Enamel Tech Talk

EFFECT OF FIRING ENAMEL

When I look at buttons and see something "different," I try to figure out how it was done. This is what I was doing when viewing button 101. The owner asked me whether this was possibly Basse Taille, as the white concentric rings were part of the base. I was not sure, so I asked Tom Ellis, technical support at Thompson Enamel and my book's enamel editor. Tom's response was as follows:

"The way I read the enamel below [button 101] is that the black was applied and fired first. The white was applied over the black and when it was fired, the shock of the heat (which happens in every enamel firing) broke the white glass into concentric circles. Most often as the enamel softens, these breaks fuse back together, but when the metal is on the thicker side, it takes longer for the enamel to soften and fuse the fractures back together. Because of the time it took the black to come back to a uniform mass, the cracking in the white had already taken place and the black filled in the areas of the cracked white, preventing the white from coming back together. . . . Thinner metal will heat up faster, the enamel heats up faster and fills in cracks before the craze lines are made permanent.

"It could also have to do with the large metal center and the soldered finding on the back. This part and the outer band of metal on the piece may have been thicker than the rest of the piece, causing the metal in the center to heat up slower than the rest of the metal in the piece. Variations in the thickness of the metal where enamel is applied and around the areas of enamel can cause stress in the enamel due to the differences in the rates of expanding and contracting with heating and cooling. Thicker metal (as in the center area and/or the fact that it is in the center—and the outer part of the piece will heat up faster than the center mass of the piece—translates into the outer part of the piece will expand and contract at a different rate (faster) than the center of the piece (slower expanding and contracting)."[1]

This explained it to me. I was confused by the concentric lines, but this would make sense because of the interior metal disk. Button 102 is a similar version of the same button. Although it does not have the same concentric lines, it does have the hint of them, which means that this was not a design choice, but one of those unexpected things that happens when one enamels!

A note on buttons 101 and 102: These may be classified as Copper Colonial (metal) buttons and not enamel buttons by some judges; thus, they may not be a good choice for an enamel award.

FORMS OF ENAMEL

Enamel comes in three forms: grain (or frit or 80 mesh or jewelry enamel), liquid, and painting types. All materials used for painting are not enamels. However, they are used in many buttons for the Émaux Peints technique and so will be discussed here. Enamels come either lead bearing or lead free. I believe the lead-bearing enamels have more sparkle (like the difference between a crystal goblet and a plain glass one), but there are many beautiful lead-free enamels on the market today.

Grain Enamel

All grain enamel (figure 2.2) starts with a base of clear glass called flux (also called fondant). Flux is a fusion of silica, soda, lime, and a small amount of borax, which is then heated to the correct consistency. Various formulas of flux, each used for different procedures, are manufactured. Coloring agents, which are metal oxides, are then added. Older enamels were limited in color. Some older enamel colors came from iron (sea green and a yellow); tin (opaque white); copper (turquoise); cobalt (royal blue); manganese (violet); silver and antimony (yellow); gold (crimson). Today more

---

101. Eighteenth-century chased copper with wide inner enamel border. Concentric circles are caused by heat shock when firing.

102. Similar button as 101 but shows the concentric circles are different; thus, they were not a design element but a result of the enamel firing.

Figure 2.2 Jar of blue enamel, 80 mesh, which actually includes all sizes from 40 to 400 mesh. *Note:* 80 mesh means 80 holes per linear inch in a screen.

colors and oxides are available. Examples of today's oxide colors include chromium (green); uranium (fine yellow) (button 103); and iridium (steel gray and black). Grain enamel is usually applied by sifting either through a screen or with a brush or spatula after it has been made into a paste or sludge by mixing it with water and possibly a holding agent. In this book, when the term "enamel" is used without a qualifier, it means grain enamel. Please take note of the term "metal oxides," as that will be important when discussing painting materials.

Liquid Enamels

Liquid enamels are a fairly new invention dating from the twentieth century. They were originally developed for commercial use for items such as road signs, washing machines, stoves, and tubs. These were mostly opaque colors. However, art enamelists quickly began incorporating these materials into their work, especially the type called "crackle" enamels (page 52). Liquid enamels all have clay in them and are applied by dipping, pouring, brushing, or spraying. Liquid enamel is also formulated to give the glass physical characteristics such as impact and heat resistance, usually for commercial use. *Note:* This material is not related to the Motiwala Brother buttons termed "Liquid Enamel" (page 34), which were created with transparent enamels, not with the material liquid enamels.

Painting Materials

A few different materials can be used for painting on enamel, which are described below.

Finely Ground Grain Enamel

The smallest grains of all enamel can be used for painting. The most known in the button world would be "Grisaille White," also called "Blanc de Limoges." This is a specially formulated white used in the technique of Grisaille. Other uses of this form of painting material could not be ascertained by looking at a finished piece.

Overglazes and Underglazes

These materials are most often used to paint Émaux Peints buttons (button 104, plus buttons 105 and 106 on page 32). In the beginning, the usage was called Onglaze painting. The powder form was originally used in the seventeenth century, and the pre-mixed forms are modern developments. Some contain glass, and some do not. Those that do contain glass, though, will not provide a nicely even coat over bare metal as grain enamel does. Thus, these are never used directly on the metal substrate; both types need to be painted on a prefired enamel surface. Because they

---

FLUX VERSUS CLEAR ENAMEL TERMINOLOGY

All older texts will call clear transparent enamel "flux." Another older name is fondant. This is not to be confused with soldering flux, which is a totally different material. In this book, the term "flux" means clear transparent enamel (or transparent clear enamel). Why the two names? Some enameling manufacturers today are trying to change the name to "transparent clear," so enamel flux is not confused with soldering flux.

---

103. Cloisonné button using a yellow called Forsythia, which contains depleted uranium, by Karen L. Cohen.
104. Émaux Peints / Sgraffito woman with Paillons.

105. **106.**

cannot be used directly on the substrate, when they were first used in the seventeenth century, the technique was considered a painting technique *on* enamel rather than an enamel technique *with* enamel. Today the enameling world considers this an enamel technique and doesn't differentiate.

107.

After firing any of these with a flux topcoat, one cannot tell which type of material the enamelist used, unless the artist states this point, as in button 107.

Overglazes have more glass and less pigment than the Underglazes and fire glossy. Today there are a few companies that make these. One type is called China Paints, which are also used in porcelain painting. Other major brands are Ferro Sunshine Paints and the Thompson Enamel lead-free Overglaze Painting Colors (900E series).

There are two types of Underglazes—one that contains a small amount of glass and one that contains no glass; both fire matte (button 108). Underglazes do not spread (i.e., they remain stable) when fired under transparent enamels, and thus the term "under" is applied to them. These are best used for details, but many enamel painters today prefer them for all their painting. Because of their stability, they are also useful for emphasizing a Basse Taille design by using black Underglaze in the design's low spots (button 109). Both types of Underglazes can be mixed with powdered glass at the enamelist's bench, before use, and thus become Overglazes and fire glossy. If not mixed with glass, to become glossy, they are typically covered in a layer of flux.

Overglazes and Underglazes come in two forms:
- **Powder Form.** Both Overglazes and Underglazes come in powder form and must be mixed with a painting medium such as water or oil for brush application. In earlier times, oil was always used. Besides the mixing medium, Overglazes and Underglazes contain varying amounts of glass and mineral pigments (aka ceramic pigments, metal oxides, and/or stains). These are the same materials used to color glass and pottery glazes. Most of these are man-made inorganic minerals. The first known was "Egyptian Blue" from finely ground slag of smelted copper mixed with lime and heated.[2]
- **Pre-Mix.** Modern Overglazes and Underglazes come in pre-mixed form. The Overglazes come as watercolors or acrylics. The Underglazes come in pen, pencil, crayon, and pastel form. *Note:* Most of the Painting Materials fire flat (i.e., with no height or texture), but the modern acrylics do allow for some texture.

In general, the term used in the book for all Overglazes/Underglazes is "Painting Materials." The finely ground grain enamel is relevant in this book only to Grisaille.

Covering the top of a painting with flux (i.e., clear enamel) protects the Painting Materials, as they are very thin and could scratch even though they are fully fused to the underlying enamel layer. When applied to Underglazes, flux has the added effect of making them appear glossy. More information about topcoats can be found starting on page 68.

108.

109.

---

105. Antique Polychrome portrait with irregular openwork plated metal border.
106. Antique Polychrome portrait with twisted ribbon and floral plated metal border.
107. Realistic Émaux Peints squirrel, hand cut from copper sheet, using unleaded enamels and Underglazes with a flash fire flux topcoat, by Karen L. Cohen.
108. Antique Limoges-style head, primarily using transparent enamels and Overglazes but with Underglaze hair, with Liquid Gold accent and multiple enamel borders.
109. Realistic Basse Taille cougar with a henna design (by Judith C. Lanza), etched into copper, with black Underglaze in recesses and enameled with opalescent white, by Karen L. Cohen.

WHY SOME ENAMELS CRACK

Enamel Tech Talk

Painting Materials are finely ground powders that are mixed with a medium before application, normally with a brush. The medium can be water or oil. In earlier times, various oils were always used, but today water and/or water-based mediums are also popular. If using oil, the choice of oil may depend on the desired consistency (i.e., a thicker or more fluid mixture). In any case, before a piece is fired, the medium must be completely dried (i.e., all liquid removed). If it looks dried but is really not yet fully so, cracking of the paint can occur (button 110). This does not feel like a crack in the button, but one can visually see the separation of the color. There are other reasons the paint might form craze lines, such as drying the piece too quickly, using 18 or thicker gauge copper, the stress caused by the metal and enamel expanding and contracting at different rates (see the ETT "Effect of Firing Enamel," page 30), or differences in the composition and application of subsequent layers.

110

Consider button 111, which is a rare button with both matte and glossy aspects. It would have been difficult for the button to have been made matte by glass etchant, as the sections between the glossy areas probably would never be as clean as this example. Although it cannot be known how this was done, it seems reasonable that the enamel field was a matte enamel and most of the painting was done with Underglazes, thus firing matte. No flux topcoat (page 68) was fused on. However, the pink transparent enamel and the Liquid Gold (page 34) accent both fired glossy.

111

TYPES OF COLORS

There are three basic types of enamel colors: transparent, opaque, and opalescent. Each has its own characteristics described in this section. All three types are found in buttons, both antique and modern. One could say that transparent-opalescent-opaque enamel is a sliding scale of see-through. Transparents can be totally seen through; opalescents can be somewhat seen through; opaques cannot be seen through at all.

Transparent Enamels

As one would expect, transparent colors are those that can be seen through to the layer below. That layer can be another color (any type), foil or other embellishment, or the metal substrate. Thus, one way to "mix" a transparent color is to layer it over another color. Figure 2.3 shows test samples done by one enamelist using an opaque color as the base and various transparents on top. In this way, she could see what various combinations would look like before committing to using them in her pieces. Button 112 shows a button that uses an opaque lilac to block out the Basse Taille pattern of the substrate, with transparent blue and purple over it.

Transparent colors can be mixed together to get a new color *if* the original colors are close, as in two greens. However, if you try to mix a red and a blue, you will not get a purple, as in paint; instead, you will get a speckling effect.

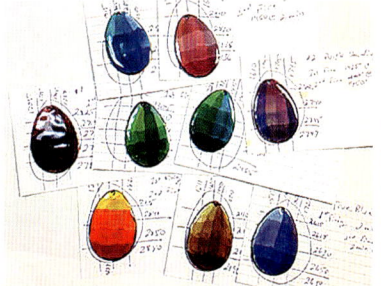

112

Figure 2.3
Tests of transparents overlaying opaque enamels by Pam East, enamelist and educator.

---

110. Antique Polychrome "faux textile" design, by André Keim. Notice the separations in the enamel paint.
111. Antique Émaux Peints, matte (Underglaze) and glossy, woman's head with Liquid Gold accents. Mounted in cut steel edged border frame.
112. Basse Taille / Cloisonné button. Opaque lilac was used as a first layer of the flower to block out the pattern with successive layers in transparent enamel shading, by Karen L. Cohen.

THE MATERIAL: ENAMEL

Another characteristic of transparent colors is that the metal beneath is reflected through the enamel. Thus, if you use, say, a blue transparent on silver, you get a true blue (silver reflects "white"), whereas, when used over gold, you'll get a green cast (gold reflects yellow and yellow + blue = green) (figure 2.4). In addition, the larger grains of transparents are clearer (i.e., more transparent) than the smallest grains (called the fines) of the same enamel. Thus, when working in certain techniques, the enamelist will "grade sift" out the smaller grains. Being clearer allows for a more brilliant reflection from the metal beneath.

Figure 2.4 Color tab for Thompson Enamel color #2530 transparent Water Blue, which shows the color over various layers: directly on copper, over flux, over white, over silver foil, and over gold foil.

The clarity characteristic is easily demonstrated in the Motiwala Brothers (page 100) Basse Taille on silver buttons (button 113). The button world calls these "Liquid Enamel" because they look fluid. The reason they look fluid is because of the beauty of the engraved silver reflecting though the transparent enamel. Any enameled piece with engraving (by hand or engine turned for Guilloché—as opposed to flat metal—will always be brighter because the engraving allows the light to reflect at different angles, thus making the enamel more brilliant. The brilliancy of transparent colors on silver is the reason I started enameling in the first place.

Another place where this reflection is apparent is in the Limoges-style (page 56) of Émaux Peints buttons (button 114). In these cases, the "metal" that is being reflected is foil, not the metal substrate of the button.

One more general characteristic of transparents is that the more layers of the same color, the deeper the color gets. Thus, an enamelist can shade with the same transparent color by having more layers of that color (button 16, page 4). However, each layer must be thin; otherwise, the enamel gets cloudy (button 115).

The warm transparent colors (like red and orange) and opalescent white usually turn brownish when fused directly to silver; this result is a chemical reaction (button 116). Thus, not all transparent colors look good directly on metal, as is the case with many colors directly on copper. To fix this issue, a layer of flux is fused on first. In addition, the various fluxes all look different over copper, as shown in figure 2.5. Button 117 shows a button with flux as the field on copper (also see button 262, page 66).

Figure 2.5 Three fluxes fired directly on copper. Note the golden color in the 2015 sample—this enamel includes a small amount of iron oxide (which adds a slight tint of yellow) but is still considered a clear.

113. Basse Taille on silver, by Motiwala Brothers (frequently called Liquid Enamel).
114. Antique Limoges-style Émaux Peints.
115. Design of small lumps of enamel covered in too thick a layer of clear that fired cloudy, by Herman Lowenstein.
116. Champlevé / Basse Taille, by G. E. Walton. The orange on this button has the look of being directly on the silver and thus turning brownish, not a clear bright orange.
117. Realistic artist palette with flux field, by Janet White.

Opaque Enamels

As expected, opaque enamels cannot be seen through and reflect no light bouncing off the metal. Because of this characteristic, one use of these materials is to block something in a previous layer (button 112, page 33). They can be blended side by side with another color (button 118). However, unlike transparent enamels, they cannot be mixed to form a new solid color. Mixing two or more opaque enamels will always produce a speckled effect. This might be the look the artist wanted (buttons 119 and 120) or used to represent stone, rock, or sand. It is also useful as the base for objects such as pears (button 121), which have a speckled look.

Opalescent Enamels

Opalescent enamels are semitransparent. They reflect some light, but not all. Thus, what is underneath an opalescent enamel may be visible (buttons 122 and 123) but will not be as bright as transparent enamel. Think of a pearl, which appears to be all one color but somehow seems to have depth or a glow to it. Opalescents are made of two immiscible glasses (two that don't mix, as oil and water)—one being the matrix and the other distributed as droplet shapes that, when smaller than the wavelength of light, form the opalescent (glowing) effect. Opalescent enamels can be used to produce a "Faux Opal" in enamel (page 72). This material is different from opalescent glass and should not be compared with it.

Opalescent colors also work well in Plique-à-jour, as the color is more visible without light behind it (button 124); yet, with light behind, the color will become more brilliant. Opalescent enamels have been mentioned in older enameling books, so they are not new, but not many buttons seem to have them (button 125). Today opalescent white is used for the field or underpainting for enamel painting, especially for portraits. Pâte (page 57) enamel was described as a translucent enamel,[3] not opalescent. However, both Pâte and opalescent white (button 126) shared the characteristic of adding vitality to skin tones. And neither was used directly on the substrate; Pâte was used over opaque white, and opalescent white is used over flux.

118. Antique Champlevé shaded opaque enamel winged dragon with multiple outer borders.
119. Antique Champlevé with speckled green and white enamel with curvilinear circle segment border. The outer border looks like two greens and white, possibly in equal proportions, but the center looks like dark green and small white lumps in unequal proportions.
120. Antique Speckled enamel Champlevé outer border and edge border of cut steels. Back shows pressed design. The mixture of black to white enamel is probably 1:1.
121. Silver Cloisonné focal pear with fine silver balls, by Karen L. Cohen. The base enamel of the pear was enameled with a mixture of opaque and transparent enamels to make it look mottled.
122. Cloisonné butterfly with opalescent white backdrop over other colors that show through slightly, using gold mica luster on the white with fine silver balls and Encrustations on the black dots, by Karen L. Cohen.
123. Antique Basse Taille / Polychrome painting with wide outer border featuring gold Paillons and Liquid Silver; the center has an underpainting of white opalescent enamel that partially covers the Basse Taille.
124. Plique-à-jour button with opalescent enamels, by Diane Echnoz Almeyda.
125. Antique Champlevé Polychrome with opalescent pink enamel in the hat and an ornate outer frame border.
126. Limoges-style / Guilloché (moiré pattern) with opalescent white used as an underpainting for the woman with Encrustations in her headdress, by Diana Wieler.

CHEMISTRY OF ENAMEL

There is a lot of chemistry involved in the process of enameling. One can work for many years creating beautiful pieces, having learned only a fraction of the information available on this topic. However, knowing at least some of the chemistry allows enamelists to figure out problems they might be having or how to combine various enamels to accomplish something they want. I will not go over all the ins and outs of this topic, but three concepts are important to buttons as described in this section.

Counter Enamel

Because of the coefficient of expansion (COE) of the substrate metal and the enamel on it, the two materials cool at different rates. Because the COE of each is not the same, the enamel can pop off the piece if the correct sized materials are not used. Up until the turn of the sixteenth century, thicker metal was always used because the concept of counter enamel was not known. But at the turn of the century, someone figured out that thin metal could be used if enamel was also put on the back of the piece. This enamel on the back is called "counter enamel" and is used to counterbalance the stresses of cooling so that the enamel stays in place. The general rule is that the counter enamel should be the same thickness as the enamel on the front. The type of enamel used for counter enamel should be compatible (close fusion flow, COE, and softening point) with the enamel on the front.

One might ask when the counter enamel should be added. I can only speak for myself as an enamelist: I usually counter enamel as the first step. But there are times when I'll counter enamel at the end of a piece. The decision is based on how the piece will be held in the kiln for firing. For example, if I am using the Scrolling technique (page 61), which is a type of marbling while the piece is in the kiln, I want the piece to be flat on the firing screen to give it maximum support. That requires no counter enamel because any enamel touching the firing screen would stick to the screen. Another time I add counter enamel at the end is when I'm working on a bowl-shaped form and I'm decorating the inside of the bowl. In this case, I'll want to have the inside facing up. If it was already counter enameled, then the stilting of the piece would put trivet marks on the counter enamel. Without the counter enamel, the bowl could just sit on the firing screen. When done enameling the inside, I can counter enamel and fire it upside down, thus eliminating trivet marks.

Sometimes "scrap" enamel is used for counter enamel. This is a mixture of enamels that otherwise would have been discarded. Typically, it has a speckled appearance (button 127), as previously described when mixing opaque enamels together. But if the back will show, many make the counter enamel look pretty. Some older buttons have incredibly beautiful, even pictorial, counter enamel (button set 128).

COUNTER VERSUS COUNTER ENAMEL TERMINOLOGY

A button that is rare or unusual is sometimes given an extra point in National Button Society (NBS) competition. This point is called a counter. This form of the word "counter" should not be confused with the term "counter enamel," which is enamel on the back of a piece used to stabilize the stresses on the enamel and metal during the cooling process. When meaning the latter, it will always be labeled as "counter enamel."

127. Counter enamel using scrap enamel with a glued-on shank.
128. Antique Polychrome buttons; backs show unusual mounting and counter enamel.

Soft versus Medium versus Hard Fusing Enamels

A soft enamel fuses before a medium one and a medium one before a hard one, being on a continuous scale. This is important to know in order to avoid certain chemical reactions. Hard enamels should be fused under soft ones, if layering, and fired first in different areas of the same piece. One modern enameling technique, Pull-through (page 64) (buttons 129 and 130), does this the opposite way (soft under hard enamel). Of course, this method was first considered an error, but it is now used as a technique.

The softening temperature of an enamel is not its firing temperature—just the temperature at which it begins to soften. This measurable temperature and its fusion flow number (a number that indicates flow or how viscous or non-viscous an enamel is at a given time and temperature firing) can be used to determine whether an enamel would be considered soft, medium, or hard. A high softening temperature and a low fusion flow number would be considered hard. A low softening temperature and a high fusion flow number would be considered a soft enamel, and medium is between the two. This point is very technical but is important for most enamelists to understand when working on complex pieces.

Another place this issue comes into play is when a piece of glass formed on its own (e.g., molded or lampworked) is fused onto an enamel piece (button 130). The separate piece of glass must be "harder" than the enamel in order not to lose shape when it's fused to the enamel. To the untrained eye, this material might be considered an enamel buildup like an Encrustation, but there are clear signs of the differences. For more information, see the sidebar "Enamel Buildup or Glass Fused onto Enamel?" on page 71.

Firescale

Firescale occurs only on copper and its alloys, such as brass. It happens because the copper oxide that is in the metal turns reddish or black when it is heated. This effect cannot be seen under opaque enamels but is a consideration when using transparents. In either case, though, the edges of the enamel might show firescale. However, firescale started being used as a design element in the 1950s by metalsmith Oppi Untracht.[4]

The first firing of a transparent color on copper must be done a certain way so that the copper oxide is taken into the solution of the enamel. This is a mouthful but means that the firing has to clear the oxide by drawing it into the enamel. Figure 2.6 shows the same piece fired three times to show various stages from being underfired to being completely fired. Obviously, if you want to put a pretty color (say, green) over the first underfired piece on the left, the green will have the red-brown base color show through it, and you will not see the color you may have wanted. This is not an issue of right or wrong; it is more about control and what you are trying to achieve. If a transparent color is not cleared in the first or second firing, it may not ever fire to completion, with the remainder of firescale showing randomly in some areas. In many cases, underfired clear and transparent colors directly on copper are considered errors and should be avoided.

Totaly Underfired   Partially Underfired   Fully Fired

Figure 2.6 Three firings of the same piece with clear transparent enamel on copper. Notice that the oxide eventually gets cleared out.

Consider button 131. The face shows multiple spots of reddish firescale. One could say it works in this instance because they could be birthmarks (or am I stretching this point?).

Firescale will also form on any exposed metal that is not enameled. Button 132 was made by pressing very thin brass. This process thins the metal at the intersection of the high and low points. When enameling is completed,

---

129. Pull-through on copper with fine silver twisted wires and balls and flower wafers, by Karen L. Cohen.
130. Pull-through on Palmach shaped copper with millefiori, fine silver balls and twisted wire, and gold mica luster, by Karen L. Cohen. The millefiori, which is harder glass than enamel, is fused before other elements that fuse faster.
131. Champlevé plaquette over square openwork filigree metal with enamel finished corners. Note firescale!
132. Antique Champlevé domed (contour) button with inner border of cut steels and outer enamel border of laurel leaves. Detail shows a black firescale edge around the high points of metal.

at the intersection of the enamel and the high point, there is a very thin line of black—this is firescale on the metal (see detail of button 132). Louis-Eliè Millenet says, "The pickling [an acid bath] of a champlevé article requires careful attention, as any trace of oxidation [firescale] left . . . would sully the purity of the enamels, particularly light shades, producing an unpleasant dark line around the edges of all the spaces."[5] However, in the case of this button, I like the black line, as it helps outline the images. Another button to view is button 223 (page 58). Look around the Faux Opals on the border—all the black you see is firescale.

METAL SUBSTRATES

In general, enamel forms a chemical bond with its metal substrate. However, in years gone by, alloys were sometimes used that required a mechanical bond between the metal and the enamel. To aid in this process, the metal was roughed up. Today, with the use of purer metals, that step is not necessary. In fact, many enamelists want their metal to be as brightly polished as possible when using transparent enamels. That being said, not all metals can be enameled successfully, even with a mechanical bond. This section describes appropriate metals for enameling.

Metals Compatible with Enamel

A few types of metal can be used for enameling, but the most popular ones used in modern times are copper (and some of its alloys), silver (both fine and sterling), and karat gold. However, gilding metal (95 percent copper, 5 percent zinc), low-carbon steel (carbon content 0.02–0.04 percent), aluminum, and stainless steel (400 series) can also be used. The basic metals of copper, silver, and gold all use the same formulation of enamel (sometimes called jewelry enamel, previously referred to as grain enamel), whereas other metals, such as aluminum and steel, might need different formulations. In older texts (ca. 1911), you may find pure metals, which today we call fine silver and fine gold, referred to as "virgin" metals.

Many art enamelists today use low-carbon steel as a substrate for enameling. Of course, steel has been used commercially for many years for such items as signage, appliances, and more. The first coat of enamel on steel is specially formulated to chemically bond with the steel and is called ground coat. After the ground coat, other appropriate enamels can be used. However, on stainless steel, a mechanical bond with liquid enamel can be made by first roughing up the metal surface.

Brass was used extensively in older enamel buttons that were pressed into designs for Champlevé. Brass is an alloy of copper and zinc. Zinc is problematic in enameling, as it causes enamel to pit and chip without being able to be repaired. A small amount of zinc is useable, but not more than roughly 5 percent. It stands to reason that the craftspeople of the day made sure that their brass alloy would allow fusion with enamels even if they had to develop a special alloy just for this purpose (button 133). *Note:* A high-expansion enamel could be formulated for enameling brass. However, most enamels sold to artists today will not work with brass and will pop off after cooling.

A modern form of metal is called "metal clay" (button 134; button 432, page 96). This is not clay but a material composed of powdered metal (silver, copper, gold, or bronze) and a binder. It is malleable and can be manipulated like clay (e.g., hand formed, molded, extruded, etc.), but, once fired (a process called sintering), the binder burns out and the resulting material is all metal. The detail of the design remains after sintering, but the piece gets smaller, depending on the metal clay used (they all reduce in size differently). This is a great way to work with metal even if the enamelist is not a traditional metalsmith.

133

134

133. Antique Art Nouveaux Champlevé / Émaux Peints button. Notice the pressed design showing on back.
134. Basse Taille on silver clay, by Joy Funnell.

FINE SILVER VERSUS STERLING SILVER

Although both fine silver and sterling can be used for enameling, there is a difference between them. Fine silver is as pure as you can get (it's labeled .999). Sterling is an alloy made with copper (it's labeled .925) to give it strength and is thus better for silver jewelry like ring shanks. In the United States today, most enamelists using silver will use fine silver, whereas in England they mostly use sterling or another silver alloy.

The .925 mark on sterling silver indicates that a piece is 925 parts pure silver and 75 parts copper. Silversmiths in England and France began stamping sterling silver objects with this purity indicator in the fourteenth century. The mark became a requirement in the United States in 1906.

Because of the copper content in sterling, for enamel to result in the transparent color normally associated with bright silver, the artist must "depletion gild" the sterling, which means preparing a layer of fine silver on the surface. This task is accomplished by a repeated heating/pickling/brass brushing process. Another method involves nitric acid baths. But in either case, the enamel color you use is important. Some enamelists prefer to stay with the transparent cool colors on sterling to eliminate any adverse reactions the warm colors might have.

Stop Warping

Flat metal frequently warps in the kiln. To avoid this outcome, the metal may be made rigid by either doming or turning the edges inward toward the front or the back. This was done in earlier times (and today as well) and is why many enamel buttons are dome shaped. In addition, to inhibit warping, counter enamel is used.

Buttons as Enamelware 3

Enamel buttons are glorious to behold and often intricate enough to invite study. Because enamels are such a specialty art form and new developments are always occurring, studying enamel buttons provides for what contemporary enamelist Jean Vormelker calls "the triple-L"—Life Long Learning. Even for longtime enamelists, there is always more to learn. The previous chapters of this book dealt with the history, the materials, and the process itself. This chapter will provide details about enamel techniques and embellishments on buttons and how you can distinguish these attributes. The information in this chapter is relevant to all buttons with enamel, whether they are classed as National Button Society (NBS) enamel buttons or not. The information is also relevant to other types of enamelware such as boxes or jewelry.

It's important to point out that in the NBS button-collecting world, not all metal buttons with enamel on them are classed as enamel buttons. This is important to understand so that proper classification can be made. Enamel is the only distinct button material in the NBS classification system that is made from two component materials—glass and metal—that, when fused together, form a distinctive new material that we call enamel.

Enamel is also the only NBS material that can appear in three forms. It can be considered a material (of the button itself), or it may be viewed merely as a Decorative Finish (DF), and, lastly, it is sometimes used as an Other Material Embellishment (OME). Barbara Barrans explains it like this: "In the button world, buttons are classified according to their 'base material.' Thus, if the main body of the button is made of enameled metal, it is, by definition, an *enamel button*. Enamel can also be used to enhance a button in two different ways. A small amount of enameling may be added to a *metal button* to decorate it, like paint. In this case, the enamel is not the dominant element or focus of the design. Used in this way, the enamel becomes a DF on a metal button. A common application is enameled borders [button 501 in appendix A].

"Enamel may also be used as an OME on other base material buttons. In rare cases, an enameled plaquette can be mechanically attached to a button of a different base material. Because the base material is what determines material classification, that button is not classified as an enamel. If the plaquette is attached to a *non-metal base button*, it is strictly viewed as OME. An enamel plaquette attached to a casein button is still a casein button [button 496 in appendix A]."[1]

Like other materials, the shank may be attached directly to the enameled metal piece, or an enamel plaquette might be set into a separate metal mounting. Both constructions are enamel buttons by definition. Two main requirements for determining what is "an NBS enamel button," as defined by the *Blue Book* classification (BB), are as follows: (1) the enamel must be the *focus* of the design *and* (2) the *shank* must be attached to the enameled metal base (or its metal mounting). Thus, if an enamel plaquette is the focus and mounted in/on a *metal base*, that button is classified as an NBS enamel button.

All buttons shown in the chapters of this book are NBS enamel buttons, whereas appendix A shows buttons that include enamel but are not classed as NBS enamel buttons.

Be aware that some buttons were created to look like enamel, or might be called enamel, when they aren't. I call this group of buttons "Enamel Look-alikes." These are discussed, with button examples, in appendix B. Included is Cold Plastic Enamel (CPE) and how to tell it from real vitreous enamel.

There are terms used in enameling that are used differently in the button world. Since the focus of this book is on enamel buttons as collectibles, I have endeavored to use terms as would be most familiar to a collector (rather than an enamelist). For clarity for both enamelists and collectors, here is a list of the meanings of terms used in this book:

- Instead of *"enamel background,"* I will use *"enamel field"* to refer to the enamel covering the substrate on which a design may be placed. This is so collectors will not be confused by "Enamel Background buttons" (page 83).
- Instead of *"finish,"* I will use *"topcoat"* to refer to how the top of the enamel is completed.
- Instead of *"pierced,"* I will use *"non-filigree"* to refer to types of Plique-à-jour whose framework is not Filigree. Traditionally, these are called "pierced" Plique-à-jour, even when methods other than metal piercing are used, such as casting, computer-aided design work, and more. However, in the button world, "pierced" and "openwork" are synonymous and refer to the actual openings in the button itself—whereas, in enameling, "Pierced Plique-à-jour" refers to any Non-filigree Plique-à-jour. Note that some Pliques do have openwork as part of their design.
- Instead of *"Silver Overlay,"* I use *"Silver Deposit,"* as defined on page 80.

> This chapter is organized by how I, as an enamelist, view the various aspects of enamel buttons. That is, it is my view of what is a technique versus what is an embellishment. This organization may not reflect the BB; thus, when competing, the collector should go by the most current BB. There are other aspects of enamel buttons, such as openwork and borders, that are about the button, not the enamel. I address these in the section below called "Other Characteristics of Enamel Buttons." Appendix F organizes a list of all characteristics so the collector will have one checklist that can be used for treasure hunting enamel buttons.

WHAT TO BUY

In the spirit of button collecting, always buy what you love. When buying for competition, this rule might be compromised by buying what you need to fill a specific category. However, the checklist in appendix F can also be used for collecting to get "one of each type" of button available.

PERSPECTIVE AFFECTING FOCUS

Please realize that the focus of a button relies on the perspective of the viewer. As an enamelist, I see the enamel before I see anything else on the button. This perspective sometimes creates issues about recognizing when something is not classified as an NBS enamel button. More about this topic can be found in the December 2011 *NBB* article "Focus Pocus," by Barbara Barrans.[2] Button 135 is an example in which the focus is split between the glass center and the enameled metal petals surrounding it. In the button world, this is considered a "combined material" button. In competition, the entrant would have to decide whether to use it as an enamel button with glass OME or a glass button mounted in metal with an enamel border. A button like this one could be successfully used either way, as judges typically give BOD (benefit of the doubt) whenever reasonable and this button exhibits qualities of both fairly equally.

135. Antique multiple material contour button of glass mounted in metal bordered with a double row of Basse Taille enameled petals.

TECHNIQUES

In loose terms, the button world "construction" is equivalent to the enamel world "technique." There is a wide variety of enameling techniques, some centuries old and some modern. A few of the modern techniques were known in earlier times but considered errors and thus avoided. Other modern examples were not known because they use materials that were developed since the mid-twentieth century. The late modern enamelist Bill Helwig said that if you can repeat the same error three times, you have come up with a new technique. And so new techniques are always being developed. The following pages describe techniques found in buttons or those that probably will be in the future—they are in alphabetical order. Note that more techniques exist, and thus this list is not exhaustive, but I've included those that are represented in buttons or expect to be in the near future.

Some of the techniques have recognizable design styles that are listed with each major category so the collector can recognize the similarities and differences. "Design style" has three meanings: pieces created in a certain location such as Canton Émaux Peints; a look achieved by using particular materials such as Limoges-style Émaux Peints; or a variation of the technique such as Guilloché, which is a specialized form of Basse Taille. I do not include individual studio artist styles, as these are shown in chapter 4, "Enamel Button Artists, Producers, and Purveyors."

Basse Taille (bäs tä' ya)

The term "*Basse Taille*" is French for "low cut," which means enamel in low relief. The term "*En Basse Taille*" can also be used. This was an early technique used by the end of the fifteenth century (page 4). The main concept of this technique is that the metal *substrate* is texturized, which can be seen through the transparent enamel covering it. However, opaque and opalescent enamels can also be used in parts of a piece. If any area of another technique has a texturized substrate, such as in a Champlevé (button 136) or Cloisonné, the button would be considered a combination of Basse Taille and the other technique.

You might ask whether it matters how the substrate texture is achieved. The answer is: It doesn't! There are many ways to achieve a design in metal, including chased, engraved, repoussé, engine turned (Guilloché), roll printed, etched, hammered, stamped, and cast (button 137). Read more about roll printing below.

You might ask whether the design makes a difference. It doesn't! Any texturized metal substrate denotes Basse Taille, whether it is a set of lines (button 136) or a curvilinear pattern (button 138). Button 139 shows a contour button that is covered in enamel, which is also considered Basse Taille.

ROLL PRINTING

Roll printing is done with a rolling mill (figure 3.1) whose purpose is to compress metal into a thinner and more uniform shape or to impress a pattern onto the metal. There are also different sets of rollers for rolling mills that allow wire to be drawn into shape, like from round to square. When impressing a pattern onto metal, almost any substance can be used. Examples are prepurchased texturized metal, etched metal, thick paper with a design cut out of it, and rice paper that has a texture. Some of these can be reused, but some, like the paper, cannot.

Figure 3.1 Rolling mill used to compress metal or press a pattern into sheet metal; reprinted from my book *The Art of Fine Enameling* (2nd ed., 2019).

---

136. Antique Basse Taille / Champlevé on silver with central garnet and steel ball OMEs.
137. Antique Basse Taille / Champlevé cast realistic Tudor Rose, by John Millward Banks, Birmingham, 1907.
138. Antique Basse Taille with curvilinear pattern.
139. Antique Chinese silver Basse Taille flower with back marking showing made in China.

METHODS SIMILAR TO ENGINE TURNING

At least three methods exist that can be confused with engine turning. These are described here.
1. Before engine-turning machines were invented, metalsmiths used hand engravers to cut designs into metal. The method was called **Bright Cutting**, which is characterized by repeated patterns. This was also done in pewter, and Bright Cut Pewter buttons are available.
2. **Flinking** (*Flinqué* in French) is also hand engraving and was done in the same era as engine turning. Flinking was used when the shape of the piece caused the use of the engine-turning machine to be too expensive or very difficult to do. However, Flinking is not as uniform as engine turning.[3]
3. It is possible to have a metal plate with a Guilloché pattern on it, which can be pressed into sheet metal using a rolling machine or equivalent. However, when enameled, although the result looks like Guilloché, it will not show as brilliant a reflection as the real thing. In enameling, this is not considered Guilloché—just Basse Taille. So, how can you tell the difference? The untrained eye might not be able to. However, this method is modern, so only new buttons might be done this way, and ideally the artist will label them as such.

Design Styles of Basse Taille

Basse Taille sur Fond Reservé. This little-known style is a combination of Basse Taille and Champlevé, originally done by Renaissance goldsmiths. Designs such as animals, birds, and arabesques were impressed into thin metal leaving a reserve of metal left at the original level. Contemporary enamelist Michele Raney (page 103) uses this technique (button 140).

Guilloché (gee yoh shay). This is a specialized form of Basse Taille. The word "*Guilloché*" is French for "engine turning," which is how the texture is applied to the metal. Engine turning is the mechanical cutting of lines on material to create a design and was first used on metal in the eighteenth century. Because the pattern is engraved with a sharp tool and on an angle, the reflection of light through the transparent enamel on top is enhanced, and its brilliance can be seen as the piece is moved from side to side. This is how Fabergé got the gorgeous patterns on his eggs and frames. Because of the process, which is hand initiated and slow to complete, purchasing engine-turned metal (that which is not yet enameled) is quite expensive, and thus the resulting Guilloché will also be expensive. In addition to the buttons in this section (buttons 141, 142, and 143), you will find many Guilloché buttons throughout this book. For more information on engine-turning machines, see the ETT "Engine-Turning Machines for Guilloché" (page 44).

Japanese Silver Basse Taille. The Japanese worked in a variety of enamel techniques. One was Basse Taille on silver (buttons 144 and 145, page 45). As these are all silver enamelware, they can be described as Gin-jippō (appendix E). These may be hard to differentiate from Gin-bari (page 60), which is done on embossed foil.

---

140. Basse Taille sur Fond Reservé on silver, by Michele Raney.
141. Antique Guilloché enamel with complex gold Paillons and a cross-wrapped, ribbed inner border of silver and a single amethyst set in a silver bezel. Tig Lichty, engine turner, says there is no official name of this Guilloché pattern, but he calls it "Sunray2x with a Barleycorn reverse" (S2B).
142. Antique Guilloché (moiré pattern) enamel on silver with opaque Émaux Peints floral design, by Heinrich Levinger.
143. Guilloché (spiral pattern) button with gold foil seahorses and fine silver twisted wire and balls, by Karen L. Cohen.
144. Japanese silver Basse Taille, with fish roe design, that looks similar to Gin-bari.

Enamel Tech Talk: ENGINE-TURNING MACHINES FOR GUILLOCHÉ

There are three forms of engine-turning machines used for enameling: the straight-line engine (creates patterns in a line—see figures 3.2 and 3.3 for example patterns), the rose engine (creates patterns radiating from a central point—see figure 3.4 for example patterns and figure 3.5 for the machine setup), and the brocade machine (can create multiple patterns—see figure 3.6 for an example pattern). Most Guilloché buttons have rose engine designs, but ones with straight-line designs can be found (button 348, page 83).

According to Tig Lichty, an engine turner currently residing in Oregon, "Brocade work is a somewhat contentious form of Engine Turning and receives its name from the finely engraved background pattern that resembles the finest of brocaded lace. It is an engraving method that follows a pattern much like Rose (round) and Straight-Line Engine Turning and, in fact, uses a type of rosette to create the brocaded background pattern. Rather than a 2-D pattern, it follows a 3-D pattern and transfers the design to the work through a pantograph-like system. The major contention of Brocade work is that the cutter transitions in and out of the engraving to create the design while the Rose Engine and Straight-Line Engine moves the cutter from left to right and back again to create patterns. Because of the Brocade Engine's ability to follow multiple patterns and a rosette simultaneously it can potentially create much more intricate patterns than either Straight-Line or Rose Engines."[4]

There was a fourth form of engine-turning machine, the geometric lathe, invented in the nineteenth century. However, because so few were made, these have never been used by enamelists.

Engine-turning machines are no longer manufactured. Thus, an artisan wanting one will have to either purchase one from a retiring artisan or build their own. Most engine turners will not create these metal designs for others, but there are a few today who do, which is lucky for modern enamelists.

Figure 3.4 Rose engine design examples, by engine turner William Brinker.

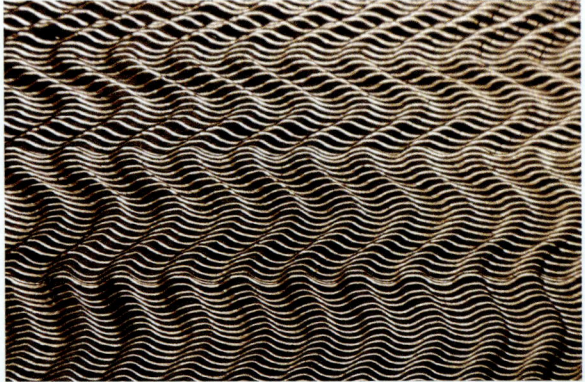

Figure 3.2 Straight-line engine design of a Chevron pattern (in the center), by engine turner Tig Lichty.

Figure 3.5 Rose engine set up, by engine turner William Brinker; from the book *The Art of Fine Enameling* (2nd ed., 2019) by Karen L. Cohen.

Figure 3.6 Brocade engine design named *La Danse de Salomé*, by engine turner Tig Lichty. Button 398, page 89, is a finished button using this pattern.

Figure 3.3 Straight-line engine design of a moiré pattern, by engine turner Tig Lichty. This is the most popular pattern of Guilloché.

145

In general, in the Basse Taille buttons, the relief work is higher than Gin-bari, and the metal, being silver, does have a different look than the silver foil of Gin-bari. Experience will help the collector recognize the difference.

Motiwala Brothers "Liquid Enamel."
As mentioned in the section on Motiwala Brothers buttons (page 100), their buttons called "Liquid Enamel" are actually silver Basse Taille with hand engraving (button 146).

146

Champlevé (shän lǝvā')

French for "raised field" or "raised plain," Champlevé is a technique in which enamel is inlaid into depressions in the metal. First done in the third century CE by the Celts decorating their shields, this technique has been one of the favorite forms of enameling. It is one of the three forms of enameling that always leaves metal exposed without enamel (the other two are Cloisonné and Plique-à-jour). As with most techniques, any type of enamel (transparent, opaque, or opalescent) can be used in Champlevé (button 147). If one or more depressions have a texturized base, then the piece is both Champlevé and Basse Taille (button 136, page 42).

You might ask whether the method of forming a depression makes a difference in the piece being called "Champlevé." It does not! An abundance of antique Champlevé buttons were made with a die or stamp; on some you can see the stamping on the back (button 148). However, many other methods exist, such as—but not limited to—engraving, etching, casting (button 149), hammering, and pierced and soldered metal (see the ETT "Pierced and Soldered Champlevé" for more information).

147

148

149

PIERCED AND SOLDERED CHAMPLEVÉ

Pierced and soldered is a metalsmithing technique in which two pieces of metal are used. The top layer has a design cut out of it (called piercing) and is then "sweat soldered" to the bottom layer. The two together thus form a solid piece with depressions for enameling Champlevé.

To pierce a metal design, a drawing of the design is first attached to the metal (usually with glue). Where the design needs to be cut out, a hole is drilled into the space to allow a jeweler's saw blade to be inserted; thus, a cut line from the edge need not be made. When the space is finished being sawed out, the blade is removed and inserted into the next hole. This process is repeated until the design is completed, at which time it will be filed and finished.

Sweat soldering involves flowing solder all over the reverse side of the top layer and then soldering it to the bottom layer. If the piece will be enameled, at least hard solder must be used. If the piece will be enameled and uses sterling silver, then, when using 22 gauge for the top and 18 gauge for the bottom, counter enamel is not needed. Surprisingly, if fine silver is used, the piece must still be counter enameled to stop cracking.

---

145. Japanese silver Basse Taille, with fish roe design, that looks similar to Gin-bari.
146. Basse Taille on silver, by Motiwala Brothers (frequently called Liquid Enamel).
147. Antique openwork Champlevé with rococo border.
148. Antique Champlevé with cut steel, showing stamped back.
149. Antique silver Champlevé (frequently called Japanese Enamel on Silver button).

FRAMED CHAMPLEVÉ

There are many cast, die-stuck, or stamped buttons that have a central depression inside a metal frame (i.e., a border) (button 150; button 517, page 113; and button 105, page 32). Technically, in the enamel world, these pieces would be called Champlevé, regardless of how the central depression is enameled. However, these do not represent the fullest expression of the technique. Good examples of Champlevé are designs that include raised metal between sections of enamel (button 147, page 45, and button 148, page 45).

I will call the examples with a single central depression "Framed Champlevé" to distinguish them from buttons with more detailed interior Champlevé design noted as good examples above. However, these Framed Champlevé buttons are perfectly wonderful to collect for the central design—for example, button 150 is a Grisaille button.

Note: Because there are so many of them and this technique is not an important part of studying the button, I have left this point out of captions.

CHAMPLEVÉ MASQUERADING AS CLOISONNÉ

At times it's difficult to tell the difference between Champlevé and Cloisonné. Sometimes the design could be called "the poor man's Cloisonné" because the exposed metal was designed to resemble wires by appearing to be the same thickness. However, there is a way to tell the difference. I wrote about this subject in an article titled "Champlevé Masquerading as Cloisonné," which appeared in the May 2021 issue of the Western Regional Button Association (WRBA) journal *Territorial News*,[5] but more information is provided here.

Six things to consider:
1. Look where the metal "wires" attach to each other: If there is a seam (which with wires there would have to be), then it's Cloisonné. However, if there are no seams, it's Champlevé. There is one caveat to this point: In earlier times, wires for Cloisonné were soldered on, and it's possible that the solder filled in the seam so that, after grinding and polishing, it looks like there was no seam. Button 171 (page 49) is an example of wire seams that have been filled in with solder—look at the bird's beak.

    Consider buttons 151 and 152. In button 151, although the lines in the butterfly wings don't touch (so it could be wire), the lines in the flower show no seams. But in button 152 the seams, where the wires abut to either themselves or the next element of the design, are clearly visible.
2. This method is not definitive but is usually the case—wires in a Cloisonné are typically very thin (0.005–0.010 inches), but metal lines in a Champlevé are usually not this thin. Buttons 151 and 152 show this quality as well.
3. Look for two of the same buttons. Cloisonné by definition is a hand fabrication technique, but Champlevé can be done by hand or by mechanical means (for example, as in casting or die striking). That is, each Cloisonné piece is done by hand, but Champlevé pieces can be reproduced mechanically. If looking at two of the same design, if the metal work (not the enamel color) is exactly the same, it has to be Champlevé.

---

150. Antique green Grisaille head with plated metal rococo border.
151. Champlevé enameled button.
152. Cloisonné enameled button using leaded and unleaded enamels, with fine silver substrate and wires, using fine silver and gold foils with fine silver balls and twisted wire, by Karen L. Cohen.

CHAMPLEVÉ MASQUERADING AS CLOISONNÉ *(Continued from page 46)*

4. Look for how the "wires" are used. Consider button 153. Look at the jar—it has wires that form the outline of the base with two vertical lines that go up to the lid. But there is also a wire that goes across these two verticals. In a Cloisonné, it is necessary to have that piece be a separate wire, as one wire cannot go in two directions at the same time. But in a Champlevé, this most likely would be a set of solid lines. Thus, this button is clearly Cloisonné. One way to figure this question out is thinking about the puzzle of One Line One Stroke—that is, can you trace the lines in a diagram, never lifting the pencil, and without going over any line twice? If you can't, then wires could not be bent to form this figure and the piece has to be Champlevé.

5. Look for short straight lines of metal. If so, the piece is most likely Champlevé. Remember that Cloisonné is a hand technique and the wires are ribbons—thin rectangular wire standing on edge. Think about this: How could a thin straight wire stand on edge without falling over? There are ways to get wire in a straight line in Cloisonné (advanced technique), but not when it is between two other lines (button 154).

6. Look at the line thicknesses (button 155). If any one line is both thin and thick, most likely it is not Cloisonné. The only way to get a wire to be multiple thicknesses is by hammering or reshaping it. Although this is done by some contemporary enamelists, there is no evidence of older Cloisonné buttons having this characteristic. In addition, this button's metalwork shows no seams. Thus, it is Champlevé.

Design Styles of Champlevé

Deccan. The central southern India city of Deccan (also spelled Dekkan) was known for its fine enamel work on gold, primarily for the court of the Nizams in Hyderabad. With Indian independence in 1947, a new craft was established with Deccan buttons. Some buttons were made with no enamel and some with paint decoration. Many silver and enamel buttons were characterized by floral patterns (button 494, in appendix A, page 108), which are frequently metal buttons with enamel DF. However, many Deccan NBS enamel buttons exist, like buttons 15 (page 4), 156, and 157.

Jaipur. The capital of the Indian state of Rajasthan is Jaipur, the largest city in the state. Its previous name was Jeypore. Jaipur is known for its gold enamel Champlevé jewelry with vivid red enamel. Some buttons were made there, but these are scarce (button 158).

---

153. Antique Cloisonné ginger jar with much pitting.
154. Antique Champlevé / Basse Taille using both transparent and opaque enamels.
155. Antique matte finish Champlevé / Émaux Peints on plated metal.
156. Champlevé silver button from Deccan, India, imitating a Multan (page 48) button. The back mark shows that it's Deccan.
157. Champlevé silver button from Deccan, India.
158. Champlevé / Basse Taille gold Jaipur enamel. The shape suggests that it may have originally been a cufflink.

Japanese Enamel on Silver. This is a name given to a certain type of enamel button from Japan. This style of enamelware was first created by Japanese enamelist Hiratsuka Mohei and his family in the late nineteenth and early twentieth centuries. The original technique was used on swords, boxes, vases, and other items, which were engraved with other metal-sculpting techniques such as repoussé. However, later works—called variations by Fredric T. Schneider—were created differently but with the same look. Schneider says, "In many cases . . . so those pieces [variations] are fundamentally sophisticated champlevé work."[6] As these were all done on silver, they can be described as Gin-jippō (appendix E).

Buttons with this look have been reproduced, probably cast, as can be seen in buttons with the same design (buttons 159 and 160). Although these are not enameled exactly the same, you can see the metalwork is the same. Although they do sometimes show a "seam" on the side of the button (possibly a solder seam), that seam could be the casting seam that was not cleaned up. Thus, these buttons are one variation that Schneider was talking about and are a shallow form of Champlevé (buttons 161 and 162).

161

162

159

160

The best example to show that these are Champlevé is button 161. You can see that the flowers are "cup" shaped, which can be described as a shallow depression. In addition, there is a small rim of silver around the enamel, thus implying that the enamel is lower than the rim and therefore in a depression. Normally we think of Champlevé as enameled in a depression that goes to the base of the piece. However, the definition of Champlevé is only that the enamel is in a depression. In button 161, there are four levels of metal forming multiple levels of depressions, and only some are enameled.

Kashmir. Kashmir, located in northern India, also made Champlevé enamel buttons, typically using the deep blue enamel of the area (also called Indo-Persian) (button 163). Although button 164 started out life as a button made for wear with Western-style clothing, it was converted to a brooch, as can be determined because the shank was removed but is still visible (and the pin finding added on top of it). Buttons in this region with shanks were probably made for Western wear, as buttons for Indian clothing were typically made as studs.

163

164

Multan. Situated on the bank of the Chenab River in the Punjab province in Pakistan, Multan is the country's seventh-largest city. Multan was also spelled Mooltan in the nineteenth century, which might be found on back marks of buttons. The city was a major cultural center whose history goes back to antiquity. In the mid-nineteenth to early twentieth centuries, Multan was known for its

165

---

159. Antique Japanese Champlevé, same as button 160 (frequently called Japanese Enamel on Silver).
160. Antique Japanese Champlevé, same as button 159 (frequently called Japanese Enamel on Silver).
161. Antique Japanese Champlevé (frequently called Japanese Enamel on Silver).
162. Antique Japanese Champlevé (frequently called Japanese Enamel on Silver).
163. Champlevé on silver, thought to be from Kashmir, made in the twentieth century. Note the two holes in the back of the button. These are vent holes to allow air to escape during the heating process.
164. Champlevé button, probably from Kashmir, India. This button might be considered a metal button with enamel DF, so it's a poor choice to use in an NBS award (competition).
165. Champlevé Multan button. Earlier examples of this style were normally in one or two colors using their typical blues. Multan cufflinks were oval, not circular, indicating that this button was converted to use as a cufflink sometime after its initial life as a button.

Champlevé silver enamels, including buttons (buttons 165 and 166), which were typically for use by the West.

Taille d'Epargne. French for "sparing cut," Taille d'Epargne (button 167) is a specialized form of Champlevé that is sometimes called "black enamel tracery" or Taille d'Espargne. The technique was used in old buttons but is hard to find. It was used in medieval work for adding ciphers and monograms to ornate pieces,[7] in the eighteenth century for inexpensive jewelry such as bangles and mourning jewelry, and in the nineteenth century in mass-produced Birmingham pieces. It differs from traditional Champlevé in that the depressions are very shallow.

Cloisonné (kloi' zənā' or klwa zô nā')

The word "*Cloisonné*" is French for "cloison," or "cell." It is an enameling technique characterized by wires being bent and formed into shapes, by hand, to form the base design of the piece (buttons 168 and 169). The shapes can be fully enclosed cells or just line designs. Cloisonné is the first documented enameling technique. This is the technique most people have heard of, although it is not as common in buttons as Émaux Peints.

The wires are usually what is called ribbon wire (standard rectangular wire, also called flat wire, around 0.040 x 0.010 inches) but really can be any thickness or shape, such as round wire (button 170), square wire (button 171), or twisted wire (button 172). Multiple sizes of wire can be used in the same piece (buttons 169 and 171). In fact, thinner wire is better to use for more detail, and heavier wire can be used elsewhere. Some artists don't connect the wires to form cells; they just use wire as a design element in, say, an abstract design.

There are many forms of the Cloisonné technique. Most Cloisonné buttons have enamel and wires that are flush, thus making the wires look inlaid (see the ETT "Steps of Cloisonné"). However, when twisted wires are used, the enamel is normally lower than the top of the wires, as twisted wires cannot be ground down without losing their look, but this approach can look good even if not the norm (button 173). Other forms can also be created. If this area is of interest to you, see my book *The Art of Fine Enameling* (2nd ed.), particularly the Cloisonné Project/Variations/Technique Gallery sections. The one attribute normally agreed on by Cloisonné artists is that the wires should not have enamel on them.

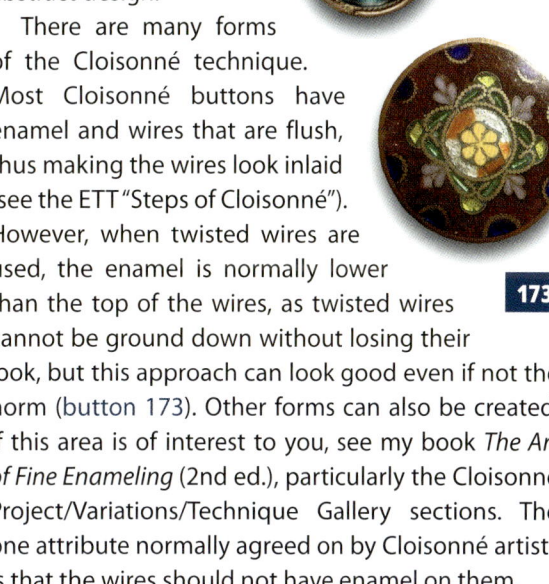

---

166. Champlevé Multan silver button.
167. Antique Taille d'Epargne with enameled bug whose wings are Encrustations.
168. Rare antique Cloisonné butterfly pictorial. Note the fine silver wire work used as part of the design.
169. Silver Cloisonné / Guilloché (spiral pattern) with nonuniform wires with gold Paillons border and decoration, by Karen L. Cohen.
170. Cloisonné on copper using round wires, by Chris Litt.
171. Antique Japanese Cloisonné bird with nonuniform wires mounted in twisted brass wire frame. Although the seams are not evident in this button for all wires, the thinness of the wire is a clue to its being Cloisonné. In addition, at the time of this button's creation, wires were soldered onto the base, and thus the "no seam" look could be due to solder filling in the spaces (look at the beak).
172. Antique Chinese Cloisonné on silver using twisted wires. This is a verbal button with the character for "long," usually used in conjunction with another word (such as in "long life").
173. Antique Cloisonné with ground-down twisted wires and foil. Note the difference in the look of these twisted wires compared to button 172.

Enamel Tech Talk

STEPS OF CLOISONNÉ

Cloisonné can be done on any enamel-friendly metal base and with any type of enamel—transparent, opaque, or opalescent. The steps are always similar to those shown in figures 3.7a–h; each step below, except the first, which doesn't have any enamel, shows the piece after being fired. The descriptions tell what has been done to the enamel in each photo.

After forming, the wires can be attached to the substrate in a few different ways. One way, often used in earlier times, is to solder the wires onto the substrate. The other method is to cover the substrate with a layer of flux, then use enamel adhesive to set the wires in place, and lastly fuse the wires to the flux. This is how most artists do it today. There are other ways, but these are the two basic methods.

Figure 3.7a The base metal is prepared, which may take a few steps. In this case, an engine-turned piece of fine silver (one step) is domed (next step). Doming helps make the finished piece sparkle more by allowing the light to reflect off the substrate metal at various angles. This engine-turning design was done on a brocade machine.

Figure 3.7b This step shows the piece after four firings: First, counter enamel is fired on, then flux is fired onto the front, and then another layer of counter enamel is fired on the back. These layers stabilize the piece and provide a surface for the wires to be fused. The fourth firing fuses the wires on. This fusing was done in one firing for this piece but could have been done in multiple firings, depending on how the artist wanted to work. Note that any wires that go to the edge of the piece should initially be long enough to hang over the edge. These over-hangs eventually get removed but ensure that the wire goes to the actual edge of the design.

Figure 3.7c This step shows the first layer of enamel fused to the piece. The application method is wet-packing. Every color used can be put down on each layer and fused at one time, but some considerations can change this general rule. Exceptions include wet-packing opaques and hard enamels. Hard enamels should be fused first so as not to ruin the firing of a softer color. One to two layers of an opaque color may be wet-packed and fused, but then their cells may not be completed until the transparent cells are done so that the opaque color does not spill over into a transparent cell, where it would be noticed. In addition, after all the enamel is added for one layer, the piece must be dried and then fired.

Figure 3.7d This is an optional step—inlaying foil into the design. The layer in which the foil is placed is also up to the artist. There are two ways to get the shape for inlaying foil into a cloison. One is to use small pieces of foil and "mosaic" them together, which was done in this case; this method provides a crinkly look. The second way is to cut one piece of foil to fit the entire cloison; the shape can be formed from taking a "rubbing" of the wire shape and using that as the cutout pattern. Foil is put down with an enamel adhesive and allowed to dry before firing. Enamel in non-foil areas can be added during this firing.

Figure 3.7e This stage shows the second layer of enamel, which is the first over the foil step. This step is repeated as often as needed to allow the enamel to reach slightly over the wire. When the color of a cell is what the artist wants, flux or a light tint can be used to fill in the remaining space.

Figure 3.7f This step shows the tenth firing of enamel, where the enamel is slightly over the wires, which is hard to see in this photo. Note that by now the wires that were extended off the edge of the piece have already been removed.

Figure 3.7g This photo shows the piece after it has been ground down and sanded to make the enamel and wires flush and to remove scratches caused during the rough grinding/sanding. This step is similar to shaping and partially polishing a cabochon gemstone or a piece of wood. That is, a rough grit is used to shape, and then finer and finer grits are used to remove scratches. I normally use diamond, but other materials can be used for this process. In all cases, water is used to keep down the heat and remove particles from the process.

Figure 3.7h The finished jewel. The polishing stage can be done one of two ways, which are described in the "Enamel Topcoats" section starting on page 68. Because I like putting embellishments on the top, I must do a flash fire. The embellishments I like to use are twisted wire, metal balls, flower wafers, and Paillons, all shown in this piece. The finished piece with its setting is shown in button 398, page 89.

CLOISONNÉ VERSUS GENERAL ENAMELWARE TERMINOLOGY

It should be noted that many people call all enamelware "Cloisonné," which is not a generic term but only one technique. Button 174 shows a mislabeled set of buttons. Thus, one must be wary when hearing the term "*Cloisonné*" to describe an object or when reading an article or book title. In addition, people have named processes using the word "*Cloisonné*" to represent objects having the Cloisonné look. Here are three examples:

- Shotai is a form of Plique-à-jour from Japan (appendix E). When I was at the Inaba Cloisonné Company in the late 1970s, I was told this was Crystallized Cloisonné. This name was applied because the process is much like Cloisonné, but the copper metal base is removed after the enameling is completed. It is not thought that this method was used to make buttons.
- Ferdinand Barbedienne (1810–1892), a famous bronze-founder in Paris, developed a technique for enameling he called Cloisonné sur Font to simulate Chinese Cloisonné. Barbedienne used plaster of Paris molds with embedded wires that were cast in bronze and enameled. It is not thought that this method was used to make buttons. His studio, Barbedienne & Cie of Paris, also created true Cloisonné.
- Consider a Cloisonné wire design that is cast before it is enameled. The resulting casting, when enameled, is considered Champlevé, as no wires were used for that object. If the original design was also enameled, then the original would still be considered Cloisonné.

Design Styles of Cloisonné

I can identify three styles in Cloisonné buttons, all Asian. Keep in mind that each enamelist has his or her own "style" of artwork and these might be recognizable also; see chapter 4, "Enamel Button Artists, Producers, and Purveyors."

Chinese, Traditional. This style is characterized by traditional Cloisonné (wires and enamel are flush) with Chinese designs. Because of the time period in which they were made, there is pitting in the enamel (buttons 175 and 176).

Chinese, Twisted Wire. This style is characterized by twisted wires (buttons 177 and 178). At least sometimes the shank was a double loop (button 178). Remember that when using twisted wires, the enamel will not be flush with the top of the wires because that would require that the wires and enamel be ground, which would change the look of the wires (button 173, page 49).

174. Cropped sheet of souvenir Champlevé buttons from the Inaba Cloisonné Company in Japan, incorrectly labeled Cloisonné. There were originally six matching buttons on this card, all being Champlevé (see the sidebar "Champlevé Masquerading as Cloisonné," page 46, for more details).
175. Antique Chinese Cloisonné bird on branch with pitting.
176. Antique Chinese Cloisonné with pits in the enamel.
177. Chinese Cloisonné with twisted wires on silver with hexagonal outer border.
178. Cinquefoil-shaped Chinese Champlevé and twisted-wire Cloisonné on silver, verbal button with central character meaning "Longevity." The back shows a double loop, as was done in button 177. This style is typical of the shanks on Chinese silver buttons.

Japanese. I discussed the provenance of this Cloisonné design style with various Japanese, Chinese, and Korean enamelists and appropriate museum curators. Gregory Irvine, the retired curator of the Japanese collection at the Victoria and Albert Museum in England, who is also the author of two books on Japanese enamels, provided the answer.[8] In addition, Fredric T. Schneider writes about the artist in his book on Japanese enamels.[9] This style of Cloisonné was created by Kyoto artist Takahara Komajiō, the most widely known maker of traditional Kyoto enamelware. His own studio was in production between the 1890s and 1910s (which helps with dating these buttons). The designs are characterized by two sizes of wire (thin ribbon wire and square wire), similar colors, repetitive spiral wires in the thinner size, and usually soldered-on wires (buttons 179, 180, and 181; see also button 171, page 49).

Although Komajiō was the original designer, it's possible that other workshops copied his designs. It's not clear whether Komajiō's or other workshops made the buttons we collect today, but they are certainly Japanese designs. Some Cloisonné designs of this style, like the bird-man button (button 179), have Egyptian elements. Irvine surmises that these pieces were made for export to Alexandria to take advantage of the Western interest in Egypt that occurred in the early twentieth century. He arrived at this conclusion and e-mailed me: "There is a pair of cigarette cases in the V&A collection that I have dated to 1900–1910 on the strength of a little note that they came with. The boxes have the label of a dealer in Alexandria."[10]

Crackle Enamel

Crackle Enamel (buttons 182 and 183) is a modern technique using a special liquid enamel palette. These enamels come in a range of colors that can be mixed like paint, are currently called Liquid Form Enamel Colors, and are manufactured only by Thompson Enamel. When these were first developed in the twentieth century, the commercial enamel industry considered this crackling a defect. However, art enamelists quickly adopted this effect as a new technique. Crackle Enamel creates a random pattern of twig-like elements and cannot be completely controlled. See the ETT "How Crackle Enamel Works" for information on how the cracks occur.

HOW CRACKLE ENAMEL WORKS

Liquid Form Enamel Colors will "crackle" only when applied over a fused specialized base coat with low expansion (here's that chemistry kicking in). When heated in the kiln, the shock of the heat makes the liquid enamel form cracks (it has a clay base and is like mud drying in the heat of the sun), and at this point the base enamel flows up into the created cracks and prevents the liquid enamel from flowing back together—the result is a twig-like pattern. Note that if the liquid is too thick, no cracking will occur in those areas.

---

179. Antique Japanese Cloisonné Egyptian-style "bird person" with two size wires and some pitting.
180. Antique Japanese Cloisonné stylized plant life pattern with two size wires, mounted in twisted brass frame.
181. Antique scallop-shaped Japanese Cloisonné with ornate scrollwork and two sizes of wire.
182. Realistic openwork pig using pink Crackle Enamel on a clear base with a fine silver ball held with black enamel for the eye, by Karen L. Cohen.
183. Realistic openwork elephant on a Crackle Enameled ball, movable, by Janet White.

Émaux Peints (emo pan)

Émaux Peints buttons use the technique of painting with enamels, mostly using Painting Materials (buttons 184, 185, 186, and 187), but also in some cases with transparent enamel (buttons 188 and 189). Painting was first perfected in Limoges, France, in the sixteenth century and went through multiple stages of development, as described starting on page 6. Although this technique originally started with colorizing images using transparent enamels, its final development in the seventeenth century was with using Painting Materials, called Onglaze painting. Today many enamelists work with Painting Materials, and some work so fine they might use a magnifying glass to help them see better, especially in portrait work.

Painting Materials are applied with a brush, and multiple layers/firings can be used to build up the design. The enamel field on which the painting is applied is a medium-to-hard fusing enamel so that the Painting Materials do not sink into it. Most of the portrait painters today use opalescent white as the field, but many other types of painting are done on opaque white. At least at the turn of the twentieth century, Genevan and British enamel painters were using an enamel field of Pâte enamel (page 57). Both opalescent white and Pâte seem to exhibit similar characteristics for such elements as skin tones and flowers (see "Pâte" section for more information).

In 1911, Genevan enamel painter and manufacturer of enamels Louis-Elliè Millenet said there are two ways to paint. One is like watercolor painting, which is always done on a white field (which is also used as the highlights) and is not covered with a clear topcoat. The other is more like oil painting, making the colors thicker, and is covered by a clear flux topcoat.[11] It's not certain whether buttons were done with both methods. This topic warrants future study.

The painting can be done over an opaque or transparent field, or it can be done over Basse Taille or Guilloché; see the ETT "Enameling over a Patterned Substrate" (page 54) for more information on this process.

There are two basic forms of Émaux Peints: Monochrome (one color) and Polychrome (multiple colors). The following is information about these two forms. This is then followed by a list of design styles of Émaux Peints.

Monochrome (buttons 190, 191, 192, and 193) designs are usually, but not always, done over a white field, similar to painting on a white canvas. One color is used, but tints of the color are incorporated for shading. Any of these tints (or the field color) can be on top of one another to give the desired effect. The use of tints distinguishes this method from

184. Eighteenth-century Monochrome / Sgraffito on copper mounted in metal.
185. Antique Émaux Peints with outer Art Nouveau border with Encrustations.
186. Antique Émaux Peints / Champlevé head with cut steel embellishments in plated brass. You can see the white underpainting at the edges of the image almost all around, but mostly on the right. Also notice the firescale (thin black line) around the entire image.
187. Antique Monochrome framed in brass border with cut steel.
188. Antique Limoges-style enamel set in a twisted design frame border.
189. Antique Grisaille / Limoges-style head.
190. Antique Monochrome black and white enamel architectural scene with cut steel border, as well as some Sgraffito in the trees and water.
191. Antique Monochrome / Champlevé dog head in pebbled "cutout."
192. Antique Monochrome figure of man with cut steel OME border.
193. Antique sepia tone Monochrome, using black as outline (acceptable for Monochrome), framed in ornate plated metal rococo leaf border.

En Grisaille, which used a build-up of only white fine grains of enamel. Another way to distinguish Monochrome from Grisaille is the presence of brushstrokes, as Monochrome designs are done by stroking with a brush as in regular painting, whereas Grisaille is done differently. See the next page for more information on telling

Monochrome from Grisaille. Polychrome is a painting with more than one color. It can be done with Painting Materials (buttons 194, 195, 196, and 197) or with transparent enamels (button 198).

ENAMELING OVER A PATTERNED SUBSTRATE

Sometimes Émaux Peints and Cloisonné designs are created on top of Guilloché (button 199) or Basse Taille (button 123, page 35). When that is done, the artist must decide whether the pattern should show through the painting. If not, then a base of an opaque/opalescent enamel or foil must be laid down first to cover the pattern. Either decision is valid, and both look good; the choice is the artist's vision of the piece. Consider button 126 (page 35), a button by Diana Wieler: She has chosen to show the pattern through the hair but not through the rest of the image in this Limoges-style Émaux Peints button.

Design Styles of Émaux Peints

Canton. These Polychrome Émaux Peints enameled buttons were created in Canton, China. The antique versions (buttons 200, 201, and 202) are characterized by always being counter enameled, using pastel colors, being made typically in size small and sometimes medium, and having loop metal shanks. The modern examples are usually back marked "China."

En Grisaille (n gri zāl'). Grisaille (formally En Grisaille) is a style of Émaux Peints, developed in Limoges, France, in the sixteenth century. It can be colored but is generally monochromatic. In enameling, there are different names for this technique depending on the field color; see the sidebar "Other Names for Grisaille-Type Enameling" (page 56).

---

194. Antique Polychrome with black and Liquid Gold border, by André Keim. Note the distinctive blue cross hatching in the design. Uses Painting Materials for color.
195. Antique linear shaped Polychrome marine scene, set in brass. Uses Painting Materials for color.
196. Polychrome flowers mounted in silvered metal; uses Painting Materials for color.
197. Antique Polychrome / Basse Taille enamel with foil Paillons border. Uses Painting Materials for color.
198. Antique oval-shaped Limoges-style head with Liquid Gold details mounted in scalloped frame with twisted-wire edge border.
199. Guilloché (basketweave pattern) / Cloisonné on fine silver with gold Paillons and fine silver twisted wire and balls OME, set in sterling silver with freshwater pearls, by Karen L. Cohen. Note that foil covers the pattern in the red area and opaque enamels cover the pattern in the paisley bases, while the pattern comes through other areas of the design.
200. Antique Canton enamel with counter enamel.
201. Antique Canton with counter enamel.
202. Antique Canton enamel mounted in metal.

Enameled Grisaille (buttons 203 and 204) is a buildup of layers of a special white enamel called Grisaille White, which is finely ground and can be applied with a brush. In an Émaux Peints Monochrome design with a black field, multiple tints of black (grays) are painted, but in Grisaille, only thin layers of white are built up on the field to form the highlights (more white) and shadows (less white). Note that with nonblack fields, the shadows are variations of the field color (button 205).

If the shadows are not "tints" of the field color, then what are they? Understanding this point will help the collector differentiate between Monochrome and Grisaille.

Can you read this:

7H15 M3554G3 53RV35 7O PR0V3
H0W 0UR MIND5 C4N D0 4M4ZING 7HING5!

If you can read this statement, it is because of the phenomenon described by Gestalt psychologists: Your brain interprets what your eyes see and creates your perception of the world. Your brain fills in missing information. When applied to color, this phenomenon is called Optical Mixing. This is what happens in the "grays" of Grisaille—they are not actually grays, but rather black (or the field color) with varying amounts of white speckles over it. The mind interprets this combination as tints of gray (or the field color). *Note:* The white speckles are the finely ground grains of the Grisaille White used to paint the image. Remember that the enamel is fired, so the "speckles" may be muted some and not sharp dots.

Consider button 205, which is a great example of studying the difference between Monochrome and Grisaille—look at the shadows. The shadows of the back landscape are bluish because the layer of white on the field is thin and so the transparent blue shows through (blue with white speckles). The figures, however, are Monochrome, with a white underpainting, and the shadows are done with black Painting Material, using various tints of black/grays.

Buttons are small canvases, and thus a Grisaille image on them may not be too sophisticated. That is, the number of layers needed to produce the result may be minimal (two to three), so the image may not have as much depth as a large Grisaille. As a result, it is difficult to determine whether some images are Grisaille or just Monochrome. Consider button 206. Today, some in the button world say it's a Monochrome, and some say it is En Grisaille. Which is it? I have asked three modern enamelists who specialize in Grisaille. One said definitely Grisaille, and the other two say it's a bad example of Grisaille, perhaps done by a novice. I think this is one of those minimal pieces—probably only two layers of white.

GRISAILLE TERMINOLOGY—ENAMEL VERSUS PAINT

In both enameling and painting, there is a technique called Grisaille. However, they are not the same. In enameling, Grisaille is done with layers of a special finely ground white enamel (Grisaille White) to build up the highlights and shadows; no tints are used. But in painting, tints of the field color are used to achieve the highlights and shadows.

203. Antique Grisaille enamel with Liquid Gold (gilded) set in metal.
204. Antique Grisaille waterbird.
205. Antique Monochrome / Grisaille: a black and white Monochrome couple with blue Grisaille field with Liquid Gold, frame border of brass with cut steels with ornate back design.
206. Antique Grisaille bird with cut steel border.

OTHER NAMES FOR GRISAILLE-TYPE ENAMELING

Grisaille means gray and really means a white buildup on a black or dark base. At some point, though, the white buildup was used on various fields, and other terms, in the enamel world, were used to define the difference. The definitions that follow come from Bill Helwig, known as the "king" of modern Grisaille.[12]

- **Grisaille**—white is built up on a dark field. This method is characterized by the shadows being perceived as tints of the field.
- **Camaïeu** (also En Camaïeu) (kâm ay' euh)—today the term refers to a white buildup on any non-dark color or transparent field, which could be multiple colors. This is characterized by the shadows being perceived as tints of the field color(s). However, initially this technique was slightly different. In the later part of the eighteenth century, En Camaïeu was developed in Geneva as a special form of Grisaille to be trompe l'oeil to simulate a cameo carved into a shell (button 207). The grains of enamel had to be ground finer so that when mixed with an oil base it produced a grainless image, especially needed for miniature silhouettes.[13]

Button 208 provides a good study to define what is Grisaille versus Camaïeu. This button has a blue transparent enamel over foil field, but if you look at the shadows of the cherub's body, you will see they are black—this was done with a black underpainting for the white enamel buildup and thus is Grisaille (white layers over black). Note, though, that the cherub's wing and some white flowers are Camaïeu—these have the white buildup on the transparent blue field and thus blue shadows.

- **Impasto** (im pas'tō or im pä'stō)—white is built up on bare copper. The bare metal substrate around the image can eventually be enameled with a color or just flux, artist's choice. This is characterized by the shadows looking like firescale.

Limoges-style. "Limoges-style" is a term not defined, widely known, or understood in the NBS button world. It is not used/defined in the *Blue Book*. But from talking with dealers and classification judges, and viewing quite a few buttons, I understand which buttons are considered Limoges-style. This term is not to be equated with the term "Limoges School enamels," which includes more than what button people consider Limoges-style (like Grisaille). Limoges-style is painting *with* enamel (buttons 209, 210, and 211), like the first three periods of enamel painting development, as described starting on page 6. This means use of foil colorized by transparent enamel. Some Painting Materials might be used for details. Limoges-style images were never covered with a flux topcoat.[14] The use of transparent enamels over the foil gives these buttons their luminous look. Once Painting Materials began being used for painting in the seventeenth century (as in Pâte, described in the following section), the images take on a different look, which is less flashy, although still beautiful. Some of the antique Limoges-style buttons were back marked, but not all. No known Limoges-style buttons were made in the sixteenth century, and most were probably done after the Limoges School Revival in the nineteenth century.

207. Eighteenth-century Camaïeu, classic mythological cherub on a lion mounted in metal.
208. Antique Grisaille (cherub) / Camaïeu (wing and flowers) with Liquid Gold on a foil and blue field. Another version is found in volume 1 of *The Big Book of Buttons* (plate 14a, page 66).
209. Antique Limoges-style with Liquid Gold accents of a woman with peacock headdress mounted in wide plain frame (frequently called Peacock Princess).
210. Antique Limoges-style set in metal with an edge paste border.
211. Antique Limoges-style portrait with Art Nouveau and pearl borders.

Pâte. It is not known when Pâte enamel buttons (buttons 212, 213, and 214) were first created (see more about dating below), but they are defined by a special enamel, called Pâte, used for the field. In addition, they are painted with Painting Materials, not transparent enamel colors. This quality dates them to no earlier than around 1630, but it could be much later based on one enamel company that started manufacturing in 1835 (see section "Geneva," page 14); it's not clear whether this was the only company making this type of enamel. Typically, Pâte enamels have no foil and often have a very smooth topcoat (i.e., hand polished—page 68). The special enamel field frequently has a greenish tint called "mellow yellow" (button 212) in the button world. Subjects are often either portraits or flower designs.

Millenet says, "Pâte enamel, sometimes called antique white, has a composition entirely different from that of the other ordinary white enamels. Pâte enamel can be made in pure white, but it is usually preferred with a slight ivory or greenish tint [Author's note: This could fire the mellow yellow noted earlier]. It has the further peculiarity of being to some degree semitransparent, and as this under certain circumstances might be a drawback, pâte enamel is not usually applied directly to the metal but on one or even two coats of ordinary white enamel, which serves as a base. The essential property of pâte enamel is that it is to a certain extent penetrated by the colours, to which it imparts great freshness and vivacity. This property is taken advantage of in the cast of portraits, particularly of young women or children, which gain infinite charm and purity in the carnations [skin tone]. Flower paintings on this class of enamel are full of life."[15]

When Millenet says "penetrated by the colours," he is referring to Painting Materials that were used for coloring. Note that his book refers to this painting as a painting technique *on* enamel rather than an enameling technique, which it is considered today.

Pâte enamel was formulated in two ways—one allowed for a clear topcoat, while the other did not. The clear topcoat could be only one layer, or perhaps two or three layers, which would be hand polished to produce the "very smooth" surface. Those without a clear topcoat would allow for relief on top.

I have not been able to determine when Pâte enamel started and then stopped being manufactured.

PÂTE VERSUS PÂTE DE VERRE VERSUS PÂTE SUR PÂTE TERMINOLOGY

The word "*Pâte*" means "paste" in French. The three art forms that use this term are differentiated by the following:

- **Pâte**, in the button world, is a style of the Émaux Peints technique. This was done on buttons (button 212).
- **Pâte de Verre** is a glass molding technique that can be used with enamel. This was done with buttons (button 304, page 75).
- **Pâte sur Pâte** is a porcelain technique, developed in 1850 and popular between 1885 and 1915. It involves the buildup of white porcelain slip on an unfired base. Once the buildup is complete, it is carved away for the fine detail and eventually fired. Jasperware sometimes can look like Pâte sur Pâte but is quite different. Jasperware images are molded, but Pâte sur Pâte is a hand sculpting process. It most closely resembles the enamel technique of Impasto (like Grisaille but on a bare copper substrate). This technique was done on buttons (button 516 in appendix B).

Probably the word "*Pâte*" was a marketing name by the Dufaux company for a particular line of enamels. Historian Erika Speel does note that in previous years a special white enamel for portraits was obtained from Venice[16] that was described as being like "fresh milk" and was a slightly translucent enamel. This describes the Pâte enamel in Millenet's book, except for the version(s) that were tinted with green. Therefore, the same type of enamel, from another manufacturer, probably was being used and not named Pâte. Thus, it would be hard to date those buttons, except for those with the mellow yellow greenish tint—these probably were created between 1835 and 1958 when the company was in business. But certainly all of them had to have been made

---

212. Antique Pâte (mellow yellow field) with two collet-set diamonds.
213. Antique Pâte (mellow yellow field) with back mark "E. M. Paris."
214. Antique Pâte (mellow yellow field) with back mark "E. M. Paris."

after 1630, when Painting Materials, not transparent enamels, were being used.

Today, most enamel painters use opalescent white as their field. I could not ascertain when and why this transition from Pâte to opalescent white occurred. Further study is needed to better understand the similarities and differences among the Venetian version, Pâte, and today's opalescent white.

Persian/Iranian. At the request of the government, the country's name was changed from Persia to Iran in 1935. Minakari, their name for enameling, means "miniature of fire." Now centered in the Iranian city of Isfahan, most enamels are of the Émaux Peints technique, many using Sgraffito (page 65) in the borders. Today enamels are done on copper, silver, or brass, although years ago gold was also used. They have two styles, as shown in buttons 215, 216, 217, and 260 (page 65).

Russian. Russian enamelists have been painting with Painting Materials for a few hundred years and originally started using the Pointillé method. The examples shown use typical colors (buttons 218 and 219). The back of button 219 shows a typical shank style of Russian enamel buttons. Today the enamel painters use opalescent white as their enamel field.

Enamel Buildup

Enamelists around the world have used the technique of building up enamel in relief for centuries. A buildup is defined as multiple layers of enamel that are fired to be higher than the rest of the enamel. This result varies by the degree of buildup, so that some examples are more obvious than others. Different cultures have different names and uses for the technique. What follows is an overview of the various buildups.

The button world defines an enamel buildup, called "Encrustation," as they did in England; however, the English call this Beaded Enamel.[17] Howard Chapin says, "Incrusted enamel is that in which the enamel is charged directly on the metal surface without any raised metal edges to hold it. It is generally used in small daubs or beads to reproduce the effect of precious stones."[18] Encrustations are mainly used as a design element to represent stone cabochons (button 220), using transparent or opaque enamels typically in gemstone colors. In the button world, Encrustations can be on the enamel surface (buttons 221 and 222; button 167, page 49) or the metal part of a button (button 223). Van Cleef & Arpels, an international jewelry company, calls this Cabochonné enameling.

---

215. Persian Polychrome domed Plaquette mounted in metal.
216. Teardrop- and spindle-shaped Persian enamel buttons with delicate hand-painted designs where the green was sgraffitoed to reveal the underneath white enamel. Silver mounts. The spindle includes a fine roped border.
217. Persian-style Émaux Peints with Sgraffito border.
218. Polychrome mounted in German silver, probably verbal, by Russian enamelist Vladamir Dolbin; photo credit JoNel Kurtz.
219. Russian Émaux Peints mounted in metal with twisted border. The shank is typical of a Russian enamel button.
220. Openwork faux Filigree Champlevé / Émaux Peints floral heart design with Encrustations.
221. Cloisonné with two types of wires (twisted and thick rectangular), foil under the red with Encrustations and silver sheet and balls on top.
222. Filigree Plique-à-jour with central Encrustation, by Diane Echnoz Almeyda.
223. Antique Émaux Peints with opalescent Encrustations that look like milky opals (Faux Opals, page 72).

"Moriage" (pronounced more-ee-a-gay) is the Japanese term for a buildup of enamel. The Japanese used it to add interest in a design (for example, over a design of loquat fruit so the fruit is raised off the base enamel). Contemporary enamelist Merry-Lee Rae has popularized the modern usage of this term for any general enamel buildup (button 224) in her classes.

French enamelist Camille Fauré (1874–1956) is well known for his Art Deco style and developed a form of enameling with large, raised enamel sections. His sculptural enameled technique, called the Fauré method, is taught today and thus might be used in buttons of the future. Typically, Fauré's use was a sculptural design covering almost the entire piece.

The Battersea-style enamels also used a form of buildup for dramatic effect (button 225). Notice raised swirls and dots that are gilded. In larger items like boxes, the same type of designs could be left white, which was the color of the underlying enamel. The dots in button 31 (page 9) are left white. Read the ETT "Battersea-Style Designs" to learn how they may have achieved these results.

When enamel buildups are placed over foil Paillons such that the outer rim of the Paillons still shows, they are called Pierreries (pi-ir-ez) in both the button world and the enameling world (the word "*pierre*" is French for "stone") (buttons 226, 227, 228, and 229). These were frequently used in eighteenth- and early nineteenth-century buttons. Because Paillons are no longer manufactured, they are hard to locate today, but some Studio Button artists have found them, so watch for Pierreries in modern buttons as well.

BATTERSEA-STYLE DESIGNS

Some of the Battersea-style buttons included a raised gilded design, sometimes as borders (button 31), typically using scrolls and dots (button 225). This result was accomplished by using a hard-fusing white enamel, which was formed while wet into the shape desired. After drying, the piece was fired and these areas were frequently gilded by using Liquid Gold[19] and fired again. A technique called "enlevage à l'aiguille" was a method using a needle-like tool to help sculpt enamel into place. This was done during the Limoges School painting development and thus known at the time of Battersea-style enamels. The book *English Painted Enamels* by Therle Hughes and Bernard Hughes says that "on many of the finest Bilston and Birmingham [Battersea-style] enamels the final touch of ornament consisted of irregular rococo scrollwork surrounding the painted reserve. This scrolling was in raised enamel, brilliantly gilded."[20] Thus, it is documented in another reference that the raised designs were done with enamel (Encrustations). In modern times, the material MUD (page 75) could be used to form these raised designs.

---

224. Fine silver Foldformed leaf button with ladybug. Note the flux Moriage dew drops, by Karen L. Cohen.
225. Eighteenth-century Émaux Peints Battersea-style floral with encrusted Liquid Gold designs.
226. Spindle-shaped copper with Paillons and Pierreries, by Karen L. Cohen.
227. Eighteenth-century enamel with Pierreries, mirrored glass mounted in wide plated metal frame.
228. Eighteenth-century octagon-shaped enamel with Pierreries/Paillons and a brass border.
229. Antique Basse Taille Pierreries and Paillons in rare dimi steel cup, most likely French, possibly a Bressan; back marked with a diamond having "V•F" inside.

Eutectic Effect

A eutectic is the combining of metals whose resulting alloy has a melting temperature of less than either of the included materials. This result can happen with a few different metals, but in enameling the biggest problem is when silver and copper are combined in one piece (like when a Cloisonné is done with silver wire on a copper substrate). This was considered an error and much to be avoided until modern enamelist Jamie Frechette (1907–2021) wrote an article for *Glass on Metal* magazine on how to use this mixture as a design element. Thus enamelists today are using this oddity.[21]

The Eutectic Effect was further developed by modern enamelist Averill B. Shepps, using enamels containing chromium to control the effect. Many times the enamelist will just let the material "do its thing." Eutectic effects present themselves as silver-looking blobs and can be left as is (with firescale on them), polished, or enameled over. Button 230 shows the Eutectic Effect over a copper etching that affected the flow of the eutectic.

230

Gin-bari (geen bär' e)

Gin-bari is a foil technique invented by Tsukamoto Jimbei in 1894 as a less expensive imitation of Basse Taille.[22] Typically, the foil is embossed with a pattern, but in all cases the foil totally covers the base. The metal substrate can be any enameling metal, but typically a less expensive metal, like copper, is used. Note that this foil—today called Gin-bari foil—is thicker than most silver foil used in enameling, as it has to hold up to an embossing procedure (see the sidebar "Leaf versus Foil versus Sheet Metal," page 77). Traditionally, Gin-bari was embossed using zinc engraved plates. Today we employ other methods as well. See the ETT "Steps of Gin-bari" for how Gin-bari is made.

Gin-bari is not a specialized form of Basse Taille. In Basse Taille, the *metal substrate* is texturized, whereas, in Gin-bari, *foil* is texturized and fused to an initial

JAPANESE TERMINOLOGY

Appendix E is a list of Japanese enameling terminology. Please reference this appendix for more information on Japanese terms.

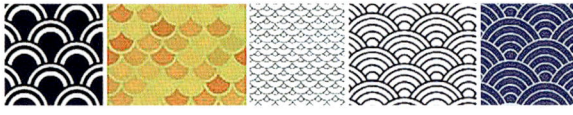

Figure 3.8 Examples of Japanese fish-scale patterns.

layer of enamel. Often, a repeating design will be used to fill the base design. Examples of repeating designs include fish roe (Nanako in Japan) (series of dots) (button 233) and fish scale (figure 3.8).

Design Styles of Gin-bari

Low Relief. In low-relief Gin-bari, the embossed design is virtually all one level and may be used for a field with Cloisonné or another technique (buttons 231 and 232).

231

232

High Relief. The embossed design is at least two levels, with the foreground being the higher, more prominent design and colorized appropriately, usually with transparent enamel (buttons 233 and 234).

233 **234**

---

230. Copper Eutectic over an etching, Basse Taille by Karen L. Cohen, reprinted from the book *The Art of Fine Enameling* (2nd ed., 2019).
231. Antique low-relief realistic Gin-bari with Cloisonné, a rare antique realistic button.
232. Low-relief Gin-bari with Cloisonné.
233. Antique high-relief Gin-bari with dragon mounted in silver. One can feel that the dragon is higher than the area behind it.
234. Antique high-relief Gin-bari.

STEPS OF GIN-BARI

The Gin-bari foil is first punctured with very small holes to allow the gases to escape during the firing that fuses the foil to the first layer of enamel. The ETT "Foil Application" on page 77 explains how to do this.

Next, the foil is embossed with a design. The foil can be embossed by either roll printing or the artisan "rubbing" the design onto the foil. Other methods might also be possible, but the point is that silver foil is embossed with a raised design, which is then enameled.

Lastly, the foil must be fused onto the piece. To do this, a soft enamel is applied to the metal substrate and fused. The foil is attached to this layer with a holding agent and fired. When the foil is fused onto the initial enamel layer, the soft enamel rises into the embossed design, holding it in place.

From there, the artist creates the rest of the piece, keeping in mind that mostly transparent enamels will be used so that the embossed design can be seen.

Graphite Pencil

Graphite Pencil can be drawn on enamel to form either an outline (button 235) or shading (figure 3.9) for a design. It has to be done on a non-glossy surface, so the enamel must first be either etched or ground. Graphite cannot be fired too high or for more than a couple of firings; otherwise, it starts to fade and can be fired out completely. Sometimes a clear coat of enamel is fused over this material as the artist's choice.

Figure 3.9 Graphite Pencil on copper to show how shading can be done. This is a tile, not a button, by Studio Button artist JB Ebert from my book *The Art of Fine Enameling* (2nd ed., 2019).

High-Fire Techniques

There are a few high-fire techniques, which require that a piece be fired above 1600°F.

Scrolling

Scrolling is a modern marbling high-fire technique, probably started in the twentieth century. Usually, enamel lumps (and possibly enamel threads) are placed over a thick base layer of enamel and fired in a very hot kiln (1650°F) until molten. Then the enamelist, using heat-resistant gloves and a pick, pulls the molten enamel around while it is still in the kiln. The most notable button artist working with this technique was Herman Lowenstein (page 99) (buttons 236 and 237), but Ada Snow Smith (page 104) also said she used this technique. In addition, modern enamelist button maker Helene Carter (page 87) (button 238) uses grain enamel with Scrolling to achieve designs more like Turkish Ebru marbling for paper and fabric. Scrolling is also discussed in relationship to the difference between CPE and enamel (appendix B).

Consider button 239. On first inspection, this example might seem like Scrolling, as the center is mixed colors. But I think the center is a millefiori that was tilted on its side and overfired to make it run. The millefiori shown is similar to one that could have been used.

---

235. Copper enamel using Graphite Pencil, gold foil, Painting Materials, and flower wafers, by Karen L. Cohen.
236. Hexagonal copper enamel using the Scrolling technique with flux field and metal bug fused on, by Herman Lowenstein.
237. Scrolled enamel with metal fused on, by Herman Lowenstein.
238. Scrolled enamel sew-through, by Helene Carter.
239. H. Lowenstein studio button with probably an overfired millefiori center, which looks similar to the millefiori next to it. This button was not scrolled but may be confused with the Scrolling technique. Note that the colors are not intermixed, as would be the case when marbling—they just look squished together; there is an indent in the center that looks like maybe Lowenstein stuck his pick into the center when it first came out of the kiln but didn't move the enamel around. This button is on a copper penny.

Webbing Design

A new (twenty-first-century) high-fire technique can be done when using a soft enamel under a harder one, much as what is done in Pull-through (page 64). However, this high-fire technique requires Pull-through to go through another step: it includes another layer of enamel that is fired between 1600°F and 1650°F. The result is a series of random "cells" or a webbing design (buttons 240 and 241; button 372, page 85). There is no formal name for this method, but I call it "High-Fire Webbing Design."

Plique-à-jour (plĕk'ä zhŏŏr' or plē ka zhōōr')

French for "membrane through which passes the light of day," Plique-à-jour (also referred to as just "Plique") was one of the first three types of enameling. It is a technique in which a metal frame is created with openings, which are then filled with enamel. Plique is the most difficult form of enameling because the lack of a metal backing means the artist must take care that the enamel does not drip off. How this technique is done today can be different from in earlier times. In the past, a backing such as foil or a mica sheet was used to stop the enamel from running out the back. This process can be used today as well, but typically it is not. See the ETT "Enameling Modern Plique-à-jour" for today's method. In addition, it takes many firings to fill an opening with enamel and thus takes a long time to finish a piece.

Other names for Plique-à-jour are "email à jure," "à jour cloisonné," and "email de plite." Russians call this open-braid work. Japanese say Shotai for their version, which is described in appendix E. The German term is "*Fenster email*," and the Norwegian term is "*vindusemalje*."[23]

To tell whether an enamel button is Plique-à-jour, turn the button over; if you can see the enamel through the openings (button 243), then it's Plique-à-jour. If the enamel is set in metal, it is not Plique-à-jour, as these enamels are never set in a solid backed mounting. Plique-à-jour enamels resemble a stained-glass window more than any other enameling technique. The enamel used can be transparent or opalescent, but opaque is not typically used because then the light would not come through. However, if opaque colors are used, the piece would still be called a Plique-à-jour (button 242).

Two enameling presentations are used in Plique-à-jour buttons; either can be used with the various framework styles. One is that the enamel is relatively flat (button 243), and the other is that the enamel is built up (buttons 242 and 244) in the opening like a large Encrustation. See the sidebar "Built-Up-Style Plique-à-jour" for information on how antique Plique-à-jour buttons could have been made. Note that both can be done today as well, though not necessarily by the same methods. See the ETT "Enameling Modern Plique-à-jour" (page 64) for how enamel is added to a Plique-à-jour frame. A few modern enamelists have made Plique-à-jour buttons, and some were imported from China (button 245); see chapter 4, "Enamel Button Artists, Producers, and Purveyors."

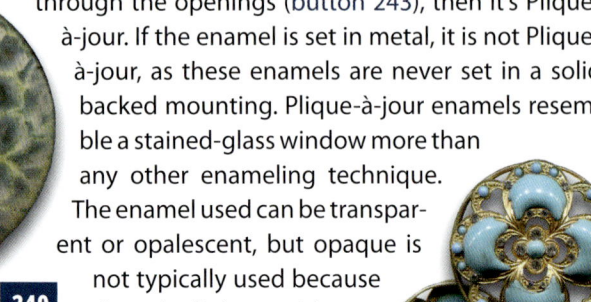

240

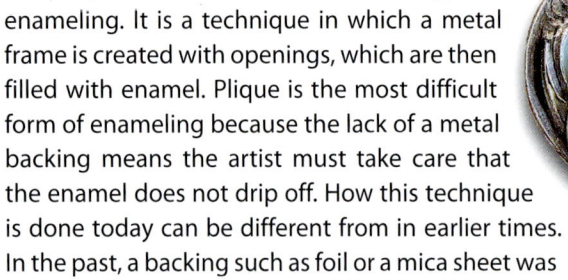

241

243

242

244

245

---

240. Webbing Design with opaque base on copper using gold Paillons, flower wafers, and fine silver balls, by Karen L. Cohen.
241. High-fire Webbing Design with a transparent base on silver at bottom of button, using black decal of a bronco rider and gold bird Paillon, by Karen L. Cohen.
242. Antique atypical opaque Plique-à-jour tetrad design with paste OME.
243. Rare antique pictorial Plique-à-jour, with gemstone eyes and white metal base. The enamel is matte, due to the way they enameled Plique-à-jour in earlier times.
244. Antique opaque openwork Plique-à-jour cross/tetrad pattern with built-up enamel and outer edge bead-like border.
245. Modern Plique-à-jour button from China (page 88). Because of the use of twisted wires, the enamel is lower than the wires.

Design Styles of Plique-à-jour Frames

Two main styles of metal framework hold the enamel: Filigree and Non-filigree. Note that the Non-filigree version is traditionally called "pierced" in the enamel world, but since that word is used in the button world to denote openwork, I have chosen to call it Non-filigree. In addition, there are modern methods to produce Non-filigree frames that do not require "piercing" but are still called "pierced" in the enamel world. Thus, this tag works for all Non-filigree forms of Plique-à-jour. These are described below.

Filigree Framework. In this style (button 246), a frame is constructed by forming wires (straight or twisted) into a design and then soldering together. The forming of the wire is similar to bending wires for Cloisonné. Typically, antique Filigree buttons do not include built-up areas of enamel (but may). In modern times, Studio Button artist Diane Echnoz Almeyda does both styles of enameling (buttons 247 and 248) in both frame types of Plique-à-jour.

Non-filigree Framework. In this style, the frame contains openings in the metal to form a design in which the enamel is placed. It does not include the bending of wires for the frame but might have had some wires added in an opening while enameling. Traditionally this style was done by cutting sheet metal using the jeweler's technique of "piercing" (buttons 249 and 250). See the ETT "Pierced and Soldered Champlevé" (page 45) for how piercing is done. However, this framework can also be created by casting (button 243) or using metal clay (page 38). The model used for casting could be from a wax model, a hand-fabricated metal piece, or a Computer Aided Design (CAD) model. Other methods are sure to be invented in the future. Button 251 was created using a method of Non-filigree Plique-à-jour, perhaps a casting.

BUILT-UP-STYLE PLIQUE-À-JOUR

Many of the antique Plique-à-jour buttons have a buildup of enamel in the spaces. I have two theories on how this result was accomplished. Both are possible, but it's not clear whether both methods were used.

In 2019, Button Bytes discussed how these could be created using a technique called Gripoix, which is a lampworking method of melting glass rods into open metal spaces. Although this is a lampworking technique and not a typical enameling technique, it still fits the definition of "glass fused to metal." Gripoix was first done in 1868, so the date of a Plique-à-jour button would help determine whether it could have been done this way or by some other method. To see this method, go to YouTube and search "Gripoix."

In 1911, Millenet wrote about how his contemporaries enameled Plique-à-jour. It is quite different from how it's done today, as they frequently (but not always) used a backing of foil (platinum, gold, or copper) or mica throughout the process to ensure that the enamel didn't fall though and then removed the foil/mica at the end. The description does say that the top was not always abraded to be even and sometimes left "undulating" to impart "a robust characteristic appearance to the enamel."[24] I assume that means that it can be built up. Removing the backing many times caused the enamel to turn matte, and it was left that way (button 243).

---

246. Antique Filigree Plique-à-jour pinwheel with decorated blades alternating with twisted wire C-scrolls. Note that this is not an openwork enamel button, as nowhere does the enamel totally surround any openwork area.
247. Filigree Plique-à-jour with built-up enamel, by Diane Echnoz Almeyda.
248. Filigree Plique-à-jour teardrop with outer twisted ribbon wire border and inner green border of twisted round wire with fine silver balls, by Diane Echnoz Almeyda.
249. Non-filigree Plique-à-jour with openwork, a stamping design around the openings, and built-up enamel.
250. Arts & Crafts–style Non-filigree Plique-à-jour within engraved metal-dominant frame with built-up enamel. Not an openwork enamel button, as the enamel doesn't totally surround the openings.
251. Antique Non-filigree Plique-à-jour pictorial bow with paste in the interior and border.

ENAMELING MODERN PLIQUE-À-JOUR

Enamel Tech Talk

Prior to enameling a Plique-à-jour frame, the enamel is grade sifted to remove the smallest sizes (remember that this process allows transparent enamels to be more transparent). In preparation for wet-packing, the enamel is mixed with water and an enamel adhesive to help hold the enamel in place. A brush, spatula, or dropper is used to apply the enamel around the edges (figure 3.10) to allow surface tension to hold it, somewhat like soapy water in a bubble maker. Before the filled sections get too dry, the piece is underfired to ensure that enamel does not drip out the back. More enamel is added, filling more holes as needed. When the enamelist thinks all cells are filled, a fully fused firing is done. Then the piece is checked to see whether any holes remain. If so, more enamel is added and the process repeats. If no holes are left, the piece is stoned and sanded to make the enamel and metal flush. If twisted wires were included, though, the stoning steps are harder to do, and more care has to be taken so that the twists don't look flattened. In these cases, it's customary to leave the enamel lower than the wires. After sanding, the piece is polished with either hand polishing or a final flash firing.

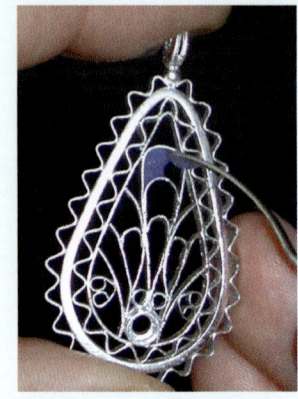

Figure 3.10 Diane Echnoz Almeyda adding enamel to a Filigree cell for the modern method of enameling Plique-à-jour. From my book *The Art of Fine Enameling* (2nd ed., 2019).

Pull-through

This modern technique (also called Break-through) is similar to Crackle Enamel in that the top layer has a reaction to the layer underneath it, which then forms a random design. The designs are different, however. Pull-through is primarily achieved by layering a soft enamel under a harder enamel. When firing, the base layer becomes molten before the top layer, which then flows up and surrounds the grains of enamel on the top, causing a dotted effect. The only controls on this process are to make the top layer thicker (less dotting) or heat it for longer (more dotting). This effect may have been known a long time ago but was likely considered an error and thus avoided. Note that in appearance it differs from Crackle Enamel in that Pull-through (buttons 252 and 253) creates dotted designs and Crackle makes twig-like designs (button 182, page 52).

Reticulated Foils

Reticulated Foils is a modern foil technique developed by Bill Helwig in the mid- to late twentieth century. It is a method of combining both gold and silver foil in layers and firing for a long time (10–15 minutes) until the foils fuse together into a texture, called reticulation. On top of this step, transparent enamels are added to take advantage of the resulting patterning. Sometimes, instead of just being a backdrop (as in button 254), the reticulation may be embellished and outlined to be the focus of the design.

Ronde Bosse

Also called "Émail en Ronde Bosse," "En Ronde Bosse," or "Encrusted Enamel" by the art world (not to be confused with the button world use of the word "Encrustation"). This means enamel in high relief and has been used since the fourteenth century. Ronde Bosse is named after the French for "in the round" and describes a three-dimensional object in high relief that is enameled (buttons 255, 256, and 257). These pieces are usually enameled with opaque enamels, but transparents and opalescent colors were also used. Gold was frequently the base metal, along with precious stones and pearls in articles first used in the church and later for personal adornment.

252. *I Love Cats*, Pull-through field on copper with flower wafers and a gold foil cat, by Karen L. Cohen.
253. *Moonlight*, Pull-through field on copper with silver foil stars, by Karen L. Cohen.
254. *Froggy Jumping*, copper button using Reticulated Foil and Sgraffito techniques, with flower wafers, fine silver twisted wires and balls, and gold foil frog on top, by Karen L. Cohen.
255. Antique Ronde Bosse openwork enamel with interrupted paste border (frequently called St. George and the Dragon).

256

257

The House of Fabergé used this technique. Herman Bangeman, in his July 2004 article in the *NBB*, says, "The buttons that collectors call Hungarian jewels are sometimes embellished with ronde bosse enameling."[25] These are also called Austro-Hungarian and court jewels, although their origin is not known (see buttons 25 and 26, page 8).

ENAMELING IN RELIEF

Enamel Tech Talk

The button literature says that it's difficult to enamel in the round, which is true. But there are things that can be used to make this endeavor easier. When enameling a design in high relief with different design elements, as in figures, the wet-packing application technique would be used. However, large wide areas can be sifted. In the wet solution, the enamelist would use an enamel adhesive to aid in holding the enamel in place when it is fired. In addition, the enamelist would probably underfire the piece until the end to ensure that the enamel stays where it is wanted and does not drip into other areas. Furthermore, soft enamels or high-fusion-flow enamels would probably not be used, as these would move around too much. When enameling a fully three-dimensional piece, in addition to the above notes, the piece could very well be enameled in sections, continually rotating the piece to keep even coverage. Again, underfiring is best until the last firing.

Separation Enamel

Separation Enamel (SE) (buttons 258 and 259) was developed by Thompson Enamel in the mid-twentieth century and is thus a modern technique. It is a liquid enamel formulation that changes the viscosity of the enamels to cause various layers, previously fused, to separate so that the underlying enamel layers can be seen around the edges of the applied SE design. Originally this method was for lead-bearing enamels, but it is now available for lead-free enamels.

The most successful outcome is when there is a good contrast between the typical three layers of enamel, each being fired between layers. The bottom base layer should be a light transparent or flux, followed by a dark transparent, followed by a light opaque. Then the SE is painted on the surface in a design of the artist's choosing and fired. The result is controlled by the thickness of each layer and the type of enamel used—softer underlying enamels give a feathered line whereas harder underlying enamels give a sharper edge.

258

259

Sgraffito

Sgraffito (buttons 260 and 261, as well as 262 and 263, page 66) is scratching through raw enamel, either grain or liquid. Doing so allows underlying enamel or metal to show through or a light color enamel to be sifted into the lines (button 254—the yellow lines in the blue near the top). This technique was used in antique buttons to help define a design (button 190, page 53—see the lines in the tree foliage and water), rather than as the main design element. Sgraffito has been popular with art enamelists since the 1950s, and a method that incorporated some Sgraffito was used in Limoges School painting and was called enlevage à l'aquille.

260

261

256. Antique realistic Ronde Bosse cicada with colorful counter enamel.
257. Antique Ronde Bosse realistic frog on a lily pad toggle button.
258. Contour three-hole sew-through flower button using the Separation Enamel technique with fine silver balls, by Karen L. Cohen.
259. Copper enamel using Separation Enamel in a spiral design with black transfer/decal of birds on a wire, by Karen L. Cohen.
260. Persian Polychrome landscape with Sgraffito in green border, set into octagonal frame with twisted wire border. This landscape is not typical of the Persian style (page 58), but the rope border of the mounting and the Sgraffito is.
261. Antique square-shaped Monochrome, signed "DF," with Sgraffito in various places.

Many Sgraffito lines are just that—lines. But sometimes you can use a shaped tool to pull enamel off the design before it's fired. An example is probably button 184 (page 53). I believe the tree leaves and the shrubbery around the tree was done with Sgraffito. That is, black was put down where the leaves and shrubs should go. Then a tool, like today's rubber shaper tools for clay, was used to pull some black off the image and make the areas look more like foliage. Of course, we can't be sure how this was done, but that is what the result of using a shaper tool would look like. However, button 264 was done with a brush.

Stenciling

As in stenciled painting, enamel stenciling uses a cutout, either the negative or the positive image, to block out an area to which the enamel is applied (button 265). Stencils can also be used by tracing the image with a graphite pencil or special pens, which can be fired onto enamel. Studio Button artist Ada Snow Smith stated that she did work in this technique.

Two similar specialized forms of Stenciling were developed at the turn of the twenty-first century by American enamelist Jan Arthur Harrell. She called one version Embossed Gold (button 266) and the other Burnt Gold. Both can be done with either gold leaf or gold foil, and in this case, unless it is noted, it is hard to tell which was used. In any case, the main difference is that Burnt Gold is done directly onto a copper base, whereas Embossed Gold is done over enamel.

Transfers/Decals

As per the online Cambridge dictionary, a decal is "a picture or design printed on special paper that can be put onto another surface, such as metal or glass." Thus, the button world use of the word "transfer" is a form of decal, and, in fact, those from Battersea Enamel Factory (page 8) were the first decals ever used in enameling. Besides Battersea-style transfer buttons, the Motiwala Brothers (page 100) also made many buttons using transfers, and in modern times, it is not unusual for enamelists to use transfers, either ones they print themselves (see the ETT "Modern Transfers") or commercially purchased decals (button 267).

Another transfer method is silk-screening, which can be done directly onto an enameled surface or made into a decal that can then be transferred to an enamel surface.

Original transfers were monochrome outlines or images (buttons 268, 269, and 270). See the ETT "Original Transfers" for more information. Black, red, blue, and sepia were used for the transfer of design. Then, if the transfer was an outline, Painting Materials or transparent enamels could be used to colorize the image. The enamel field was sometimes enhanced with pink, yellow, or green enamels.

262. Flux field over copper, with red enamel that has been Sgraffitoed to form stripes with a millefiori center, by Herman Lowenstein.
263. Realistic button—the hedgehog's ear was done with Sgraffito, and his spikes were done by Scrolling, by Helene Carter.
264. Realistic cross with Sgraffito done with a dry brush, by Karen L. Cohen.
265. Stenciled blue design on clock face with movable hands, by Janet White.
266. Heart-shaped copper using stenciled Embossed Gold technique using gold foil, by Karen L. Cohen.
267. Transfer on enamel by Joy Robbins; photo credit JoNel Kurtz.
268. One-of-a-kind eighteenth-century transfer enamel on copper made by Scovill Manufacturing Co. This piece was a gift to Lafayette during his trip to the United States. It's rumored that the chip in the center, revealing the copper base, occurred because Lafayette always carried this button in his pocket with other objects.
269. Nineteenth-century Transfer / Polychrome flower on plated metal with a shaped rococo border, back marked "Paris EM." See button 272 for a closeup.
270. Antique Monochrome enamel transfer mounted in metal with cut steel border. Notice the dotty pattern, which shows it's a transfer.

TRANSFERS VERSUS HAND PAINTED

How does one tell whether a button is a transfer/decal or was painted using the Émaux Peints technique? Here are some ways to differentiate. Other ways may exist, but this list provides a general overview.

1. Check two buttons with the same design. If the two buttons are exactly the same, then it must be a decal, because someone hand painting the same design would never be able to create two exactly the same.
2. Many full-color decals are digitally printed or silk-screened. When magnified, they can look pixilated (button 271).
3. Antique buttons using the transfer printing method, when magnified, will show the image as a series of irregular dots (button 272).

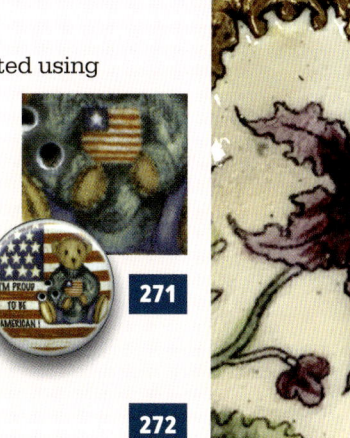

ORIGINAL TRANSFERS

Originally transfers were accomplished by taking a heated detailed engraving plate, applying colored enamel ink, printing onto tissue paper, applying the paper to an enamel base, and firing. Sometimes the paper of the transfer was removed and sometimes not.

There were two types of engraving plates. One had a stipple method, which was created using an etching process. This was eventually completed with hand engraving and frequently used in portraits (somewhat like our presidents on money bills). The other was standard hand engraving, which was used in various ways, including lettering. Sometimes the stipple plates were used to put down the design in oil, which, while still sticky (not quite dry), was dusted over with pigments, shaken so what didn't stick to the oil fell off, and then dried completely before firing. Today we call this method "sift and tap." This type of transfer use was usually not overpainted with colors, although other transfers were.[26] More information on Battersea-style transfers can be found in the book *English Painted Enamels*.[27]

MODERN TRANSFERS

In modern times, new decal paper was developed to allow an iron-toner copier or laser printer to output an image that can be used as a decal. These fire a sepia brown color (button 273) and can be made easily by artists. Printing onto special paper for circuit boards etching, like PnP paper, can also be used for decals, and they fire black.

Today decals printed for fused glass, porcelain, or enamels can be used in enameling. They are printed with enamel fines (any color), gold, silver, or Painting Materials. To print them, they can be silk-screened or printed either digitally or by press. Four-color decals need to be preheated, in something like a toaster oven, to burn out other substances before fully firing onto an enamel (button 274). One type of modern decal is Dicro Slide, which is made with the coating for dichroic glass. These can be further processed to get what is called Dicro Slide Frit, small pieces of the coating without a backing that look like multicolored glitter (button 275).

---

271. Transfer and verbal, three-hole sew-through button, by Karen L. Cohen.
272. Detail of button 269. Notice how the outline is a series of dots while the remaining image was hand painted.
273. Transfer / Émaux Peints button, by Mona Ledwin.
274. Left: Transfer image after preheating. Right: Button after firing in the kiln. By Karen L. Cohen.
275. Black and gold transfer/decal of a Hoopoe bird on branch, also using Dicro Slide Frit multicolored decals, by Karen L. Cohen.

ENAMEL TOPCOATS

When completing an enamel, the artist must decide on the topcoat to best represent their design. In the enameling world, this element is called the finish. So as not to be confused with the button world term "Decorative Finish (DF)," I will use the term "topcoat." That being said, the default topcoat, and most common, is a glossy surface. As most enamels fire glossy anyway, no extra firing would be needed. However, sometimes a piece is ground, which produces a matte surface. In addition, some enamels or Painting Materials fire matte. For these situations, a topcoat must be designed. There are at least two non-glossy topcoats and at least two ways to get a glossy topcoat. This section describes these methods.

Glossy

Glossy topcoats are the most common for enamel. This can be accomplished one of two ways—with extensive grinding (hand polish) and without (flash fire). Which is better? The hand polish provides a much more brilliant surface, which is the smoothest possible topcoat. If creating two pieces with the same design, one with a flash fire and one with a hand polish, you would clearly be able to tell the difference. But it may be difficult if not comparing two pieces. Which should the enamelist use? That could depend on the enameling technique used and other considerations. More on this subject follows.

Émaux Peints pieces cannot be directly ground for a hand polish because the paint is thin and would be removed by the grinding/sanding process. Although the colors fuse into the enamel field (i.e., they are stable), the paint is so thin that scratching could remove some color. Thus, a clear coat is frequently added to protect the painting and to brighten and harmonize the colors.[28] This is called the "Geneva Method," "crowning," or "fluxing"—and, at least by the second half of the nineteenth century, it was a basic part of the process for enamel painters. Émaux Peints enamels were finished with no topcoat, a flash fire with flux, or a hand polish. With a clear coat on top, it's like looking through thin glass, thus giving the illusion of depth—which is one way to see whether there had been a clear coat on top of a painting.

Flash Fire

This is the easiest way to complete a piece. A flash fire is a fast fire in which only the top layer of the enamel fuses, but the underneath need not. This process allows the surface to become glossy. It can be done with or without an additional layer of enamel.

One topcoat of flux over a painting is sufficient to protect the image. In early texts on enameling, this method is mentioned. "Crowning" (final layer of flux) would be fired as a flash fire. For extra brilliance, however, antique buttons could also have one or more layers of flux and then be hand polished (see below).

When a piece is ground/sanded, the artist must decide whether a flash fire or a hand polish should be done. This would mainly be for techniques such as Cloisonné, Champlevé, or Plique-à-jour. With these techniques, if the piece has no surface embellishments, then the artist could use either a flash fire or a hand polish. But if the enamel has surface embellishments in relief (button 121, page 35), then a flash fire is necessary, as a hand polish would destroy the relief. Do note, though, in a Cloisonné with a flash fire, one can feel the wires slightly, as the enamel sinks a bit with each firing. As an example, look at figure 3.11. These images show the same piece (a Cloisonné jewel) in two stages: a flash fire on the left and its completed hand polish. This artist uses a flash fire as part of his hand polishing technique.

Figure 3.11 Two images of the same jewel by contemporary enamelist Don Viehman showing the difference between a flash fire and a hand polish. Observe the circled area. In the left view (the flash fire), the wire looks puckered because, even though after the grinding/sanding the enamel and wires were even, after the flash fire the enamel sinks just a bit. In the right view (the hand polish), the wires and enamel are totally even and very smooth.

Hand Polish

A hand polish is typically used with those techniques that grind/sand the top of the enamel, usually to be flush with the metal surrounding it, as in Cloisonné, or over a painted enamel (but not Grisaille or Limoges-style). The top might also be ground to get an even topcoat so the reflection will be more consistent, which provides a more brilliant appearance. Smooth/even reflections are important when viewing something that is shiny—the piece looks more impressive because the image is more precise and not distorted. Take, for example, a star sapphire gemstone. When rotating the stone from side to side, the star moves perfectly as six straight rays. With an uneven surface, the rays would wiggle.

Abrading the enamel requires taking the grinding/sanding to about 600 grit. If left at that stage, the piece would have a satin finish, not quite matte but not high gloss; one could flash fire at this point. To go to high gloss, the sanding would continue to 1200 or 1500 grit, and then a compound like cerium oxide would be used. This surface is superior to a flash fire because a regular enamel surface has microscopic pores. With each finer grit of sanding, the pores get smaller and smaller, and the scratches of previous grits get removed. Finally, the last compound polishes the smooth surface to a high gloss. In techniques such as Cloisonné and Champlevé, one cannot feel the separation between the metal and the enamel. Figure 3.11 shows the difference. How do you tell the difference on a button? It might be difficult, but if the top is extremely smooth, as in many Pâte buttons (page 57), that would be your clue.

Matte

A matte topcoat (buttons 276, 277, and 278) can be accomplished in a few ways. Most typically today it is done with a glass etchant (like Amour Etch or Etch All) painted on or dipped into, which takes only 10–15 minutes. The other way is to grind and then sand the top to about 400 grit. To get an Émaux Peints piece to be matte, multiple clear coats would have to be added first, as the etchant directly on the Painting Material would remove some of the design. In earlier times, "sandblasting" (or the use of highly caustic hydrofluoric acid) was the method to matte enamels. By at least 1911, a liquid called "mate-email" was available that was fast to use, was safe, and resulted in better matte surfaces.[29] See the ETT "Matte Enamels" for more information.

Today we have glass etchant resists to cover areas not to be etched. In 1911, they used a "thick coat of resinous matter such as bitumen, pitch, gutta-percha, or even suitable varnishes or wax" as a resist with the "mate-email" to shield areas they wanted to be left glossy.[30]

Sugar Fire

An underfired topcoat is another way to achieve a non-glossy surface to an enamel. It is not smooth, like a matte enamel, but bumpy (somewhat like the look of Coralene). This is called a Sugar Fire topcoat (button 280, page 70; button 399, page 89—the photo shows the Sugar Fire topcoat over the sun better than the rest of the piece). Sugar Fire "softens" the look of the enamel image by making it appear hazy. This is a modern method. Though doable years ago, it probably was not employed. It is popular today with art enamelists.

In a Sugar Firing, usually a light transparent enamel or flux is applied with either a 100- or a 200-mesh sifter

MATTE ENAMELS

Some enamels are formulated to fire matte. These might have quartz or clay in them to reduce the gloss. Other enamels are low-acid resistant, which means that if they are put into an acid solution, they will go matte and may never fire glossy again. Lastly, pure metal oxides for painting fire matte. What was used in antique enamels is not known, but similar enamels must have been formulated, as shown by button 111 (page 33). See button 279 for an example of black enamel that went matte in acid.

---

276. Antique matte Champlevé / Emaux Peints with C-scroll pattern design.
277. Antique matte Polychrome head with Champlevé outer border.
278. Antique matte scarab set on wide pictorial outer border.
279. Turn-again pattern with Faux Opal center using fine silver balls and twisted and round wires, by Karen L. Cohen. The field was made matte by putting the button in acid; note that the Faux Opal did not turn matte in the same acid bath.

in a very thin layer and then fired until it just starts fusing (figure 2.1a, page 29), stopping before it's fully fused, thus leaving a grainy surface. Depending on how long it is fired, the amount of graininess will vary. If opaque enamel is used instead of transparent, the Sugar Fire will be just a texture on the enamel surface.

and 282) of the button. Embellishments found on the metal portion of a button are cut steel, paste, gemstones, pearls, and more. In addition, sometimes enamel might be fired onto the metal, creating gemstone-like Encrustations (button 289, page 72).

Dichroic Extract Powders

Dichroic Extract Powders are the pure form of the coating found on Dichroic Glass. They are available in various colors. They can be applied to an enamel in the last firing to provide a brilliant dichroic effect.

Gemstones

Gemstones of all types are typical embellishments to any piece of decoration. If the gem is hard enough to be fired in a kiln, then it could be fused into enamel. That includes synthetic stones such as Cubic Zirconia (CZ), which does come in colors. These can be fired directly into the enamel and held in place by surrounding enamel (button 283).

Most natural stones, except for diamonds, cannot be heated to high temperatures. However, the coefficient of expansion of diamonds is dissimilar enough to enamel that, when fused into enamel, it causes craze lines around it. Although these probably would not further crack, it most likely is not what the designer intended. Thus, to add any type of natural stone to the enamel surface without firing or gluing them in, a bezel or prong setting can be fused into the enamel and the stone set after the enameling is completed. In addition, diamonds can be bought preset in something like a tube setting, and this entire setting/diamond combination unit can be fused into the enamel; other methods exist. Alternatively, the stone can be part of a pin shank (button 284).

EMBELLISHMENTS

In enameling, we consider anything other than enamel itself or Painting Materials to be Material Supplements (also called embellishments). These may be under the enamel or on top. However, in the button world, Decorative Finishes (DFs) and Other Material Embellishments (OMEs) lie on the top of the enamel or on the metal surface of the button. For enamelists, all DFs and OMEs fall under the same group as Material Supplements. It is not for me to say what the classification of these embellishments are, especially if they are not on top of the surface, so I leave that for the classification committee to determine.

In this section, I address embellishments listed in alphabetical order without regard to prominence. Keep in mind that some of these are used only in the modern era, so they may not be on older enamel buttons, but I list them so you will know when you see them in the future. Of course, new materials might also be developed. I start with those embellishments found on the metal surface of the button, not the enamel itself, as these are part of enamel buttons but not part of the enamel.

Embellishments Not on the Enamel

In the button world, Decorative Finishes (DFs) and Other Material Embellishments (OMEs) added to an enamel button can be either on the enamel itself or on the metal portion (buttons 281

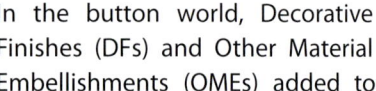

280. Émaux Peints reminiscent of Chinese Brush Painting of a cherry tree branch and blossoms with three bird Paillons using a Sugar Fire topcoat, by Karen L. Cohen.
281. Antique oval Monochrome figure with outer cut steel border.
282. Antique enamel head mounted in six-lobed openwork metal frame border with graduated paste.
283. Fold-formed fine silver button using leaded transparent enamels, black decals of dragonflies, Dicro Slide Frit decals coming off the dragonfly's tail, flower wafers, fine silver twisted wire and balls, and a pink CZ, by Karen L. Cohen.
284. Antique Polychrome floral design with Sgraffito fish-scale design outer border and pin shank diamond center. Note that the back has a similar design.

Glass

Many forms of glass (figure 3.12) can be fired onto enamels, including lampwork, molded glass, and specially formulated materials containing glass. These embellishments are discussed below.

Figure 3.12 Enamel lumps, Dichroic Frit Flakes, pulverized Goldstone, and seed beads.

Balls

Glass balls (a bead without a hole) can be fused into enamel (button 285); they can be opaque or transparent glass. Typically, they are of a harder glass, so during normal firing they will not flatten out. However, if totally overfired, they could start flattening (or at least sinking more into the underlying enamel). A very beautiful button with glass balls is button 10 (page 2).

Reflector balls (button 286) are a type of glass ball used to reflect light. They are the essential components added to make highway line paint reflective. They come in three sizes, and all can be fused onto enamel.

Beads

Glass seed beads can be fired into enamels—but only high-quality, non-dyed beads. Sometimes they will be fired with the holes facing up (button 287, page 72;

ENAMEL BUILDUP OR GLASS FUSED ONTO ENAMEL?

How can you tell whether something is a separate piece of glass fused onto the enamel or an enamel buildup (see definition on page 58)? If it's a separate piece of glass, that glass would normally have been a harder glass (i.e., it softens at a higher temperature) than enamel. Thus, when heated at normal enamel temperatures, it retains its shape (sharp edges, cupped form, etc.). When enamel fuses, it slumps to a puddle on the surface, forming a flat bottom and, with enough enamel, a domed top like an Encrustation. When glass is fused onto the enamel, it will fuse at the point of contact, but the part that is not at the point of contact will retain its shape, creating a shelf, "overhang," or "undercut." In addition, any sharp edges it may have had will stay fairly sharp (may round slightly but not completely).

> *Note that glass balls fused onto enamel have curves/undercuts, which really are just the smallest cross section of the sphere (**button 10**, page 2). Lampwork-shaped glass can also be fused in (**button 292**, page 72).*

There is one exception to the overhang rule—fusing enamel lumps/chips onto enamel. These are technically not enamel "buildups," but they do form mounds, usually with irregular shapes and no undercuts (button 297, page 73). Tom Ellis says this: "Lumps have much less surface area than ground enamel which has a lot of surface area—each individual grain of enamel has its own surface area. When enamel gets hot enough to soften . . . it tries to reduce its surface area to the very least amount possible. It pulls to the greater mass. In lump form this would take place as the material heats to softening temperature. If the temperature increases, there is a point where gravity and fusion flow influences the enamel shape—it becomes a 'puddle.'"[31] An enamel buildup would not result in the irregular shapes as seen in the button (button 297, page 73).

There is one other caveat: Enamel chips can be made in small spheres when fired in a special way, but fusing them to an enamel surface is delicate. Thus, fusing a mass of them together is difficult. In any case, these are not buildups of enamel.

---

285. Realistic Gin-bari frog using glass balls as eyes and metal ball OMEs, by Karen L. Cohen.
286. Realistic copper poodle using reflector balls as its "pomps" and white fusible paint for an eye, by Karen L. Cohen.

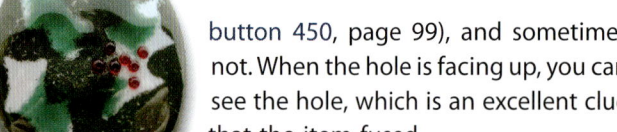

button 450, page 99), and sometimes not. When the hole is facing up, you can see the hole, which is an excellent clue that the item fused was a seed bead! Moreover, if the bead is of a larger size and the hole is up, it can also be fused with a smaller seed bead sitting in the hole to give a dot effect (button 288; button 412, page 92).

287

288

Faux Opals

Opals are semiprecious stones that cannot take the heat of the kiln. However, opals can be simulated with enamel in one of three ways. One was done more than a century ago (button 3, page viii). In 1899, Cunynghame says, "The dissolved gold [obtained from another procedure] can of course be used to color enamel with. With care, the imitation gems can be made parti-coloured. By using flux with 10% of arsenic in it opal intaglios can be imitated."[32] This coloring, to any experienced enamelist, cannot be achieved by just an enamel color. Thus, it was exciting for me to find out how this may have been done.

For the second approach, consider button 289, which has milky, opal-looking Encrustations on the border. This is probably opalescent white enamel directly on the brass substrate, thus reflecting the brass from its base, which shimmers.

289

The third method is using special enamel lumps called Opal Jewel Effect lumps by Thompson Enamel. This technique was developed by Irmgard Carpenter, wife of Woodrow Carpenter, the deceased owner of Thompson Enamel. Basically, a Cloisonné wire is bent to the shape desired and fused into the enamel field. On the next firing, gold and silver foils are laid inside the wire and fused. Then transparent enamels are fused on top of the foil.

Lastly, the Opal Jewel Effect lump is added on top of this and fused at a higher-than-normal temperature (around 1470°F). Assuming it produces a high enough dome (if not, add more), it is fired again at a lower temperature (around 1430°F) so that it becomes somewhat milky. The result looks like an opal (button 290).

290

Goldstone

There are two forms of Goldstone, which I suspect are the same type. However, one is premixed with enamel, and one is not. The original was an enamel made in Japan, called Goldstone or Tea Goldstone Enamel. It has powdered metal (usually copper) added to enamel and provides a "glitter"-type effect (button 62, page 15).

The other is a glittering glass, sometimes called aventurine glass. Goldstone may be confused with a semiprecious stone but is man-made. It has been used in older buttons (button 296). If crushed to a fine powder (.425mm), it can be mixed with flux or other enamels to look like glitter (button 291). This effect is called "flimmer" by the Germans.[33]

291

Lampwork

292

Lampworkers are glass artists who use a torch to form glass into desired shapes. Glass comes with various coefficients of expansion, and all of these may not be compatible with enamel. But if they are compatible, any shape formed by this method can be fused onto enamel. Normally the glass is a harder glass than enamel, so its shape does not change when fused into the enamel surface. It would probably be best to do this fusing at the last firing or two (button 292).

---

287. Stenciled holly leaves with red seed beads as berries, by Linda K. Reynolds.
288. Detail of a fox movable button with yellow and black seed beads for the eyes, by Janet White.
289. Antique Émaux Peints floral with hexagonal border of opalescent Encrustations (Faux Opals). Note firescale around the Encrustations.
290. Cloisonné/Guilloché (moiré pattern) triad-like design with Faux Opal, by Karen L. Cohen.
291. *Maharaja's Pet*, realistic elephant button using crushed goldstone mixed with enamel for the blanket and headpiece using fine silver balls, twisted wire, and flower wafer, by Karen L. Cohen.
292. Enameled button embellished with (probably) lampworked glass "petals" forming flowers, by Émaux Ardéchois. Notice the undercuts of some of the petals, where you can see shadows under these overhangs.

Lumps

Two types of lumps can be fused onto enamel. One type is enamel, and the other is harder glass. Smaller versions can be called chips, bits, or frit. This section discusses both types of lumps.

Enamel Lumps. Enamel lumps are a typical embellishment to buy from enamel suppliers. In fact, from Thompson Enamel, you can order lumps in any color enamel that they sell. Lumps come in both opaque and transparent colors and in mixtures and can be fired to be flush with the enamel field or raised into a bump. There is also a type called Venetian Lumps, which are scrolled liquid enamels and thus variegated (button 293). Lumps are used in the Scrolling technique (button 294) discussed on page 61 or as a design element by themselves (button 295). The small chips were used extensively by Herman Lowenstein (page 99) to create his signature look. They are not often found in antique buttons, but there are some examples, such as button 296. One Thompson Enamel item comes only in lump form—Opal Jewel Effect Lumps. These can effectively be used to form a "Faux Opal" (button 279, page 69).

Lumps can be used in a way that sometimes can be confused with an enamel buildup. With experience, the collector can tell the difference. Consider button 297. This button may look like a buildup of enamel to the inexperienced eye, but if that were true, there would not be all the hills and valleys of the colors. To an enamelist, this button clearly uses lumps and not the technique of building up enamel. For more information, see the sidebar "Enamel Buildup or Glass Fused onto Enamel?" (page 71).

Glass Lumps. Various types of glass lumps can be fused onto enamel. The coefficient of expansion must be compatible, but these lumps are normally harder glass than enamel and thus retain some (if not all) of their shape when fused. This type includes Dichroic Frit glass pieces (button 298) and other pieces of glass normally acquired from a glass fusing supplier. These can be small pieces with sharp edges that may somewhat round out when fused to enamel, though not completely.

Murrini and Millefiori

Murrini are canes of colored glass designs whose cross sections are used for embellishments in both glass and enamel items. Those murrini designs that look like flowers are called millefiori. (*Note:* Many people call all murrini millefiori, but "murrini" is the generic term.) Glass canes can be made by lampworking or by molding glass in successive molds with different shapes. Millefiori canes are frequently used in glass paperweights and are a mainstay of Venetian/Murano glass articles. Most glass paperweight button artists will make their own murrini to include in their buttons, especially for their signature. See buttons 299 and 300; buttons 301 and 302 (page 74); button 262 (page 66); and button 450 (page 99) for examples.

As most murrini are made with hard glass, they take a lot of time to fuse and are thus usually fused onto enamel before other embellishments (see the ETT "Order of Fusing in Embellishments," page 74).

---

293. *Artist's Palette Petite*, realistic button using enamel threads and lumps and a Venetian lump under the threads, by Karen L. Cohen.
294. Realistic bell-shaped copper using lumps in Scrolling, by Herman Lowenstein.
295. Enamel button with Separation Enamel (page 65) field, black decal of a Stegosaurus, with enamel lumps left in relief, by Karen L. Cohen. Notice the red lump on the left is not quite rounded on the top. This has the look of the lumps in button 297.
296. Antique Champlevé openwork border with unusual center of enamel chips and goldstone.
297. Champlevé / Basse Taille button with enamel lumps forming a flower-like design with an enamel border.
298. Dichroic Frit Flake pieces in this movable/verbal button, by Janet White.
299. Enamel button using multiple designs of murrini from glass canes.
300. *Six Rays*, six-hole sew-through button using three sizes of millefiori, by Karen L. Cohen.

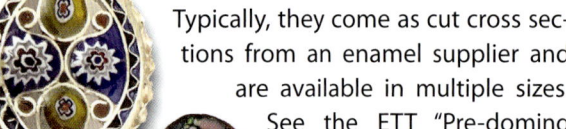

Typically, they come as cut cross sections from an enamel supplier and are available in multiple sizes. See the ETT "Pre-doming Millefiori" for information on how to prepare these for fusing onto an enamel piece.

Flower wafers (button 254, page 64) are an exception to murrini being made of hard glass. Flower wafers—canes using vitreous enamel—were developed by Tim Ellis (brother to Tom Ellis) in the early 1990s using a proprietary method. Because they are regular enamel, these do not have to be pre-domed and can readily be fused to a piece. They are one of my favorite embellishments.

PRE-DOMING MILLEFIORI

When purchasing millefiori, they are normally sent as rough cross sections of a cane (figure 3.13). These are made with hard glass, which takes a long time to fuse. Normally the artist would want their tops to be domed, but doming them while fusing them onto a piece may take too long and ruin the rest of the piece, so I always teach students to pre-dome them before use. To do this, I set many of them out on a ceramic firing plate and fire at one time so that they are available when needed (figure 3.14). They might take about 8–10 minutes to dome.

Figure 3.13 Just-purchased millefiori prepared to be slumped to dome their tops.

Figure 3.14 Millefiori domed after pre-firing and ready to be used in an enamel piece.

ORDER OF FUSING IN EMBELLISHMENTS

When creating an enameled piece, it's important for the artist to determine the order that elements will be added. Harder glass elements go in first so that softer items are not overfired. The elephant in button 303 required many firings to get each of the elements in. These are the firings needed to finish this piece:

- Counter enamel is added to the back.
- The front base gray of the elephant is fused on.
- The millefiori is fused in after being pre-domed.
- The fine silver balls are then fused in to provide the boundaries for the twisted wire to frame the blanket.
- The twisted wires are applied. These could have been done on the previous fusing, but it is difficult to get them all to stay in position if the balls are not fused in first.
- Next is the mica luster around the millefiori. However, lusters are not totally opaque, so the dark gray base affects its color. Thus, in this firing, I wet-packed a layer of color that coordinated with the luster color on the blanket and around the millefiori.
- The luster, as well as the eye of the elephant (with black Painting Material), is applied in the last firing.

---

301. Silver Filigree Plique-à-jour with millefiori, by Diane Echnoz Almeyda.
302. Realistic clover-shaped copper with millefiori, by Herman Lowenstein.
303. Realistic elephant button, embellished with millefiori, mica luster, fine silver twisted wire and balls, and black Overglaze for the eye, by Karen L. Cohen.

Molded Glass

Molding of glass has been known since ancient Rome and Egypt. The most common technique is called Pâte de Verre (pot di vair'), which became popular during the early 1900s in the Art Nouveau period. The term "*Pâte de Verre*" means "glass paste" in French. A mixture of powdered glass and coloring agents was mixed and molded. If different colors were used, then the relief parts of the mold were brushed in first. After the mold was fired in a kiln to fuse the glass, the item was removed, which sometimes necessitated the mold being destroyed. Molded glass in modern times outside of France is usually called cast glass.

Today fused-glass artists create molded glass with a binder called Liquid Stringer, which can also be used with enamel. Another material for the binder is CMC (carboxymethylcellulose). Various types of molds can be used.

If the coefficient of expansion of any cast glass is compatible with enamel, then the molding can be fused onto enamel (button 304).

SULFIDE VERSUS PÂTE DE VERRE

Sulfides are molded glass also known as Cameo Incrustations. They are usually white figurines that are encased in clear glass items such as paperweights. They look very similar to Pâte de Verre. However, even though both are glass moldings, they are not the same. Sulfides are manufactured with clay/ceramic materials mixed with a glass paste in a process using sulfur, from which it gets its name. They are encased in clear glass, whereas Pâte de Verre is glass plus colors only and not encased in glass.

MUD

MUD (button 305) is a glass material developed by Unique Glass Colors in 2009–2010 for glass fusers. It's a combination of glass slivers and a binder. When fired, the binder burns out, leaving just the glass. This process works perfectly well on enamels, but it also can be used on non-firing materials (such as wood) and allowed to air dry to rock hard. However, once fired onto glass or enamel, it is totally permanent, whereas, when allowed to air dry, it can be softened if wet. MUD comes in both white and black and can be colored with enamel in or over it. When fired, it remains in relief. To use, it's normally piped though a pastry bag and then manipulated with a brush to get the desired design. I feel it would be perfect for making designs such as in the eighteenth-century Battersea-style buttons that were usually gilded and had texture to them. This is a very new material, and not many enamelists are working with it yet.

Paste

Paste jewels were developed to simulate gemstones. In antique buttons, paste embellishments were sometimes glued into the enamel surface (button 306), as they could not take the heat of the kiln. Today, synthetic gemstones (page 70) would probably be used instead, as these materials come in a variety of colors and can take the heat of the kiln.

Threads

Threads are small pieces of what glass artists would call stringers (figure 3.15—notice some are fat and some are thin). These are very delicate and fuse quickly. Overfiring will cause them to spread. See buttons 307 and 308 for examples of their use.

Figure 3.15 Enamel threads, mostly opaque.

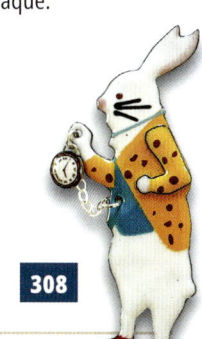

---

304. Antique rare enamel Pâte de Verre woman's head with foil embellishment.
305. Enameled button of a rose made with MUD, by Karen L. Cohen.
306. Antique Matte Polychrome basket with glued-in paste, in shaped plated metal floral outer border.
307. *Artist's Palette*, realistic button using enamel threads and lumps, by Karen L. Cohen.
308. Realistic Wonderland rabbit using threads for his whiskers and an arm made by a separate piece of enameled metal fused to the body, by Janet White.

Glow-in-the-Dark Materials

Glow materials come in both powder and decals (button 309). Both must be charged with bright light in order to glow and can be recharged as needed.

Metal

Metal is one of the two components in the base of any enamel, but it can also be used as an embellishment in various forms. Antique enamel buttons often used foil and Paillons, whereas in modern times enamelists might also use balls and wire. This section lists what is available.

Balls

In general, metal balls can be made from silver, copper, or gold by heating a small piece until it melts, at which point it pulls itself into a ball. Fine silver and gold make perfect spheres, but copper and its alloys will have a flat bottom unless made in special way. If you want to make balls of equal size, you must start with equal amounts of metal. One way to do this is to make a tight coil of wire, which is cut apart for equal-size rings.

Metal balls (button 310) can be fused onto enamel by forming a small indent in the enamel or using a mixture of the appropriate enamel color with water and enamel adhesive to form a cup in which the ball sits. These are usually done on the last or second-to-last firing because with each firing the ball will sink and thus not sit in high relief.

309

Filings and Drill Curlicues

The metal dust after metal has been filed (i.e., filings) and the curly pieces left after drilling into metal (button 311) can also be fused into enamel to give the surface a texture. The curlicues are especially good for wavy hair on a person or animal!

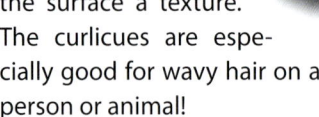
311

Foil and Leaf

Foil and leaf are both forms of thin metal but are usually very different in appearance, usage, and application. See the sidebar "Leaf versus Foil versus Sheet Metal" for how they differ. Foil can be applied at any level over the base coat of enamel, as it must fuse to enamel, not metal. Leaf is normally on top but can also be embedded. If used on the top, gold foil/leaf never tarnishes, but silver foil/leaf can. The application of foil is straightforward, but the application of leaf is more complex. See the ETTs "Foil Application" and "Leaf Application" (page 78) for more information. Foil is usually an embellishment, but it can be used to form the focus of the design (buttons 312 and 313).

312

313

One type of foil embellishment is called Paillons (figure 3.16). These are precisely cut shapes of a thicker gold or silver foil (thicker than what is normally used in enameling) that are usually embossed. They may be used singly or in groups. Although the relief side of the embossing is normally facing up, they can be used facing down with enamel inlaid into the depressions to enrich the design. These were made to simulate repoussé metal ornamentation.

Keep in mind that the term "*Paillons*" has multiple meanings (see the sidebar "Paillons Terminology," page 78). But as used here, I mean the examples as in figure 3.16. These have been used extensively in buttons, especially in the eighteenth century. Paillons are no longer manufactured, but a stash was found, so some of today's Studio Button artists have them to use on modern buttons. Typically, Paillons are used under a clear coat of enamel (or a very light tinted color), but this was a design choice and not needed for the integrity of the piece. In 1911, Millenet wrote that Paillons are normally covered with two layers of flux, the second being just thick enough to cover the high points of the relief in the Paillons.[34] The flux over the Paillons may be thick enough to then hand polish for more brilliance.

---

309. Heart-shaped copper button using flower wafers, gold foil dragonfly, fine silver balls, and glow-in-the-dark decal foliage, by Karen L. Cohen.
310. Octagon-shaped silver Filigree Plique-à-jour with silver balls on top, by Diane Echnoz Almeyda. Note that the balls on the lighter blue enamel are fused onto the enamel, but the other balls had previously been soldered onto the metal frame.
311. Movable robin in nest with metal drill curlicues in nest design, by Janet White.
312. Enamel on copper, focus of a foiled owl with some wires for accent, by Chris Litt; photo credit JoNel Kurtz.
313. Gold foil plant life, by Anita Tullis.

Foil and leaf are most often found in gold or silver. Today, leaf also comes in palladium and foil comes in platinum, but these are not frequently used. Foil can be used to provide a base design (i.e., Gin-bari) or cover an error (you would never know, as the mistake is covered!), to give the look of a silver or gold enameled piece on a copper base, to add more sparkle in a design (like in Limoges-style of Émaux Peints), or just to add a design element. Use over a copper base is common because copper is less expensive than silver (button 314; button 486, page 106). Foil (button 315) and leaf (button 316) will usually look quite different on an enameled surface, primarily because of their thickness and how they are used. Few (if any) antique buttons use gold leaf, so I included a dish (figure 3.17) to show what leaf looks like. I expect it to be used more often in contemporary times.

Figure 3.16 Example of various gold Paillons; from the book *The Art of Fine Enameling* (2nd ed., 2019).

Figure 3.17 A small enameled dish with a gold leaf design applied using a rubber stamp. Notice how the leaf is "broken." This result is typical of leaf on enamel. Foil does not usually do this.

LEAF VERSUS FOIL VERSUS SHEET METAL

Metal is milled into various thicknesses and measured in units including gauge, microns, millimeters, and inches. The following is a list of those metals normally used in enameling, but other versions—both thinner and thicker—exist; from thin to thick: leaf (0.5 microns), foil (1.4 microns), Gin-bari foil (4.5 microns), tooling foil (36 gauge), sheet metal (26–14 gauge). Please note that tooling foil is considered sheet metal even though its name includes the word "foil."

In general, leaf is so thin that it cannot be manipulated without being attached to a separate paper, as in Patent Leaf (figure 3.18), which is typically sold in a booklet of 25 sheets. Foil is thin enough that it can be cut, but mainly when formed in a sandwich between two pieces of paper. Sheet metal is sturdy enough to be held by a corner and cut with metal shears or a jeweler's saw.

Figure 3.18 Top to bottom, left to right: Patent Leaf, Gin-bari foil, gold foil, fine silver sheet.

FOIL APPLICATION

To attach pieces of foil to enamel, some enamelists say, the foil must have holes put in it to allow gases (like from an enamel adhesive) to escape during firing. To do this today, the enamelist puts the foil on a piece of 220-grit sandpaper, covers that with something soft like a piece of felt, and then uses a tool to roll over the felt, pressing the foil into the sandpaper. In earlier days, enamelists used fine needles embedded in a cork or homemade "sandpaper." Once the process is complete, if one holds the foil up to the light, tiny holes can be seen through the foil. It is now ready to be cut into shape, sandwiched between two pieces of paper. Once shaped, foil is attached to an enamel surface with a thin enamel adhesive. Other methods can be used, but this is the basic approach. The adhesive is brushed onto the enamel surface and the foil laid down on it. This is then allowed to dry completely before firing to make the foil permanent.

---

314. Cloisonné of unicorn, using flower wafers and fine silver balls and wires, by Karen L. Cohen. *Note:* The copper base was totally covered with silver foil before the Cloisonné wires were set.
315. Antique Émaux Peints saucer shape with Liquid Gold and foil in the butterfly's wings.
316. Sgraffito through gold leaf (square in the middle), with gold mica dots as a border, by Linda Lingren.

Enamel Tech Talk

LEAF APPLICATION

Leaf is attached using a material called "sizing." In enameling, the sizing must burn out completely in the kiln. Before applying the sizing, the surface should be rubbed with alcohol to ensure that it is clean. Enameling sizing is applied to the surface by any method that fits its design. Two application methods include brushing it on with a regular or specially shaped brush or brushing it onto a rubber stamp and then stamping the enamel. Once sizing is applied, it is left to partially dry to the tacky stage. Then the leaf is patted onto the tacky surface and left to dry completely. Invariably more leaf is on the surface than is needed by the design, and at this stage that is fine. When completely dry, a soft, bushy brush is swept across the design, and any leaf not attached to the sizing is thus removed. If more of the leaf needs to be removed, a bamboo skewer with a touch of alcohol can be used to rub some off, but care must be taken because too much alcohol will ruin the remaining leaf. When the desired amount is left, the piece is fired to make the leaf permanent (figure 3.17, page 77).

Another way to decorate with leaf is with Sgraffito (button 316, page 77). In this method, the leaf is applied as noted earlier, but with a special sizing. Once dried but before firing, a sharp tool is drawn through it so that the underlying enamel can be seen. A topcoat of clear can be used as an artist option.

PAILLONS TERMINOLOGY

The word "*Paillons*" has been used in a few ways. The first definition is what is usually found in a dictionary, and the others are in general usage. The second definition listed here was used more than a century ago.

1. A precisely cut ornamental design in foil, both silver (button 317) and gold, that is frequently embossed.
2. A small, shaped piece of foil used to embellish a particular aspect of an enamel design, as in the hat of a woman, as used in Limoges-style Émaux Peints buttons (button 209, page 56). In 1899, they used annealed (softened) foil to give a smooth look and non-annealed foil to give a crinkled look (button 318).
3. Any small piece of foil (button 319).
4. A small piece of flat sheet solder for metalsmiths.

Liquid Metal

Liquid metal has been used in enameling since the fifteenth century[35] and comes in gold (button 320), silver (button 123, page 35), and palladium. Gold is the most common. In the button world, the gold is called "gilded." In the enamel world, the gold is called "Liquid Gold." It is typical to find this material on Battersea-style buttons (button 321), but many other buttons also include it.

Mesh

Metal mesh comes in a variety of metals with a variety of weaves. It can be manipulated to form three-dimensional shapes or be cut to a particular shape (button 322). Mesh can also be used as the substrate for enameling (button 323). If using mesh as a substrate and using transparent enamels, it could be considered a form of Plique-à-jour.

317. Antique Basse Taille with silver Paillons forming six-lobed leaf inner border.
318. Cloisonné button with crinkled foil look.
319. Antique Émaux Peints, dress is foil-enhanced, outer border of cut steel.
320. Antique Polychrome couple with Liquid Gold inner border mounted in outer border of pastes.
321. Antique Battersea-style Émaux Peints / Guilloché with gilded (Liquid Gold) inner border.
322. Realistic Cloisonné hot air balloon with fine silver mesh used as a design element in the basket and a gold foil star and silver balls on top, by Karen L. Cohen.
323. Enamel of birds with Encrustations on a screen substrate. Image courtesy of Lion & Unicorn Auctions.

LIQUID GOLD APPLICATION TODAY AND YESTERYEAR

In the sixteenth century, enamelists ground up gold leaf and mixed it with honey and water and brushed it on. This material was sometimes called Shell Gold (search YouTube for "shell gold" on how this was made). In 1911, the gold came as a fine powder that had to be mixed with an essential oil that was a fat oil (medium for mixing painting powders to allow for slower drying) and mixed into a stiff paste. It was applied with a brush and not overly worked. After firing, it was burnished to bring out the brilliance.

Today, Liquid Gold can be purchased pre-mixed as a liquid (figure 3.19) or in pen form. As in earlier times, the liquid is applied with a brush in one application without going back over the area, but after firing it need not be burnished. Liquid Gold is finicky to work with, but, when done properly, it is wonderful to behold. It must be fired very low (below 1300°F) and on the last firing of a piece. If fired too high or for too long, it will either get craze lines or break up into a scattered pattern that might look good, but the result might not be what the artist had in mind.

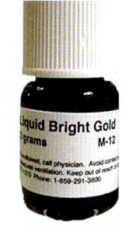

Figure 3.19 Liquid Gold

Metal Clay Overlay Silver Paste

This is a product currently exclusively made by the Aida Chemical Industries Co. Ltd., which developed a form of metal clay called Art Clay in the 1990s. Their Art Clay Overlay Silver Paste was then formulated to specifically be used on top of glass and porcelain and thus works on enamel. It is a liquid form of paste that is typically applied with a brush- or sponge-type tool. After firing onto enamel, it can be reapplied to gain some relief. It might be used to look like Silver Deposit (page 80) but, ideally, would be denoted as such to eliminate confusion. Obviously, this is a modern material and dates from the end of the twentieth century.

Metal Point

The technique of drawing with metal is called Metal Point (button 324). Copper, brass, silver, steel, or gold-filled wire or nails are used. The color each turns when fired depends on the firing temperature and time. As with some other materials, Metal Point must be done on a non-glossy, rough surface, such as after etching. It is difficult to know after the fact whether something was done with Metal Point unless the artist notes it.

Sheet and Cast Metal

Although foil and leaf start out as sheet metal, they are much thinner. Read about the differences in the sidebar "Leaf versus Foil versus Sheet Metal" (page 77). See also the ETT "Metal Embellishment Application" for how to attach sheet or formed metal to an enamel field (button 325). Any enameling sheet or cast metal can be used as an embellishment, but, as with foil, if used on the top, silver and copper metal will eventually tarnish. It may be covered with a topcoat of clear or possibly a chemical metal protector that doesn't affect the enamel. Conversely, it might be an enameled piece of metal. Metal can also be formed into a focal subject, like a bug (button 236, page 61) or border (button 141, page 43), or used as an embellishment (button 326).

METAL EMBELLISHMENT APPLICATION

Metal in the form of sheet (with or without enamel on it), wire, or balls can be added to an enamel surface with the same basic method. To do this, the enamel color for the attachment is moistened with water and an enamel adhesive and used to form a rim around the item, somewhat like an enamel bezel. This is allowed to dry and then fired. There are slight differences in the process for each type of metal, but this is a general overview. However, sometimes the added piece of metal (with or without enamel on top) need not have this bezel look but will look like it is "sitting" above the enamel, as in button 327.

---

324. Realistic flower button, by Janet White. Shading is done with Metal Point—copper (bluish) around the outside of petals and silver (yellow) in the center.
325. Realistic copper pig with attached fine silver Basse Taille wing and a silver ball for an eye, by Karen L. Cohen.
326. Copper fused onto an enamel field to form a bunch of grapes, by Herman Lowenstein.
327. Copper enameled using artist-made decal (the waves) and stenciled sun, by Janet White. The wave is a separate piece of metal added to this button without the "bezel" look.

Silver Deposit

In the glass and porcelain worlds, this material is called Silver Overlay. However, the term "overlay" has a different meaning in the button world, which mainly relates to glass over glass buttons. The *NBB* article by Herman Bangeman in October 2003 includes an excellent description of this electroformed technique.[36] He suggests it be called Silver Deposit, which implies the process of electroforming—depositing metal in articulated areas—and this is the term I use for the technique throughout this book. Some have called this approach Silver Resist, but that is a misnomer, as a resist is a material used to repel the electroplating solution. Silver Deposit enamel buttons are not common (buttons 328 and 329). See the ETT "Silver Deposit Process" for how this is done. And see the sidebar "Is It or Is It Not Silver Deposit?" for how to tell whether your button is a Silver Deposit or Champlevé. This process should not be confused with a button that has been electroplated with silver (button 330). That is, a Silver Deposit button has been electroplated on top of the enamel, but an electroplated button is one in which the metal of the button was electroplated to make it silver colored.

Today, Metal Clay Overlay Silver Paste (page 79) can be used, but the resulting art would not be called Silver Deposit because it would not be done by electroforming.

SILVER DEPOSIT PROCESS

Enamel Tech Talk

In 1889, Oscar Pierre Erard and John Benjamin Round, both of Birmingham, England, patented one method to accomplish Silver Deposit. This method involved an electroplating process in which a flux mixture was first applied to the image, forming the desired design, and then fired on. Herman Bangeman says, "The formula for their flux contained seven parts of calcined borax, three parts of sand, four parts of oxide of lead, one part of nitrate of potash, one-half part of phosphate of lime, and two parts of white arsenic. These components were melted together, cooled, and ground into a powder."[37] This powder was then mixed with powdered silver and turpentine oil (the flux mixture). After the design was fired on, the piece was put in an electroplating bath to deposit silver onto the design.

A second method was patented in 1892 by John H. Scharling of Newark, New Jersey, which uses both electroforming and etching processes. These two processes are considered opposites: electroforming adds metal, and etching removes metal. The bath for each process is similar, but the nodes that affect the process are reversed. The second method of Silver Deposit is to initially deposit silver over the entire surface as in the first method and then apply a resist to where you want the silver to stay. This time the chemical bath would etch away the silver that was not covered by the resist. This alternative process uses a resist, which explains the term "Silver Resist." Once completed, however, it might be difficult to tell the difference between these two methods—thus the name "resist" may not be accurate. Note that Scharling also developed a way to use the initial piece as a pattern for making duplicates of the same design.

Because these methods are electrically conductive, for them to work, the two nodes of the bath (anode and cathode) must be attached to metal. When done on enamel, the edge of the piece can be used to attach to the proper node. But when done on a nonconductive material such as porcelain, celluloid, or glass, Silver Deposit requires that a line of the flux mixture (or copper ribbon or wire) be applied on the back of the button that connects to its metal shank (figure 3.20). This line or tab is the key to determining whether a piece made of another material has Silver Deposit on it.

Figure 3.20 Back of a glass button with a metal line that forms the proper connection to allow for Silver Deposit.

---

328. Antique Polychrome enamel with silver deposit Art Nouveau border.
329. Antique Polychrome head with helmet and breast plate of Silver Deposit, attached edge paste border.

IS IT OR IS IT NOT SILVER DEPOSIT?

How can you tell whether an enamel button has Silver Deposit? Consider button 330 while reading this sidebar.

First, keep in mind that a deposit is *over and attached to* the enamel. It is not metal that is embedded in the enamel, as would be true if fusing a piece of metal (enameled or not) to an enamel. The difference in what this looks like will become apparent when viewing enough of them. But in general, the intersection of the metal to the enamel in a Silver Deposit is a neat, clean separation, whereas if metal is fused to enamel or the piece is enameled into a metal border, the intersection would not be a clean separation. See how the silver in button 329 looks like it's sitting on top of the enamel, whereas the silver in button 330 doesn't have the same look.

Second, because the Silver Deposit is on top of the enamel, the enamel cannot be higher than the silver, as it is in button 330. Look at the dots and "comma" design on the border—these are Encrustations.

Third, view the back of button 330, where you can see the "stamped" design from the front along the edges in the four o'clock to seven o'clock positions—this indicates the button was stamped and is thus a Champlevé.

330

Wire

Gold, silver, and many other metals are made into wires in a wide variety of shapes, such as round, half-round, square, and ribbon/flat. We have already discussed that in Cloisonné, ribbon wire is usually used. Cloisonné wires are embedded so that they look inlaid. But other types of wires can be used for embellishments. Round wire, for example, can be manipulated to make twisted wire. Either shape can be used decoratively in or on a piece (button 143, page 43; button 279, page 69).

Mica

Mica is a silicate mineral found in certain rocks, such as granite and crystals. It can withstand high heat and fires to a metallic-looking sheen. Mica comes in a few forms, such as sheet, powder, paint cakes, and decals. Sheet mica can be used in enameling to hold a piece in the kiln. However, the other forms can be used as embellishments on enamels. Mica powder (one brand is Thompson Enamel Lusters), paint, and decals come in a wide variety of colors. Normally it's used on the top surface of an enamel design in the last firing to provide a pearlized or metallic DF (button 303, page 74; button 331).

331

OTHER CHARACTERISTICS OF ENAMEL BUTTONS

The preceding sections describe many attributes of buttons relating to the enamel of the button. This section discusses attributes of enamel buttons that do not relate to the enamel, but rather to the button itself.

Borders

Borders come in many different materials and can be paired with a variety of material-based buttons. This section discusses borders on enamel buttons, not enamel borders per se. Not all buttons have borders, and some have multiple borders. Some borders are integral to the main button body, and some are added. Some have patterns, and some are plain. And some do not have to be enamel (button 335, page 82; button 351, page 83). Note that there are also enamel borders on non-NBS enamel buttons, which are considered merely an enhancement to another material-based button (appendix A, buttons 488, 500, and 501).

There are many styles of borders. This is a fairly extensive classification and worth further study. Enamel buttons can be found with various types (page 82): edge border (buttons 332 and 333), frame border (button 334; button 18, page 5), inner border (buttons

---

330. Stamped Champlevé / Émaux Peints button with matte topcoat, which has been electroplated.
331. Cloisonné on rounded triangular-shaped copper with silver wires and stylized blackberry design using purple mica powder, by Linda K. Reynolds.

335 and 336), integrated border (buttons 337, 338, and 339), interrupted border (button 362, page 84), outer border (buttons 340 and 341), pictorial border (button 342; button 461, page 101), and rim border (button 343).

EDGE BORDER

INTEGRATED BORDER

FRAME BORDER

OUTER BORDER

PICTORIAL BORDER

INNER BORDER

RIM BORDER

332. Antique Polychrome / Champlevé woman's figure with *edge* paste and *inner* Champlevé borders.
333. Antique Champlevé with openwork attached *edge* border of cut steel.
334. Antique Pâte enamel in turret-like *frame* border.
335. Antique rare openwork Champlevé with *inner* wood border and *outer* stamped border with cut steel.
336. Antique Champlevé / Émaux Peints rose with *inner* oval metal border and *outer* Champlevé border.
337. Champlevé / Basse Taille bird with an *integrated* "wings" border.
338. Antique Enamel Background mounted in an Art Nouveau *integrated* lily border.
339. Antique openwork Champlevé rose with *integrated* border mounted on screen back.
340. Antique wide Champlevé *outer* border with pearl center and green paste.
341. Antique Émaux Peints framed with plated metal rococo *outer* border, by AP & Cie of Paris.
342. Antique Basse Taille / Polychrome enamel floral with *outer pictorial* leaf border, back marked sterling.
343. Antique Gin-bari / Cloisonné flower design with a rim border.

Combined Techniques

There are many enamel buttons the *NBS Blue Book* calls combined techniques (made using two or more types of enameling). Examples are as follows. Cloisonné is often paired with Gin-bari for dramatic effect (button 344). In antique buttons, Champlevé and Émaux Peints combinations are easy to find (button 345), as are Guilloché and Émaux Peints (button 346).

Commemorative Buttons

These buttons are representative of special events in history (button 347).

Enamel Background Buttons

An Enamel Background button is one example in which the enamel is not the focus of the button. "Backgrounds," as an NBS type, are defined by their construction and have their own classification, so it benefits the collector to recognize this type of button. If a button has the construction of an enamel background but the enamel is the focus of the button (button 348), then it's not classified as an NBS Enamel Background button.

Background buttons are typically composed of three basic layered parts: (1) a metal back/mounting, (2) the background material, and (3) a focal device appearing on top of the background material, such as an escutcheon. These parts can be held together by a "reverse bezel" (button 353) (what the *Blue Book* calls a two-piece construction) and/or by rivets, pigtails, or other mechanical means. Enamel may have a slightly different construction from other background buttons because of the nature of enamel being a material fused onto metal. That is, the metal back/mounting may be enameled to form a "built-in" background (button 349). To this piece, a foreground is attached, making it two parts, rather than three.

To determine this point, one would have to inspect how the enamel background is attached. In either case (two-part or three-part), it's an NBS Enamel Background button and thus an NBS enamel button. Good examples of Enamel Background buttons are buttons 349, 350, 351, 352, 353, and 354. Notice in button 351, the focal device is pearl instead of metal and it is not centered; rather, it forms a pictorial border over the top of the enamel background sky.

As stated, these buttons all have a metal or other material pinned over the *top* of the enamel, not *fused* onto the enamel. An example of a button that is neither a background construction nor an NBS classified enamel button, for that matter, is button 489 in appendix A. This is a one-piece stamped brass button, therefore considered a metal button, which uses enameling as a DF to enhance the raised focal design of the acorns and leaves.

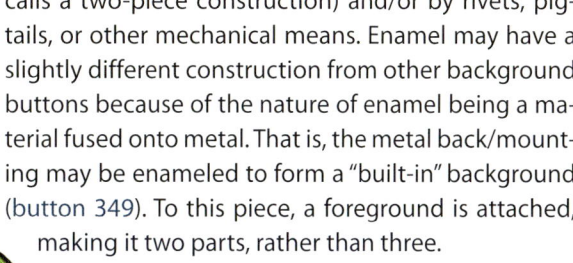
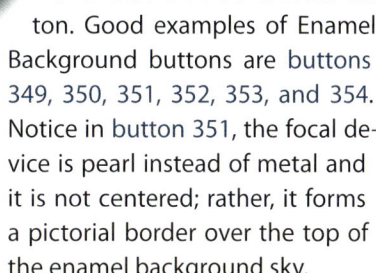

344. Antique Gin-bari / Cloisonné wisteria mounted in silver; combined techniques.
345. Antique Champlevé / Polychrome head with cut steel outer border; combined techniques.
346. Antique Guilloché / Émaux Peints ribbon and bow design; combined techniques.
347. Antique Émaux Peints button to commemorate the French Revolution, made in the late 1800s.
348. Early nineteenth-century Guilloché (straight-line engine design) with Paillons, mounted in a stylized plant life outer frame with central bezel-set faceted jewel—not an NBS Enamel Background button, as the blue enamel portion is a major part of the complex design.
349. Enamel Background button with brass Egyptian escutcheon. This button is an example of the two-part (not three-part) construction noted earlier, as can be seen in the back and side views.
350. Antique Basse Taille Enamel Background button with silver basket and bow, with marcasites.
351. Antique Enamel Background button with gold Paillons and a carved pearl foreground/border pinned with cut steel.
352. Antique Guilloché Enamel Background button with brass and cut steel "foreground."
353. Antique foiled enamel Background mounted in tooled brass bow design held together with a reverse bezel.
354. Antique Basse Taille Enamel Background Livery button with diamonds on 18-karat gold.

Mounted in or on Metal

Many enamels are set into a metal mounting. Should an enamel plaquette be on a material other than metal with the shank going into that other material, it would not be considered an NBS enameled button (buttons 496 and 497, appendix A).

The type of connection to the mounting is not important—just that the enamel is a separate piece from the mounting. Some examples of attaching an enamel to the mounting are bezel, prong or tab set, riveted, and pinned in with a pigtail. In general, the mounting in the enamel world would be called a "setting," and the enamel would be called a "jewel." However, in the button world, the enamel is called a plaquette, no matter how it is shaped or mounted. Some are set *into* the mounting (buttons 355 and 356), and some are set *onto* the mounting (button 357; button 131, page 37).

Mechanical/Movable

Antique movable buttons are hard to find and therefore good to have in your collection (button 358). Studio Button artist Janet White (page 105) creates many movable whimsical buttons (button 359).

Openwork

Openwork enamel buttons are not uncommon and usually have delicate designs. To fall into this NBS category, the button must be an NBS enameled button exhibiting openwork *and* the openwork must be surrounded by the enamel (buttons 360 and 361). A button can be an openwork button and an NBS enamel button (buttons 362 and 363; button 419, page 93) but yet not be an NBS openwork enamel button because of the requirement that the enamel has to surround the openings in some place on the button.

Pictorials

These designs are those that are not merely geometric or conventional. They include animals (button 364), plants (button 365), objects (button 366), and miscellaneous (other pictorials) (button 367). The predominance of the subject matter determines its correct pictorial class. Animals, plants, and objects are easy to recognize. The last section—other pictorials—includes basically all subject matter that does not fit into these first three categories.

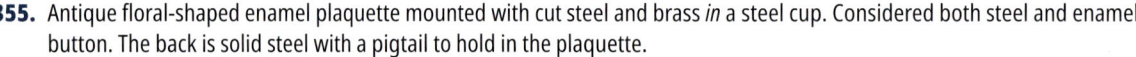

355. Antique floral-shaped enamel plaquette mounted with cut steel and brass *in* a steel cup. Considered both steel and enamel button. The back is solid steel with a pigtail to hold in the plaquette.
356. Antique Champlevé enamel plaquette mounted *in* a steel cup. Considered both steel and enamel button.
357. Antique Champlevé butterfly plaquette mounted on a tole base with added brass and cut steel embellishment.
358. Antique rare movable Émaux Peints Enamel Background button with outer Champlevé border. Center triad steel "focal" design rotates to reveal roses showing or not.
359. Movable enamel of "No Evil" monkey button with seed bead eyes and enamel threads for nose and mouth, by Janet White.
360. Antique openwork Champlevé with C-scroll pattern border and cut steel embellishment.
361. Émaux Peints of a cyclist. The openwork between the wheels makes this piece an *openwork enamel button*.
362. Antique Champlevé with interrupted paste border.
363. Antique Basse Taille with openwork folded ribbon border (not an openwork enamel button).
364. Antique Polychrome birds on branch; animal pictorial.
365. Antique dish-shaped Polychrome pansy with painted scalloped and dots outer border; plant pictorial.
366. Antique Polychrome basket with wide outer border of brass; object pictorial.
367. Antique Pâte enamel Polychrome head and curved brass outer border; other pictorial.

Sew-through

Modern examples are plentiful (buttons 368, 369, and 370), but antique sew-through enamel buttons (button 371) are hard to find.

Shapes

In collecting buttons of any type, it is good to include the three basic shapes: linear, contour, and realistic. Linear buttons (buttons 372 and 373) can be any shape, as long as they are relatively low profile and not realistic. Circular buttons are the most common form of linear shape. Others include scalloped, star, crescent, heart, abstract, oval, square, rectangular, and more. Note that a heart-shaped button (button 372) is not a realistic, as the human (or any actual) heart does not have this shape; thus, these buttons are considered linear. Realistics (button 374) are easy enough to recognize—buttons whose shapes are that of the subject of the button. Contour buttons are ones with significant height in relationship to their base/radius (buttons 375, 376, and 377; button 25, page 8).

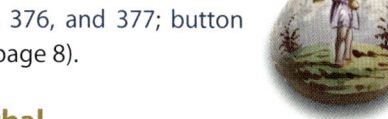

Verbal

Antique enamel buttons (buttons 378, 379, and 380) with letters/words on them (i.e., verbal) are hard to find, so this is also a good characteristic to have in your collection. Modern verbal buttons (button 381) are easier to find, as many decals today have words in them. To be a verbal, a letter/word need not be in English, and it may have characters or symbols as well.

368. *Ouroboros*, Graphite Pencil and Émaux Peints as a five-hole sew-through, by Karen L. Cohen.
369. Openwork Plique-à-jour sew-through button, by Diane Echnoz Almeyda.
370. Three-hole sew-through button with signature enamel chips, by Herman Lowenstein.
371. Antique Champlevé sew-through.
372. Linear heart-shaped pattern—High-Fire Webbing Design with gold Paillons and a central Pierrerie, by Karen L. Cohen.
373. Antique, linear shape, Cloisonné set in metal.
374. Realistic Basse Taille butterfly.
375. Champlevé contour enamel button.
376. Antique Émaux Peints in silver; contour button; by Ludwig Politzer.
377. Antique Émaux Peints; contour enamel button.
378. Antique Gin-bari verbal (character for "Happiness") mounted in scalloped brass frame.
379. Antique Champlevé verbal (single letter) button. This button is probably French; the *"N"* could likely stand for Napoleon but could be a reproduction.
380. Antique Canton Émaux Peints verbal (character for "Longevity"); the button also shows cultural symbolism of animals ("two bats bring longevity").
381. Transfer verbal enamel button with gold foil sun, flower wafers, and fine silver twisted wire and balls, by Karen L. Cohen.

Enamel Button Artists, Producers, and Purveyors

4

Many enamelists have contributed to this book, most of whose names we do not know. In this chapter, I have documented those I could, but this topic is one for future study. Included here are individual enamelists, as well as companies and retailers that make and/or commission for sale enamel buttons. Although the enamelists might have created other types of buttons, only their enamel buttons are shown here. The list is in alphabetical order and is not exhaustive. Each of the enamelists listed in this chapter is also in the index, which indexes all of their buttons in this book. Other places to look for enamelists who made buttons are in books on Studio Button artists,[1] the July 2004 *NBB* article by Bruce Beck titled "Enamels of the Modern Era,"[2] and Loïc Allio's two books.[3]

The National Button Society (NBS) defines studio buttons as those designed and fabricated primarily for sale to collectors. Most are signed and dated by the artist.

In addition to the information that follows, some buttons are shown in this book with known names but little extra information. These are as follows:

- AP & Cie (Albert Parent & Company) (button 55, page 14; button 341, page 82), Paris, France (1912–1939)
- David-Anderson (button 41, page 11), Oslo, Norway (1843–1901; company with his name began in 1876 and is still in business; various signatures can be found at https://www.925-1000.com/david-andersen_marks.html)
- Rose Marie Diem (button 82, page 21), California (1941–2023); she signed only her silver buttons, not copper ones
- Vladamir Dolbin (button 218, page 58), Russia (made buttons ca. 1996)
- Douglas Clock & Co. (button 57, page 14), England
- Joy Funnell (button 134, page 38), East Sussex, United Kingdom (twenty-first century)
- G. E. Walton (button 116, page 34), Birmingham, England (company from 1888 to 1912)
- Marius Hammer (button 17, page 4), Norway (1847–1927)
- J. Millward Banks & Co. (button 137, page 42), Birmingham, England (1863–1925/1926)
- James Fenton & Co. (button 70, page 17), Birmingham, England (1863–1954)
- Doris Hall (button 83, page 21), Ohio, then Massachusetts (1907–2000)
- Chris Litt (button 170, page 49; button 312, page 76), New Mexico (twentieth–twenty-first centuries)
- Ole Petter Raasch Olsen (button 42, page 11), Olsen, Norway (company from 1976 to the present)
- Pearce & Sons (button 72, page 17), Birmingham, England (stamp used from 1895 to 1911)
- Ludwig Politzer (button 376, page 85), Austro-Hungarian (about 1878–1905); signed his pieces LP, usually on the shank
- Joy Robbins (button 267, page 66), England (latter part of the twentieth century)
- Scovill Manufacturing Co. (button 268, page 66), Connecticut (name changed in 1979 to Scovill Inc.)
- Anita Tullis (button 313, page 76), worked around 1975
- William Hutton and Sons (button 71, page 17), Birmingham, England (ca. 1800–1918)

Diane Echnoz Almeyda, Georgia

Diane Almeyda had an early artistic education centered on music. After a short career as a court reporter, she became a stay-at-home mom. Attracted to tiny treasures and buoyed by her love of jewelry, in 1995 she started on the road to her future as an enamelist, miniaturist, jeweler, and Studio Button artist.

In 1998, opportunity knocked, and Almeyda took a Plique-à-jour enameling workshop (and many thereafter) with a Latvian-born master jeweler who later moved to the United States, Valeri Timofeev. Almeyda is a well-known Plique-à-jour enamelist of the highest quality. She started making studio buttons in 2010, creating metal Filigree and Plique-à-jour designs (buttons 382, 383, 384, and 385) as well as other types of enameled buttons (buttons 386, 387, and 388). Almeyda's enameled two-millimeter diminutives (button 387) are about the smallest you will find. She numbers her pieces and back marks them with her initials or full signature as space allows (figure 4.1).

382

Her work can be found in several private collections as well as in the Kentucky Gateway Museum. She teaches jewelry making and Plique-à-jour enameling at International Guild of Miniature Artisans (IGMA) classes and national and international workshops, and she also gives private lessons. Her work and further information about the technique can be seen on her website (http://www.plique-a-jour.com).

383

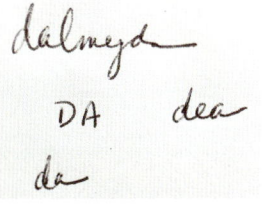

Figure 4.1 Diane Echnoz Almeyda's signatures. Not all buttons are signed because of space limitations.

385

386

384 / 387 / 388

Helene Carter, Canada

Helene Carter (b. 1970) learned to sew as a little girl. Following this interest, she studied fashion design in college and later explored weaving and felt making. She has fond memories of going through her grandmother's button jar, imagining where the buttons came from and imagining what new creations they might adorn. In 2007, she started enameling with Lorna Robin, with whom she worked for about nine years. Carter makes enameled buttons, jewelry, and home decor items, selling mainly through her studio shop and to locals, tourists, and collectors. Sometimes she gets the pleasure of seeing her customers' clothing using her buttons. She works mainly on copper and currently uses pre-1996 Canadian pennies as her base for round buttons. Carter frequently employs the Scrolling technique (page 61) (buttons 389 and 390) using grain enamel, lumps, and/or threads. Using copper cutout shapes, in addition to round, all of her buttons are sew-through and none are back marked. Her work can be seen on her website (https://www.etsy.com/ca/shop/FireWorksCopper).

389

390

382. Filigree Plique-à-jour Macintosh Rose design, by Diane Echnoz Almeyda.
383. Plique-à-jour dragon using opalescent enamels, by Diane Echnoz Almeyda.
384. Plique-à-jour chameleon using transparent enamels, by Diane Echnoz Almeyda.
385. Filigree Plique-à-jour box whose lid is a button with Encrustations, by Diane Echnoz Almeyda.
386. Enameled Émaux Peints unicorn plaquette on painted copper shield, by Diane Echnoz Almeyda.
387. Enameled diminutives, two millimeters each, by Diane Echnoz Almeyda.
388. Émaux Peints realistic gnome, hand cut from copper, three-hole sew-through, by Diane Echnoz Almeyda.
389. Scrolled heart design, by Helene Carter.
390. Scrolled realistic foot design with flower wafer, by Helene Carter.

Chinese Cloisonné and Champlevé, Modern

Around 2000, Kathy Hoppe from Wisconsin started to design and import enamel buttons from China. Some were Cloisonné (button 391), some Champlevé (button 392), and some Champlevé and Basse Taille (button 393). There were more than 20 different designs in the ones with the 2000 back mark. She also designed a set of five different clowns, Humpty Dumpty, and Santa Claus.

Hoppe has been collecting buttons since 1996, and for 11 years she was a dealer at both state and NBS shows. She has written two books: *Buttons beyond the Glass Curtain* and *Moonglows Past and Present*. In 2003, Hoppe started lampworking and making glass buttons. She also imported glass buttons from the Czech Republic. Her buttons can be found on her website (https://www.etsy.com/shop/KPHoppe).

Chinese Plique-à-jour, Modern

At the turn of the twenty-first century, Mary Libby (Bib) Neiman decided to commission a Chinese company she met at a gift show in New York City to make Plique-à-jour buttons. Neiman didn't want all the buttons to look Asian. Thus, she worked with a famous Japanese artist, George Suyeoka, who lived fairly close to her, to design some whimsical images for the Chinese company to manufacture. Suyeoka was born in Hawaii but studied at the Art Institute of Chicago and then moved to Illinois. He is now deceased. Neiman thinks that the angelfish, grapes, rose, and hummingbird are not Suyeoka's designs, but this is not confirmed.

These buttons (buttons 394 and 395) are characterized by brass twisted wires, with the outer wire being of heavier gauge, which the company thought would add strength to the frame. Unlike most Plique-à-jour items, the button backs are covered with the same enamel as the front, except when the design included openwork. Unfortunately, these are no longer being made.

Neiman has seen some buttons at auction that look similar, but she doesn't think these were made by the same company. It seems this style of Plique-à-jour button may also have been made by someone else.

---

391. Cloisonné butterfly, designed and imported from China by Kathy Hoppe.
392. Champlevé clown, designed and imported from China by Kathy Hoppe.
393. Champlevé / Basse Taille rose on lattice, designed and imported from China by Kathy Hoppe.
394. Plique-à-jour peacock with openwork, imported from China by Mary Libby Neiman.
395. Plique-à-jour butterfly, imported from China by Mary Libby Neiman.

Karen L. Cohen, Pennsylvania

Karen L. Cohen's career spanned the math and computer science fields, but she always created artwork as a professional hobby. Initially, Cohen (b. 1948) made silver and enameled jewelry, having first learned this technique as a teen at summer camp. Besides enameling, Cohen works in a variety of media and frequently takes classes in new materials because she loves to understand the process.

In 2009, at the encouragement of Susan Calkins (a longtime collector and button judge), she decided to concentrate on making Studio Buttons. To date she has created more than 1,700 buttons (enamel, fabric/beaded/temari balls, metal, and gourd) for collectors, each of which comes with a card of authentication that describes the techniques and materials used and includes each button's identifying number. Cohen creates both one-of-a-kind buttons and editions/series, which are denoted by a dash numbering scheme. Her back mark is a stylized "KC" (figure 4.2) either by hand or stamped on metal. Although she specializes in Cloisonné (button 397), she works in a wide variety of other enameling techniques such as Guilloché (button 398), Basse Taille, Émaux Peints (button 399), Sgraffito, Transfers/Decals, Pull-through, Scrolling, Champlevé, Gin-bari, Separation Enamel, and more. Her signature look on enamels is the use of relief work using twisted wire and metal balls. She also loves to use gold Paillons and flower wafers. Sometimes she works with her daughter, Judith C. Lanza, who draws henna designs for some of her Basse Taille buttons (button 109, page 32). Lastly, Cohen is now ordering custom four-color decals to fire onto enamel buttons, using

A FAMILY CONNECTION: SYNTHETIC PLASTICS CORPORATION

Karen L. Cohen's maternal grandfather, Louis Kasen, and his brother, Dan, started the Synthetic Plastics Corporation (SPC) in Newark, New Jersey. One of their product lines was buttons, and family members had buttons named after them. Button 396 shows the Karen Button, which came in a wide variety of colors in five sizes. Button collector Judy Masur is currently researching SPC for her upcoming book on this subject. Contact her at jmasur7493@aol.com.

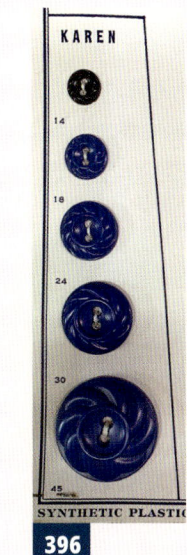

396

either subjects of her other artwork (Artisan's Collection, button 400) or photos given to her by collectors (Custom Photos Collection).

Cohen has written two books on enameling, the latest published in 2019: *The Art of Fine Enameling* (2nd ed.). Currently retired from computer work, she now sells her artwork and teaches enameling and beading at various venues to both adults and children. Her buttons and non-button artwork can be seen on her website (http://www.kcEnamels.com).

399

400

397

398

Figure 4.2 Cohen's signature, designed in Junior High School art class. She uses this mark either as a stamp on metal or handwritten in various ways.

---

396. The Karen Button, manufactured by Synthetic Plastics Corporation.
397. Cloisonné / Plique-à-jour combination using silver foil, Faux Opal, flower wafer, fine silver balls and twisted wire, by Karen L. Cohen.
398. Cloisonné / Guilloché on fine silver using leaded enamels, gold and silver foil, flower wafers, and gold Paillons set in sterling silver with cultured pearls. The Guilloché was done on a brocade machine, by Tig Lichty, and the pattern is called La Danse de Salomé, by Karen L. Cohen.
399. Émaux Peints of Chinese Brush Painting design of a wild orchid and gold foil sun with a Sugar Fire topcoat, by Karen L. Cohen.
400. *Birds on Bamboo* ceramic decal on enamel. Artisan's Collection of a Chinese Brush Painting under an encaustic painting, by Karen L. Cohen.

Marie Demicco, Maine

Marie Demicco (b. 1948) always had hands that needed to make things. For many years, she had a weaving studio, as color, texture, and movement were the voices of her craft. After a knee injury, she started taking metalsmithing and enameling classes with Pauline Warg. An enameling workshop gave her an "aha" moment—here was color and texture and movement in a whole new form! She has been making jewelry and enamel components since about 2008. Demicco loves to layer enamel: foil on the bottom, layers of watery transparent colors, and embellishments on top (button 402).

Her love of fiber arts also led her to making buttons. Demicco says, "If you put all that time into knitting a sweater, why would you put an ordinary button on it?" She started making custom buttons for her own projects, and things just took off from there. Anything goes (buttons 401, 403, 404, and 405)!

Around 2016, Demicco was invited by the Maine State Button Society to sell her buttons at their annual show, in which she participated for three years until COVID-19 hit. Up to that time, she knew nothing about the passion that people have for collecting buttons. In 2023, she started metal stamping her buttons with her name and logo (figure 4.3). Her buttons can be seen on the web (https://www.etsy.com/shop/SpurwinkRiverArts).

Figure 4.3 Marie Demicco logo, representing the estuary of the Spurwink River, which twists and turns as it exits into the sea about a half mile from her house; the two dots are for her husband and herself. She began stamping the logo onto the back of buttons beginning in 2023.

Sandy Dingman, California

Sandy Dingman's journey in the world of enameling has been a lifelong pursuit of creativity and self-expression. From her earliest memories, Dingman (b. 1956) was captivated by the art form, thanks to her hobbyist father's enameling kiln. As a young child, she watched in awe as he transformed plain metal into vibrant, colorful works of art. Little did she know that this initial spark would ignite a lifelong passion. As an adult, Dingman pursued a degree in jewelry design at California State University, Northridge, eager to explore the limitless possibilities that enameling offered. On graduation, her hunger for knowledge and desire to perfect her enameling skills led her to the prestigious Gemological Institute of America. Nature serves as a profound inspiration for her artistic endeavors, as is evident in her buttons (buttons 406, 407, and 408).

Beyond enameling, Dingman has discovered a deep passion for hand knitting and crocheting. Through this love for fiber arts, she found an opportunity to merge her two passions. She started making enamel buttons in 2015. She mainly works in kiln-fired copper using techniques of Sgraffito and Basse Taille (etched or hydraulic press) while incorporating glass seed beads, flower wafers, and found copper objects like gears. To date, all her buttons are sew-through, and none are back marked.

---

401. Champlevé (etched) reproduction of Roman cloak buttons, by Marie Demicco.
402. Enameled realistic fish copper cutout using silver foil and seed bead, by Marie Demicco.
403. Two-material button: enameled copper with ceramic cabochon (from San Miguel de Allende, Mexico) and seed beads, by Marie Demicco.
404. Stenciled enamel that artist called Batik-style, by Marie Demicco.
405. Enameled spindle-shaped copper with fused seed beads, by Marie Demicco.
406. Sgraffito enameled copper circle, two-hole sew-through, by Sandy Dingman.
407. Sgraffito enamel button with seed beads and glass balls, two-hole sew-through, by Sandy Dingman.
408. Basse Taille (etched design) two-hole sew-through, by Sandy Dingman.

Nancy DuBois, New Jersey

Nancy DuBois's (b. 1960) appreciation for sewing buttons started in her twenties and has continued to be one of the most inspiring and educational facets of her life. Her studio button journey started in 1990 when fellow button collector Eva Evans from Massachusetts, knowing that DuBois did leather working, asked whether she would make her a leather log cabin button. She did, and so began her love of crafting small works with button shanks.

DuBois works in a plethora of media, such as Plique-à-jour enameling (buttons 409 and 410); scrimshaw on shell, bone, vegetable ivory, and stone; reverse painted watch crystal buttons; "fun buttons" such as holograms, cast resin, and carved polyester buttons; and paperweight and Pâte de Verre glass (after earning a degree in glass art and industrial design). Since 1990, she has produced limited quantities of studio buttons every year. Around 40 different enamel buttons were made after 1999. Designs included butterfly, rooster, fan, hot air balloon, peacock, dragonfly, and cross. DuBois has collaborated with fellow crafts artists such as John Gooderham, Sarah Hodgson (Atley buttons), and Dana Gayner. Her favorite subjects to use for studio button designs are fables, fairy tales, flowers, insects, animals, Kate Greenaway, sunbonnet babies, moons and stars, and all manner of humorous themes.

NANCY DUBOIS NUMBERING SCHEME

Nancy DuBois signs her buttons with her initials ("*N.D.*"), the year and month they were made, and the number of that button type (such as scrimshaw, cast resin, etc.). Thus the button back mark shown in figure 4.4 was made in September 1999 and is the first of its type. Her back mark also shows limited editions by additionally including something like 3/10, which means the third button of 10 made. However, some buttons, like her "fun buttons," are not numbered and often have initials and dates on a paper label adhered to their backs.

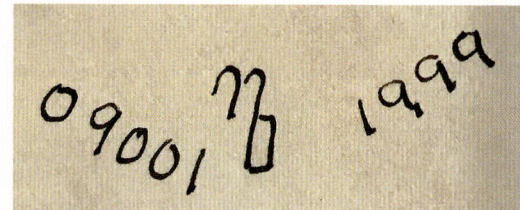

Figure 4.4 DuBois's back mark.

409. Plique-à-jour rooster in silver, by Nancy DuBois.
410. Plique-à-jour butterfly in silver, by Nancy DuBois.

Marie Elwyn, Massachusetts

Marie Elwyn (b. 1954) has been a button collector since 2004, starting with a black glass button she had kept since she was 15. In 2012, she decided to start making enamel buttons. Her back mark is a stylized "*ME*" (figure 4.5). Elwyn enamels pennies pre-1983 (but not 1983D, as these are not pure copper) (button 411) and copper shapes (button 412). Some of her buttons have shanks (button 413), and some are sew-through. Her penny buttons are not counter enameled but have painted backs.

Figure 4.5 Marie Elwyn's back mark.

Émaux Ardéchois, France

This French company made enamel flower buttons and earrings. There may be other designs, but information was unavailable. These flowers have petals made of harder glass that was formed separately and then fused onto the enamel (button 414 and button set 415). I say this because the petals are three-dimensional, and enamel does not fuse in the way these petals are formed (page 71 for more information).

Peter Carl Fabergé, Russia

Fabergé (1846–1920) was known as Peter Carl, Carl, and Karl Gustavovich Fabergé. He was the grandson of artisan Pierre Favry, one of the Huguenots who fled France after the Revocation of the Edict of Nantes (page 7). From France, Pierre went to Germany and eventually to Livonia, which was part of the Russian Empire. Registering as a master joiner, in the late 1700s Pierre first used the name of Peter Fabrier and then, in 1808, registered under the name of Peter Faber. In 1828, he adopted the surname Fabergé. His son, Gustav, was apprenticed to famous jewelers and enamelists; in 1841, he opened his own company, House of Fabergé, in St. Petersburg. Gustav's son was Peter Carl Fabergé. After a grand tour of Europe, Carl worked under the tutorage of his father's number one master, Peter Hiskias Pendin, who had taken over the business when Gustav moved to Germany. On Pendin's death, Carl took over the family business and redirected the company from making fashion jewelry of the day to making art jewelry.

In 1882, Peter Carl Fabergé realized he could not manage all the work himself. He then employed other master jewelers, who had their own firms, to work under the name of Fabergé. His most important head workmasters were August Wilhelm Holmström, Michael Perkhin, Alma Pihl (Holmström's granddaughter), and Henrik Wigström. These masters developed their own style, eventually approved by Fabergé, and signed their own work. I could only find that Holmström made buttons.

Peter Carl Fabergé is well known for his beautifully made gemstone, precious metal, and enameled eggs. His first egg to the tsar's wife was so well received that in 1885 Fabergé received the title of "Goldsmith by Special Appointment to the Imperial Crown." Because of this title, Fabergé was able to study the important Hermitage Collection, where he developed his own style, his most famous being Guilloché enameling. With the addition of his brother Agathon to the firm, other objets d'art were added to their line. Fabergé also created cufflinks and buttons.

---

411. Enameled copper penny with a millefiori, by Marie Elwyn.
412. Enameled realistic copper frog using millefiori and seed beads (notice the smaller seed beads sitting in the holes of the larger ones for the eyes and knees), by Marie Elwyn.
413. Sample of Marie Elwyn's soldered-on shank.
414. Enamel button with a three-flower design, by Émaux Ardéchois. This button was made the same way as button set 415.
415. Set of enamel buttons with petals most likely made of lampwork glass, by Émaux Ardéchois.

William Hair Haseler, England

William H. Haseler (buttons 416 and 417) was an English jeweler and silversmith, born in Birmingham about 1821. He started his own company named W. H. Haseler & Co. At the turn of the twentieth century, he worked with Liberty & Co. (page 97), as well as on his own. His company was the principal manufacturer of Liberty's Cymric line, although designers came from other studios. His pieces carry his "*WHH*" mark and the mark for having been made in Birmingham. He died circa 1909, but the company continued after his death.

416

417

August Wilhelm Holmström, Russia

Born in Helsinki, Finland, August Wilhelm Holmström (1829–1903) was a silversmith and goldsmith. He apprenticed to Karl Herold in St. Petersburg and, in 1857, was a master with his own workshop. His children followed in his footsteps, and at least his son Albert used the same mark of "*AH*." Holmström was one of the head masters of the House of Fabergé. He created many types of objects, including buttons (button 418).

418

Charles Horner, England

Charles Horner (1837–1896), born in Ovenden, England, was an important nineteenth-century jeweler. In the 1860s, he started a business in Halifax called Charles Horner of Halifax. After his death, his sons (James Dobson and Charles Henry Horner) helped continue his company with a new partner, Charles William Leach. The company went out of business in the 1980s. Company items marked with a "*CH*," though, might have been made after his death.

Primarily working in the Arts & Crafts and Art Nouveau styles, Mr. Horner was initially known for the "Dorcas" thimble (patented in 1884), which was innovative and of much higher quality than previous products. The Dorcas thimble was a silver thimble with a steel core, which better protected the finger. After World War I, the Horner company was one of the first to use casein plastics, which they branded as "Dorcasine" and used in various items they made.

The company was also known for enameled silver pendants, some using opalescent enamels, hat pins, and other items including buttons (button 419). Many of their enamels were Basse Taille with a common bumpy design in the metal (button 420). Button 421 has a similar background but is not back marked, so it's not clear who made it.

419   420

421

---

416. Enamel over silver foil set in metal, Arts & Crafts style, by William H. Haseler. This foil use is similar to Gin-bari.
417. Champlevé button sold by Liberty & Co., by William H. Haseler.
418. Antique Guilloché 1.375-inch gold buttons, framed with unusual nine-lobed diamond border of C-scrolls, by Fabergé master workman August Wilhelm Holmström after 1896 for the firm of Peter Carl Fabergé; Cleveland Museum of Art, India Early Minshall Collection 1966.490.
419. Antique Basse Taille with an openwork frame border, by Charles Horner (not an NBS openwork enamel button).
420. Antique Champlevé / Basse Taille button, by Charles Horner.
421. Antique Champlevé / Basse Taille with *interrupted* border.

Inaba Cloisonné Company, Japan

The Inaba Cloisonné Company started during the Golden Age of Japanese Enameling in 1886 by Inaba Isshin and closed sometime in the 1990s. They made beautiful enamelware, including Shotai-jippō (page 117) and other styles. They also made buttons, which were souvenirs for the Western trade (buttons 422 and 423). Their mark is shown in figure 4.6. They may have labeled their buttons as Cloisonné, but most of them are Champlevé. However, they did make some Cloisonné buttons (button 424).

Figure 4.6 Mark of the Inaba Cloisonné Company.

André Keim, France

André Keim was a French enamelist (button 194, page 54; buttons 425, 426, and 427) who back marked his work "AK" (button 427). At one time, his work was confused with that of Arthur Kim,[4] who also back marked his work "AK" (Kim is now not thought to have enameled). Keim's work is shown in volume 5 of Alastair Duncan's *The Paris Salons 1895–1914*.[5]

Dorothy Kendall, Pennsylvania

Dorothy Kendall (d. 1961) made ceramic and enamel buttons (button 428), making most in the 1950s. She was an art teacher for 33 years and worked on her artwork independent from her job. Her back mark was a "K" superimposed on a "D." She is also referenced in Jane S. Leslie's *A Reference Book on Studio Button Makers*.[6]

---

422. Champlevé by Inaba Cloisonné Company.
423. Champlevé by Inaba Cloisonné Company.
424. Cloisonné by Inaba Cloisonné Company.
425. Antique Polychrome pictorial with asymmetrical cross-hatched inner border and gold painted outer border, by André Keim.
426. Antique Polychrome / Champlevé with French verbal (The Cutter of Botz) outer border, by André Keim.
427. Antique Champlevé / Émaux Peints by André Keim.
428. Émaux Peints with Liquid Gold and with a flux topcoat, by Dorothy Kendall.

Jessie Marion King, England

Jessie M. King (1875–1949) was a Scottish designer who studied at the Glasgow School of Art starting in 1892. She worked in various media but is best known for her children's book illustrations and jewelry designs. King started designing for Liberty & Co. (page 97) around 1904, initially designing fabrics and wallpaper. Later she started designing (not making) for Liberty's Cymric silver line. She also designed buttons (button 429) manufactured through W. H. Haseler (page 93) that were not for the Cymric line (i.e., no Cymric back mark).

King's designs are of two main types—Art Nouveau (frequently silver with enamel) and Arts & Crafts (precious metals sometimes with stones/pearls or small amounts of enamel). She was influenced by both art styles and in turn influenced the world style known as "Glasgow Style."

In 1909, King married her longtime fiancé, Ernest Archibald Taylor, another artist. In 1911, living in Paris, they set up the Sheraling Atelier, an art school. However, in 1915 they returned to Kirkcudbright, Scotland, where King lived for the rest of her life. Near her house at Greengate, the couple started an artists' colony known as "Greengate Close Coterie." At the time, complete artist training included spending time there, even for extended periods.

429

Archibald Knox, England

Archibald Knox (1864–1933), while designing wallpaper and fabric for the famous Silver Studios in the United Kingdom, was not well known until he started designing for Liberty & Co. (page 97) at the turn of the twentieth century. From his association with Liberty & Co., he became known as one of the principal designers of the Art Nouveau period, frequently using designs with a Celtic feel to them. Knox was a teacher and the lead designer at Liberty & Co.'s Cymric silver and Tudric pewter lines.[7] Button 430 shows a button with the same design as a brooch designed by Knox for the Cymric line. In 1912, Knox moved to the United States to seek employment but left in 1913 and returned to his birthplace, the Isle of Man. He died in 1933. For more information on Archibald Knox, see the book *Archibald Knox* by Stephen A. Martin (1995).

430

Kokuto Co. Ltd., Japan

After World War II, Japan became a center for mass production of quality buttons for the fashion industry. Ken Kasamaki started Kokuto Co. Ltd. in 1972 and was owner and president of this Tokyo-based firm until about 2015. Ken Kasamaki is the father of Kumi Dreves, who works with Sachiko Nishida (page 101) today and owns the Yanaka Red House Button Gallery (page 106).

Kokuto was named in honor of the multitalented twentieth-century artist Jean Cocteau (the company's formal English name was Cocteau). It contracted with others to make mainly Cold Plastic Enamel (CPE) cast buttons (button 504, page 110); the firm called these "epo-ire," which means "epoxy-added." However, Kokuto manufactured for large custom orders only. It also made some enameled cast buttons, although only a small quantity, and Dreves does not have any examples of these. The buttons are not back marked. In addition, Kokuto mass-produced high-end buttons for large companies like Iris, Onda, and Mitake, which are still in business (although on a smaller scale, as the industry moved outside Japan). Iris now hosts and runs a button museum in the old headquarters building (https://www.iris.co.jp/english/about/bunka).

429. Champlevé on silver, Arts & Crafts style, identified as a Jessie M. King design, and sold through Liberty & Co.[8] Back marked *"WHH"* and *"SILVER."* The *"WHH"* is for the manufacturing company William H. Haseler. Silver loop shank, 1.125 inches.

430. Champlevé Cymric line button with central seed pearl, attributed to being designed by Archibald Knox for Liberty & Co.

Mona Ledwin, Tennessee

Mona Ledwin (b. 1957) is a lifelong learner, continually taking classes to learn new creative skills. Her first Cloisonné class was in 1995, and since then she has taken classes from several enamel artists. Today Ledwin uses not only a kiln but also a torch. In 2005, she took her first metal clay class and eventually started teaching. Because of working in this media, she makes silicone molds of the Victorian buttons in her collection (she's been collecting since 2006) and now sells these on Etsy. She often, but not always, uses scrap counter enamel (speckled) and signs her buttons with a white paint pen, which is permanent but not fired on (button 431). The shanks on her copper buttons are purchased vintage button shanks that she solders on after the enameling is completed. However, she makes the shanks for her silver metal clay buttons herself, and these are either fired with the metal clay or soldered onto the button.

Ledwin's favorite crafts are enameling, jewelry making with metal clay, and fused glass. She uses several enameling techniques including Sgraffito, Graphite Pencil drawing, painting with various Overglazes such as China Paints (button 432), and Transfers while using regular grain and liquid enamels. She especially enjoys using transfers that she prints herself (button 431), but she also uses commercial versions. As a jeweler, Ledwin hand-cuts some of her copper shapes, but she also uses commercially available ones. She has been commissioned to make club buttons as well as state button society favor buttons (button 433). She is happy to take commissions like making custom decal transfers of your pet or family members. Ledwin also enjoys teaching basic enameling. See her buttons and molds on her website (https://www.etsy.com/shop/monaledwin).

Heinrich Levinger, Germany

Heinrich Levinger (d. 1899) was an established jeweler in Pforzheim, Germany, in 1881. His company remained in business until his death. After his death, his son, Emil, reopened the business as Heinrich Levinger Company, still using his father's signature (figure 4.7). It's possible that he was the one to register a different mark (button 434) for exports to England (possibly starting in 1899). Emil partnered for a time with Karl Bissinger. Together they changed the company name to Levinger & Bissinger and continued to use the "*HL*" mark. After they split, the company went back to using the Heinrich Levinger name. During all this time, they created Jugendstil and Art Nouveau jewelry and buttons, some in Plique-à-jour enameling. Because the same signature was used by all of these companies, it's not clear who actually made each piece.

In the button world, Levinger is known for Guilloché buttons with flower paintings (button 435). However, he also produced other styles of buttons (button 436). Please note that just because Levinger buttons are known for being flower paintings over Guilloché, it doesn't mean all examples of this style are his (see button 57, page 14).

Figure 4.7
Heinrich Levinger signature.

431. Émaux Peints with artist printed decal, by Mona Ledwin.
432. Émaux Peints on silver metal clay with a frame border, by Mona Ledwin.
433. Artist-made decal button made for the 2020 Colorado State Button Society show, by Mona Ledwin.
434. Heinrich Levinger signature registered in Birmingham for Levinger imported items, marked 1903.
435. Antique Guilloché / Émaux Peints, by Heinrich Levinger.
436. Antique Matte Champlevé / Basse Taille triad design in silver with central Amethyst and twisted rope outer border by Heinrich Levinger.

Liberty & Co., England

Arthur Lasenby Liberty was a London merchant who opened his first store, Liberty & Co., in 1875, as a department store. He is quoted as saying, "I was determined not to follow exiting fashions but to create new ones." He imported ornaments, fabric, and objets d'art, especially from Japan, as British society was enthralled with their designs. In 1890, Liberty & Co. became a public limited liability company. As of today, the store still exists and is currently located on Great Marlborough Street in London in the West End.

Liberty & Co. is a retail store, not a maker of items. Thus, Liberty employed various artisans to make his wares. However, Arthur Liberty was most interested in promoting his own brand. To this end, all pieces carried the mark of "Designed by Liberty & Co." (button 439) unless displayed for publication, at which time the designer's name was used. This fact, plus the lack of contemporary documentation, causes confusion today regarding who actually made which pieces. Various people have studied this issue and have documented their findings. A good article by Anthony Bernbaum can be found at his website (https://www.peartreecollection.co.uk), and much of my information is from there.

Although many different styles of art were sold in the store, Liberty's growing association with artisans of the day moved his business to selling many Art Nouveau items, including buttons (button 440) and belt buckles, and led his company to become an important part of the growth of the Art Nouveau and Arts & Crafts movements. Because of the influence of the East, his shop became known as "East India House." Liberty & Co. was so well known that the Art Nouveau style in Italy was called "Liberty Style."

At the turn of the twentieth century, Liberty formed the Liberty & Co. (Cymric) Ltd.—a line of silver items, some with enamel. Not only is the exact year in question, but with whom he joined forces is also not clear. Many believe it was English jeweler William Hair Haseler (page 93). However, some feel it could have been Rex Silver of Silver Studios. In any case, W. H. Haseler was the major manufacturing arm of the Cymric line, and he worked with the designer Oliver Baker. The Cymric line did include buttons and belt buckles (buttons 437, 438, and 439).

Speel says, "Enamel craftsmen who supplied Liberty worked under the direction of Archibald Knox and were required to remain anonymous. They included Oliver Baker, Bernard Cuzner, Jessie M. King, Fred Partridge (who had been associated with Ashee's Guild of Handicraft), and Rex Silver."[9]

The buttons were frequently Champlevé (button 437), sometimes Basse Taille (button 439), and some came in sets (button 78, page 18). Although most of the designs have the metal and not the enamel as the focus of the button, many Liberty buttons with enamel are considered NBS enamel buttons because they include quite a bit of enamel. This issue can be confusing for the American collector, and there is no hard rule to help clarify things. In addition, at least some of the button designs were also used in other objects, such as brooches, clocks, and tea caddies. As these other items were sometimes attributed to specific designers, an association can sometimes be made as to who designed particular buttons (see Haseler; Knox, page 95; and King, page 95).

The Cymric line was influenced by the Arts & Crafts movement. This was Liberty's most successful commercial line of items, and many pieces had a Celtic feel. These were sold mainly from 1900 to 1912. The label was discontinued after 1926.[10]

---

437. Champlevé enamel button in the Cymric line, by Liberty & Co.
438. Champlevé enamel button in the Cymric line, by Liberty & Co.
439. Basse Taille on silver (possibly hand repoussé), by Liberty & Co. The back shows the Liberty back marks: "*L & Co.*" for Liberty & Company; Anchor is the city of Birmingham Assay Mark (British); Lion Passant mark means certified sterling; "*C*" mark is for the year 1902 (the year the button was made). This qualifies as Basse Taille because even though the metal texture is not "low relief," it is texturized and totally covered with enamel.
440. Champlevé enameled, shaped Interlaced pattern of a multilobed, petal-like design, by Liberty & Co.

Linda Lingren, California

Linda Lingren's (b. 1950), journey into button making began in the 1990s when she searched for the perfect buttons for a dress she had studiously made, couldn't find any, and decided to make her own. Those first buttons were square with a green checkerboard design, and they greatly enhanced the pin-pleated front of the dress.

It became her obsession to learn as much as she could. Thus, Lingren took numerous classes and workshops, including offerings by the Jewelry Arts Institute in New York City; the Revere Academy and City College of San Francisco, California; and the Crucible in Oakland, California, as well as through membership in the Enamelist Society. These and other classes allowed her to delve deeper into the intricate world of enamelwork and discover new techniques to incorporate. Additionally, she completed classes in clothing design, ceramics, drawing, painting, watercolor, sculpture, design, woodworking, printmaking, and color theory. She strives to create pieces that are not only aesthetically pleasing but also enduring and lightweight. She finds inspiration in nature (plants, insects, birds, fish, and landscapes) and the human figure.

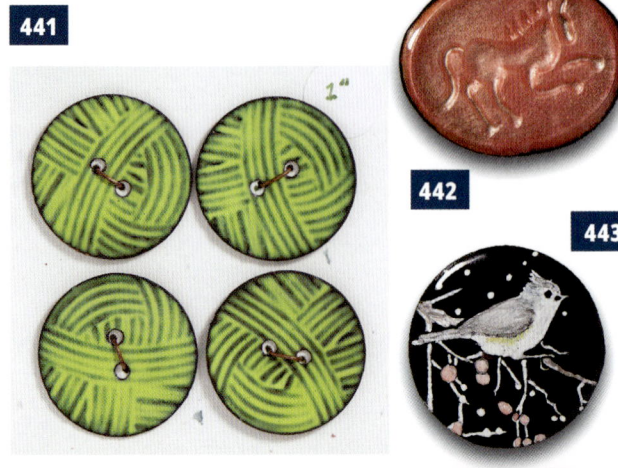

Lingren's creations fill a spectrum from enamel buttons to jewelry, in which she uses such techniques as Cloisonné, Basse Taille (buttons 441 and 442), Émaux Peints (button 443), and foil. She signs the back of her buttons with her first name and date (button 444). Lingren's work can be seen on her website (www.enamelsbylinda.com).

Phil Linley, Connecticut

Phil Linley (ca. 1926–2014) was not an enamelist but a master machinist who crafted studio buttons from various parts, either adding a shank or making a setting for a purchased focal. He also developed and sold the certified Linley Measure for button sizing (figure 4.8). Linley made buttons using a few different materials, one being enamels. His wife, Dorothy (Dot), painted silhouettes, which he also used for his focals. Linley prepurchased enamel plaquettes for some of his studio buttons. His back mark is shown in button 445, and another example of his work is shown in button 446. Linley was also the show manager for the National Button Society Conventions from 1990 through the year 2000.

Figure 4.8 Linley Measures, certified for button sizing by the NBS.

---

441. Basse Taille, realistic ball of yarn (done by a hydraulic press using black Underglaze in the recesses), by Linda Lingren.
442. Basse Taille horse design (done by carving the horse in acrylic and using a hydraulic press to get the impression in the silver), by Linda Lingren.
443. Émaux Peints of a Titmouse in winter, by Linda Lingren.
444. Linda Lingren back mark. See front of this (button 316, page 77).
445. Champlevé enamel plaquette made into a button, by Phil Linley. The reverse shows his back mark.
446. Transfer enamel plaquette set in metal, by Phil Linley.

Herman Lowenstein, Florida

Herman Lowenstein (1895–1982) wore many hats—he had a PhD in chemistry and did research in rubber, was involved in chemical warfare during World War I, worked in publishing, and sold educational materials. When he retired to Florida, he started using his artistic talents, initially in shell art. In 1975, he received a small kiln from his daughter and started enameling. After selling at some art shows, he was "discovered" by button collectors, and the rest is history.

A. T. "Mickey" Hall, a past NBS president, befriended Lowenstein and helped him understand what button collectors wanted. Through the years, Lowenstein sent Hall "thank you" buttons as gifts (button 447). When Hall moved to a retirement home, her Lowenstein collection of correspondence and buttons was purchased by Peg Swassing Meredith, who still owns many Lowenstein buttons and correspondence today. For a period of time, Viviane Beck Ertell, the internationally known dealer, represented his buttons at various shows throughout the United States.

Lowenstein created enamel buttons until 1981, which were either shank or two- to six-hole sew-throughs. His shanks were fairly unique (button 448 shows one, and others were similarly stacked but with a different shape). He enameled on copper pennies (button 448), stamped metal, and available copper cut-outs (button 449). When using pennies, sometimes he totally covered the face, and sometimes the penny face could be seen through the button's transparent field. He also etched copper for Basse Taille (button 450). As he worked in the 1970s and 1980s, he most likely used Thompson Enamel materials, maybe even using lead-bearing enamels. He is known for his designs using small lumps of enamel, which could be called "chips." He worked in Scrolling (button 294, page 73), Sgraffito (button 262, page 66), just doing a design with the chips (button 451), and Champlevé (button set 452). He used other materials, such as glass seed beads and millefiori (button 450), and he frequently used clear enamel base coats (button 450). His zodiac series is well known, and it's thought that he made 25 sets of these (button set 452). His buttons are usually back marked with "HL," but not always, and sometimes he painted the back with a goldish paint (button 453).

447. Enamel button (two hole sew-through with metal wreath), by Herman Lowenstein, made as a "thank you" to A. T. "Mickey" Hall.
448. Back of button 239 (page 61) that shows Lowenstein enameled on pennies.
449. Scrolled realistic four-leaf clover, by Herman Lowenstein.
450. Basse Taille with a flower design—millefiori as center, blue glass seed beads as petals, and light green threads as stem and leaves; field color is flux; by Herman Lowenstein. Notice the red firescale from one to nine o'clock on the rim.
451. Enameled copper circle with enamel chips fully fused into dots, by Herman Lowenstein.
452. Champlevé enamel Zodiac set on stamped metal with typical Lowenstein enamel chips design, by Herman Lowenstein.
453. Enameled copper circle with black lumps and black thread on a white field, by Herman Lowenstein.

Motiwala Brothers, India

The Motiwala Brothers of Bombay, India, established in 1921, was run by Bogwan Motiwala and probably his sons, as no brothers were ever mentioned. The Transfer enamels were the first to be commissioned, using greeting cards sent to them for the original designs. The rest was history, as the Motiwala Brothers saw the opportunity to create many other assorted materials in buttons for the Western world by using a sort of cottage industry of artists in India to develop and create these magical miniature works of art.

They made buttons for about 10–12 years in the mid-1900s. Although the family did help in the making of these pieces of art, Motiwala subcontracted with other artisans in the area. However, as in Liberty & Co. and Fabergé, all buttons are labeled as Motiwala Brothers buttons, some with Deccan back marks. The company produced buttons not only in enamel but also in other media, such as carved and painted ivory and wood, inlaid silver, shell, silver and gold wirework, inlaid glass, and many other techniques (approximately 22 in all).

They produced two main types of enamel buttons. One was transfers (button 454). Sometimes the transfers were outlines and then hand painted (button 457). They also produced a set of zodiac buttons (button set 458).

The other type of enamel button was called "Liquid Enamel" (buttons 455 and 456), but it has no relationship to the material liquid enamel as described on page 31. They were so named because they looked fluid (page 34). They are actually silver Basse Taille enameled buttons in which the substrate metal has been engraved by hand (many colorized as the original Basse Taille pieces were done, as shown on page 4).

There is more to be said about this company, and excellent articles can be found in the *NBB*.[11]

454. Colored transfer of St. Nick, inspired by a greeting card design, by Motiwala Brothers.
455. Basse Taille on silver, by Motiwala Brothers (frequently called Liquid Enamel).
456. Enamel Openwork Basse Taille on silver, by Motiwala Brothers (frequently called Liquid Enamel).
457. Émaux Peints / Transfer, by Motiwala Brothers.
458. Transfers for each in the Zodiac set, by Motiwala Brothers.

Simon Mower, England

Andrian Sadgrove, an English button dealer, commissioned Simon Mower, a British jeweler, to make three button designs in Plique-à-jour (buttons 459 and 460) in the early twenty-first century. The design not shown is of a cat on a tin roof. It is believed that six of each were created. They are back marked with the initials of Andrian Sadgrove.

Sachiko Nishida (西田 幸子), Japan

Sachiko Nishida (b. 1979) is an award-winning artist who designs fine Cloisonné and Plique-à-jour enamel with advanced metal engraving techniques. Nishida mainly creates jewelry in a very modern style, but in 2022 she started making buttons (buttons 461 and 462). She signs the back of her buttons with a stamped "Sachi" (button 463).

Born in Kanagawa Prefecture, Nishida graduated from Japan's national art university, Tokyo University of the Arts, in 2006, with a major in engraving. She has a studio in Arakawa-ku, Tokyo. In October 2021, she was awarded the top prize—the Prime Minister's Award—at the fifty-fourth Japan Enamelling Artist Association Exhibition, and in February 2022, she won the Outstanding Performance Award by the Satoh Artcraft Foundation. Nishida also serves as a director of the Japan Enamelling Artist Association. See her work on her website (http://www.n-sachi.com).

THE MAKING OF SACHIKO NISHIDA'S FIRST TWO BUTTONS

Sachiko Nishida's first buttons were created at the request of her friend, Kumi Dreves of Yanaka Red House Button Gallery (page 106). They designed the buttons together, based on images of plants and insects, using the much-loved dragonfly, with a size from five to six centimeters (roughly 2 to 2.33 inches). There are symbols to note in these designs: summer—green bamboo in Japan is fresh, and the blue dragonfly expresses the season; autumn—the sun dyes the rice ears gold and red dragonflies swim in the sky. It took four months to make these two works, starting with the base wax for the casting of the metalwork.

459. Plique-à-jour button with paste, by Simon Mower. The back mark is for seller Andrian Sadgrove.
460. Plique-à-jour button with paste, by Simon Mower. The back mark is for seller Andrian Sadgrove.
461. *Dragonfly on Bamboo.* Plique-à-jour dragonfly with a pictorial (bamboo) interrupted sterling silver border, by Sachiko Nishida; photo credit Kumi Dreves.
462. *Dragonfly and Ears of Rice.* Plique-à-jour dragonfly with a pictorial (rice stalks) sterling silver border, by Sachiko Nishida; photo credit Kumi Dreves.
463. Sachiko Nishida's back mark; photo credit Kumi Dreves.

Carolyn Noga, Illinois

Carolyn Noga was an enamelist who was making enamel beads and other jewelry when Bruce Beck met her in 1990 at the Bead and Button Show in Milwaukee and asked her to make buttons. She made somewhere around two dozen for Beck to sell and stopped after that. Most had a movable part (button 464). Noga would form the copper base of the button using a doorknob (for larger examples) or other small types of knobs (for the smaller buttons).

Glenda L. Ott, California

Glenda L. Ott (b. 1940) is an enamelist and jeweler who started making buttons in 1990 when asked to make the favor button for the California State Button Society Show. Subsequently, she made favor buttons for not only an NBS show but also other state button shows. She works in Cloisonné, silk-screening, and Plique-à-jour (button 465). In general, she didn't back mark her buttons, but those she did sign were either "GOTT" or "glo" and the year the button was made (figure 4.9).

Figure 4.9 Glenda L. Ott's back mark.

E. J. Peeler, Kansas

E. J. (Edwina) Peeler (1947–2020) was born and raised in Kansas. However, for a time she lived in Texas. She was also known as E. J. Broadhead. Peeler was an accomplished watercolorist. She had been a button collector for several years when she met Jean and Freddie Speights in Texas, and they convinced her to create buttons utilizing her talents. She made some studio buttons (buttons 466 and 467): transfers on shell and ceramic, and copper Plique-à-jour.

464. Émaux Peints on concave shape of Dorothy and Witch, by Carolyn Noga. Dorothy's head is separately attached (plaquette), and the witch head is movable.
465. Plique-à-jour realistic hot air balloon on silver, by Glenda L. Ott.
466. Plique-à-jour button in brass, by E. J. Peeler; note her stylized shank.
467. Plique-à-jour hot air balloon, by E. J. Peeler.

Michele Raney, Washington

Michele Raney (b. 1959) is a jeweler and enamelist whose innovative technique of metal design produces beautiful Basse Taille and Champlevé pieces (called Basse Taille sur Fond Réservé). Raney studied metalsmithing in the United States, as well as enameling and engraving in London. She then developed a way to make steel dies to strike her metal by hand engraving graphite and then using electrical discharge machining (EDM). Typically, she die strikes thick, 12-gauge fine silver as her enameling base. Because of the thickness of the metal, she does not need to counter enamel these pieces, but she does so if the metal gauge requires it. Unique features in Michele's technique are the depth and detail, which create a truly dimensional landscape. Her pieces require three to five firings for shading and up to 10 firings with the application of several colors. Her designs are inspired by nature and wildlife—hence the playful name she chose for her body of work: "Enanimals."

Raney has been making buttons since about 1996 but took a hiatus after five years to concentrate on jewelry. To date, she has made more than 30 buttons, using lead-bearing enamels, in the Basse Taille (buttons 468 and 469) and Plique-à-jour techniques. She back marks all her work (button 470). Her work can be seen on her website (http://www.micheleraney.com).

Linda K. Reynolds, Kansas

Linda K. Reynolds (b. 1961) had been collecting buttons for many years when she started taking enameling classes in 2019. Of course, she was inspired to make buttons! Although she typically uses the Cloisonné technique (buttons 471 and 472), she employs other techniques, such as stenciling (button 473), and uses a variety of embellishments like mica lusters and seed beads. She back marks her buttons with her initials "*LKR*" and the year (button 474). Prior to enameling, Linda took classes in goldsmithing. She has made aluminum buttons as well as jewelry made with buttons.

468. Basse Taille dragonfly, by Michele Raney.
469. Basse Taille Man in the Moon, by Michele Raney.
470. Back of button by Michele Raney showing her hand-engraved back mark. The "999" denotes fine silver, "MR" are her initials, "7/98" is the month/year of creation, and "2" is the number of the design on the front.
471. Cloisonné pear using fine silver wires on oval copper, by Linda K. Reynolds.
472. Cloisonné sunflower using fine silver wires on copper, by Linda K. Reynolds.
473. Stenciled lattice-type design with painted black outlines, by Linda K. Reynolds.
474. Linda K. Reynolds's back mark.

Ada Snow Smith, Unknown

Ada Snow (Mrs. Lawrence B.) Smith, active in the mid-twentieth century, enameled on copper and created mainly pictorial buttons such as lighthouses, Kate Greenway figures, castles, Mayflower ships, and more. At least some of her shanks were glued on (button 475). She wrote an article in *Just Buttons*, February 1977, about her enamels.[12] She said that she worked in these techniques: Scrolling (button 477), Stenciling, Sgraffito, Decalcomania (silk screen reproductions), and Émaux Peints (buttons 475 and 476). See more of her buttons in her article.

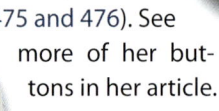

Joseph H. Spencer, Florida

Joseph H. Spencer (1925–2016) served in the US Navy during World War II as a USS *Farragut* radar man and was awarded the Purple Heart. Although he planned to be an opera tenor, he left the music field to sell school and church furniture. Then, in 1962, he met enamelist Harold Martin, and in 1970 he started working on a form of torch-fired enameling using two torches; at that time, this technique was unique to the enameling world, but he had been using it for his larger enameled sculptures. He eventually settled in Florida and opened his first enamel studio in 1976. In 1996, he was contacted by button collector Sara (Sally) Bottorf and started making enameled buttons.

Working primarily with a torch, Spencer used lead-bearing and lead-free Thompson Enamels. He preferred the lead-bearing options and often made his own tools. He called his torch firing "MTF" (Multi-Torch-Firing), "Flame Firing," or "Open Fire." He created some buttons with fused-in copper pieces (button 479) and made diminutives with millefiori (button 480), frequently using copper cutouts as a base for realistics (button 481). Spencer made shanks that were embossed with his initials "*JS*" (button 478); he always counter enameled his buttons. He loved to teach and give public enameling demonstrations, and he sold a line of mixed enamel frit blends. Learn more about Spencer at https://www.joespencerart.com.

475. Émaux Peints button, back marked and counter enameled, by Ada Snow Smith. The back shows a back mark of "Snow" and the date of "'80." This also shows that the shank was glued on. Note that the counter enamel was done with scrap enamel and shows the typical speckled look (see page 36 for more information on scrap counter enamel).
476. Polychrome button depicts the famous *Skating in Central Park*, by Ada Snow Smith. Read more about the origin of this design in the July 2017 *NBB* article "Skating in St. Moritz?"[13]
477. Scrolled enamel button, thought to be (not verified) by Ada Snow Smith; back is not signed, although the counter enamel is similar to button 475 and the shank is glued on (although a different shank) (button 127, page 36).
478. Joseph H. Spencer's mark—typically stamped onto his handmade copper shanks.
479. Enameled oval with copper clown fused in, by Joseph H. Spencer.
480. Enameled diminutive with a millefiori design, by Joseph H. Spencer.
481. Enameled realistic enameled leaf, by Joseph H. Spencer.

Janet White, California

Janet White (b. 1946) is a native Californian, long-time crafter, and late-in-life button collector whose passion is china buttons. In 2015, she began building small assemblages combining vintage metal and wood pieces. She subsequently took enameling classes to make pieces to add to the figures she was building. An enamel handbag with a lift-up flap for a lady robot gave her the idea for a movable button (button 482) and triggered her interest in combining mechanics with color and design. She wrote an article on her enameling for the *New York State Button Society Bulletin* January 2022 issue titled "Crafty Creations: Creating Enamel Buttons with Janet White."[14]

To execute her whimsical movable designs, White frequently relies on metal rivets (button 483) but also uses silver jump rings, fine chain, and copper and brass wire. She usually doesn't make one-of-a-kind buttons, but she sets no limit on her editions. For each button, she designs a card for them to rest on—this is her own reward for finishing a design. If she knows she is not making more of the design, she will number these cards like 1/4, 2/4, 3/4, and 4/4; otherwise, her buttons are not numbered.

In 2023, White started working with pine needle artist Elvira Bowers. Their joint buttons (button 484) are enamel buttons (the shanks are attached to the enamel centers) with pine needle borders. Also in 2023, White started working with Elizabeth Mott, a wood button maker, providing enamel OMEs for Mott's buttons.

White's back mark is a spiral, a design used by different ethnic groups to signify a journey. The stamp she used for the original spiral eventually wore out, and her replacement (which she bought multiples of) is somewhat different but is the one used for all her latest pieces; figure 4.10 shows two that she has employed.

Figure 4.10 Janet White's signature spirals. The one on the right is the newest.

---

482. Stenciled realistic purse with flap that moves, by Janet White.
483. Realistic beetle with movable wings and seed beads for eyes, by Janet White.
484. Transfer / Émaux Peints with artist-made decal and a pine needle border; enameling by Janet White and pine needle work by Elvira Luetke Bowers.

Diana Wieler, Canada

Diana Wieler was born on the Canadian prairies in 1961. She's had a long history in the arts, written books for teens, sculpted in miniature, and enameled. She started to make Studio Buttons in 2009 using Bronze Metal Clay. Preferring to work more with color, she decided to learn enameling in 2010. As there were no classes near her, she bought books and taught herself. Then, in 2019, she started making leather mosaic Studio Buttons and, in 2021, micro mosaic polymer clay Studio Buttons. At least one of her buttons is in the Italian button museum, Museo del Bottone.

Her favorite enameling techniques are Émaux Peints (button 485), sometimes over silver Guilloché (button 126, page 35), and Cloisonné, often over silver foil with a copper base (button 486). Although not a button collector herself, she loves creating buttons because they are small canvases and the subject matter is unlimited. Wieler primarily makes one-of-a-kind buttons, but she may make another of any particular design, as she likes changing up what she is creating. She might use commercial settings to mount her work, but usually she solders a shank on the back. Wieler does not number her buttons. Sometimes she fuses metal to the back with "*DW*" (button 487), and sometimes she paints her initials on the front as "*DJW*." She is inspired by the natural world and by other artists, past and present, especially from the Art Nouveau period. She sells her buttons on her website (https://www.etsy.com/people/thebuttonatelier).

Yanaka Red House Button Gallery, Japan

The Yanaka Red House Button Gallery was founded by Kumi Dreves in 2012. It is named after its location in Yanaka, a quiet part of central Tokyo that has a long and deep connection to art. In fact, it's made of red brick and is a miniature version of the "Red House" built by William Morris (page 17) and his friends. It features Morris wallpaper and English antiques.

Dreves originally started out as a jewelry/accessory/clothing designer and maker with a side of vintage jewelry and British antiques in 2002, when she started Adam Ltd. However, during a visit to London she saw some fabulous old buttons at an antique show. She conceived the notion of both collecting and selling gorgeous old buttons and of using vintage buttons in fashioning costume jewelry (figure 4.11). As she became consumed by buttons, she realized she needed more room. Dreves thus shifted focus and, with her husband, Tom Dreves, built a gallery/house/atelier/office/storeroom in 2012, opening the gallery that year (https://www.yanaka-redhouse.jp).

Since 2021, Dreves has embarked on a cross-cultural mission to get award-winning artisans of Japan's Meiji-era traditional export crafts (maki-e lacquer, Shibayama inlay, and enamel) interested in

Figure 4.11 Necklace made with enamel buttons, by Kumi Dreves; photo credit Kumi Dreves.

---

485. Émaux Peints button of Jackie Kennedy, by Diana Wieler.
486. Cloisonné over silver foil covered copper of Rapunzel, mounted in metal, by Diana Wieler. This is similar to the Gin-bari technique.
487. Diana Wieler's back mark.

creating new items of beauty in the form of buttons. She also hopes to help Western button aficionados better understand and appreciate those traditional techniques. Currently part of the Yanaka inventory are unsold buttons from Kokuto Co. Ltd. (page 95), which was Dreves's father's company, and some inventory that was produced by Kokuto on her request before they wound down operations. Although most other inventory is antique and vintage buttons purchased elsewhere, she also has started to commission artists to make buttons for her to sell. The two dragonfly Plique-à-jour buttons Dreves commissioned from Sachiko Nishida (page 101) are a part of this Meiji arts revitalization project. She also sells her own button-based jewelry creations. Dreves is interested in the currents of artisan techniques, personally knows some contemporary enamel artists/manufacturers, and understands the history/techniques of enamel in Japan. Her husband, a lawyer now practicing in Japan, supports her endeavors and helps as needed.

Appendix A: Buttons with Enamel DF or OME

The buttons shown in this appendix are buttons not classified as National Button Society (NBS) enamel buttons but that include enamel. The enamel may take the form of either a Decorative Finish (DF) or an Other Material Embellishment (OME). The types are separated into metal base versus other material base for better understanding.

METAL BUTTONS WITH ENAMEL DF OR OME

These buttons do not have enamel as the focus but use it only as an enhancement on the metal. The enameled surface area may be located anywhere on the button, including the border (button 488). The coverage may be minimal or extensive, as seen in some of these examples.

488. Antique openwork metal button with cut steel OME and enamel Émaux Peints DF outer border.
489. Antique brass button with Champlevé enamel DF and a triplicate acorn design. Note that this is not an enamel background, as it is one-piece construction.
490. Antique Smuggler's Button (mechanical), silver with enamel DF and gemstone OME (frequently called Austro-Hungarian or court jewels).
491. Antique combined material button of predominantly silver with enamel DF, with gemstones and pearls (frequently called Austro-Hungarian or court jewels).
492. Canadian brass uniform button with enamel Basse Taille DF.
493. Antique openwork brass button with Champlevé / Basse Taille enamel DF and cut steel OME.
494. Antique silver button with Champlevé enamel DF and pictorial back mark. Looks like Niello (appendix B).
495. Antique flat steel button with Champlevé plaquette OME attached with two cut steel rivets.

OTHER BASE MATERIAL BUTTONS (NOT ENAMELS) THAT HAVE ENAMEL OME

This type of button is not commonly found.

DECORATIVE ENAMEL BORDERS

Barbara Barrans says, "Non-metal/non-enamel base buttons may have enamel added as an embellishment or decoration in the form of a border. It may be unclear whether these added enamel borders are more properly classed as OME or as DF. Although not common, these examples are certainly worth including in your button collection. Borders made entirely of enamel might be seen as OME, similar to an enamel plaquette. Borders made of metal which are partially decorated with enamel would fit the other category of DF."[1]

496. Antique casein button with enamel plaquette OME.
497. Antique engraved and gilded pearl button with enamel plaquette OME.
498. Antique velvet background button with enameled escutcheon (coat of arms for Montenegro).
499. Antique combined materials realistic butterfly button with both jade and filigree Plique-à-jour enamel wings, with twisted wire detail and enameled body. The jade and the enamel are of equal focus in this button. Depending on how the button is classed—either gemstone or enamel—the other material would be considered an OME. However, combined material is the best classification.
500. Antique pearl mounted in metal with prong-set Faux Opal (glass) center and narrow Champlevé enamel outer border.
501. Antique fabric mounted in gilt with cut steel OME and shaped rococo enamel border DF.
502. Antique celluloid shield over star-design metal center with scalloped Champlevé / Basse Taille enamel border DF.
503. Antique smoky pearl background with a Champlevé flower plaquette (OME) and outer Basse Taille border DF, both with paste OME; photo credit JoNel Kurtz.

Appendix B: Enamel Look-alikes

This appendix discusses various materials that look like enamel but are not. They might have been made to simulate enamel but not always. In any case, the collector should be familiar with these so they do not mistake them for enamels.

COLD PLASTIC ENAMEL (CPE)

Buttons come in many different materials, which may have Decorative Finishes (DFs). Both vitreous enamel and CPE are two such DFs. These can look very similar but are vastly different in composition and use. I wrote about this subject in the July 2020 *National Button Bulletin* article "Is It Enamel or Cold Plastic Enamel?"[1] First, let me give you some descriptions:

- Vitreous enamel is glass fused to metal at high temperatures.
- CPE is a form of plastic and is usually air dried; however, it can be put into low heat to quicken the drying process. It is applied in various ways (brush, toothpick, etc.) and usually needs only one or two applications. It comes in both transparent and opaque colors. I have also heard it called "Cold Enamel" or "Unfired Enamel." Enamelists do not like that the word "enamel" is used for this material at all! See button 504 for a sample.

How can you tell the difference? There are two basic ways: one is a definitive test; the other is an eyeball test, but this method works only if the CPE is swirled.

- Definitive test: Hold a straight pin vertically and tap the surface. If it skips over the surface, then it's enamel (i.e., glass). However, if the surface is tacky, it's CPE. But be careful! You can scratch CPE with a pin (though not enamel); therefore, do not drag the pin over the surface—just tap it. *Note:* I have done this numerous times and have never scratched the CPE, but it could happen, so be careful.
- Eyeball test: Look at the color and see whether it's swirled (i.e., marbled or intermixed colors). If so, note the type of swirl. Swirls in CPE are smooth lines, but swirls in enamel are usually done from lumps, so the lines are surrounded by broader color (remains of the lumps). Liquid enamel can also be done with swirls, but again the look is different. It may take time to develop the eye for this difference. When in doubt, the pin test is definitive!

Swirling in enamel is done with a technique called Scrolling (like marbling) and is described in more depth on page 61.

Consider figure B.1 and button 505, which are enamel, and buttons 506 and 507, which are CPE. Notice the two-tone look of the swirls in the CPE buttons. I have never seen multicolored CPE swirls, but they might exist. But see that the

504. Metal button with CPE DF to look like Champlevé, by Kokuto Co. Ltd. (page 95); photo credit Kumi Dreves.

Figure B.1 Liquid enamel swirled on copper with gold decal on top. This sample, created by Karen L. Cohen, is not a button.

swirls are smooth and well blended into each other. By contrast, look at button 505 and notice how the lumps that were swirls (scrolled) in Lowenstein's button are marbled into each other, multicolored but not well blended. Now notice the piece in figure B.1, with its swirls multicolored and somewhat blended. This must be done before the liquid enamel is dried and thus before it's fired. I know of no way to change the colors of liquid enamel to look like the CPE colors to test whether I could make the blending look like CPE. All three of these styles look different. Note that the cow in button 507 is solid. It would be hard to tell whether this piece is CPE or enamel, except that the moon is clearly CPE and thus the cow would be as well. Again, the definitive test is the pin test.

FLAME PAINTING ON COPPER

This is a metalsmithing technique in which a small-tipped, very hot torch is used to heat copper with various temperatures, either to get a pattern (button 508) or to give random color (the button's back). The resulting color could fade if not sealed with some form of metal-compatible spray, which also keeps the copper color bright. You can tell this is not enamel using the pin test described in the earlier CPE section. See more about Flame Painting at https://www.coppercolorists.com.

FOIL OR METAL UNDER GLASS

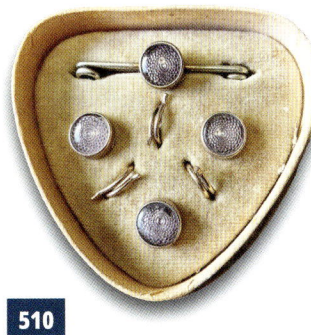

These buttons are textured colored foil under glass or colored glass over textured metal or foil, made to resemble Basse Taille enameling (buttons 509, 510, and 511). Domed glass might magnify the image, whereas enamel will not.

---

505. Scrolled copper enamel button, by Herman Lowenstein.
506. White metal peacock CPE DF with exuberant feather display accented with aurora and clear pastes. *Note:* This is one of the best uses of CPE I have ever seen.
507. Fabric with bead embroidery, using glass beads on cotton, with focal of cow jumping over the moon with swirled CPE, movable, by Karen L. Cohen.
508. Realistic turtle using Flame Painting on copper by Ev Batto (note that this artist's last name is not clear).
509. Faux Enamel (foil under glass) mounted in openwork metallic lustered metal frame.
510. Woman's boxed set of Faux Enamel buttons (foil under glass).
511. Colored glass over textured metal with raised inner metal border, made to look like Guilloché. We can tell this piece is not enamel because the dome of the glass has too high a side curve for it to be enamel.

NIELLO

Although Niello (buttons 512 and 513) was not developed to imitate enamel, it can be confused with enamel. It can also be confused with Bidriware. Niello is a black material frequently composed of sulfur, copper, silver, and lead, and it is used as an inlay in engraved metal, usually silver, in items such as jewelry, buttons, swords, and more. Niello inlaid in this way has the look of Champlevé enameling. It can also be used in larger spaces in pieces such as wall hangings. The stark contrast between the silver and the black Niello provides a beautiful look. Button 494 (page 108) is a Champlevé button with black enamel that could be confused with Niello.

Niello gets its name from the Latin *nigellum* for substance or the medieval Latin for black—*nigella* or *neelo*. Although it was common in Europe, it can also be from parts of the Near East or Asia.

PERTAPGHAR ENAMELS

Another technique of Faux Enamel is Thewa, developed in the Pertapghar district of Rajasthan, India. Another name is Pertapghar Enamel. However, pieces made in this way are not enamel at all; instead, they are glass with gold pressed into them when the glass is molten. Normally created as jewelry, button 514 is a button, probably from the late 1800s or early 1900s.

PORCELAIN

Porcelain buttons can look like enamel buttons (button 515) or not (button 516), although porcelain artists were not trying to simulate enamel. With experience, one can probably tell the difference, but it can be difficult. There is no definitive test for this material. Also keep in mind that some Painting Materials (China Paints) are the same for both porcelain and enamel paintings.

Porcelain is a form of clay, and enamel is glass fused to metal. If the button has no setting such that the back can be seen, the difference is clear—if the back is metal, it's enamel; if it's not, then it's porcelain.

The first edition of *The Big Book of Buttons* provides a way to tell the difference between porcelain and enamel when the plaquette is mounted in metal such that the back cannot be seen:[2] Tap it with a fingernail, and enamel should give a metallic sound. But porcelain or ceramic will not. However, small buttons may not be distinguishable in this way. Thus, it's not clear that this method always works.

Both enamel plaquettes and porcelain can be mounted in a metal frame. When the piece in question is set in metal, look to see whether the metal has a separation space between it and the focal. If the metal looks like it's attached to the focal,

---

512. Antique Russian Niello button.
513. Antique Russian Niello button.
514. Faux Enamel Pertabghar Enamel button from India.
515. Porcelain button that looks like it could be enamel.
516. Porcelain button with the technique of Pâte sur Pâte (page 57).

it's an enamel. Button 517 shows an enamel done directly in a metal frame so there is no separation between the focal and the metal.

This may be hard to tell, but here is something to look for: If the enamel has

517

a hand polish (see page 68), the coloring of the enamel might look like it's under glass—that is, there is some depth to the piece. In porcelain, all coloring would be on the surface, as this material is never covered with a clear coat.

517. Émaux Peints enamel button, saucer-shaped, enameled directly in the metal frame.

Appendix C: Enamel Restoration

To repair or not repair—that is the question. This question is easier for the collector to answer than for a person with a piece of broken jewelry. A chipped or scratched enamel button does not lose its value in competition, although it will affect its selling price (button 518).

There are several factors to consider. Enamels from different factories are not necessarily compatible. Because an old piece has old enamel, one can never be sure what type of enamel is in the piece. In addition, as the piece must be put into a kiln with high heat, if it includes a solder joint, it's possible the joint will open up in the kiln and ruin the piece. Most enamelists do not want to do repairs at all! But there are a couple around the United States who do. The issue is that, in general, the piece must be de-enameled and then re-enameled. As this process can be said to damage a button from its original state, most collectors will not do it. However, a person with a broken piece of jewelry may very well not mind.

A few other ways to repair enamel have been suggested. One is to use Cold Plastic Enamels (CPE). Another way is noted in the book *Oriental Cloisonné and Other Enamels* by Arthur and Grace Chu, in the chapter on repairing Cloisonné.[1] The Chus use two-part epoxy and pigments rather than CPE. Diane Ford, a button collector, has repaired Plique-à-jour using Aleene's Tacky Glue and watercolors (button 519). This glue will be affected by hot water and detergent, so use this method with caution. Lastly, if the enamel is only scratched or has a slight chip, it might be able to be refired to smooth this imperfection out, but there is still the solder joint issue, and I do not recommend taking the chance.

---

518. Antique Plique-à-jour with chips.
519. Antique Plique-à-jour / Foil Egyptian scarab repaired by Diane Ford.

Appendix D: Button versus Enamel Terminology

BUTTON TERMINOLOGY	ENAMEL TERMINOLOGY	DEFINITION
All-over pattern	Diaper pattern; diaper design is used in the book	Repeating single or combined motifs
Award	Competition	An NBS contest with defined rules for what should be included
Battersea-style/Battersea-type/Battersea/Bilsten enamels	English Painted Enamels	Enamels of the style done at the Battersea Enamel Factory but not necessarily done at the factory itself (page 8)
Construction Assorted	Techniques	The major enameling techniques used to make a button
CPE—Cold Plastic Enamel	Resin	A form of synthetic polymer, a basic material; other terms are "cold enamel" and "unfired enamel"
Counter	Not to be confused with the enameling term "counter enamel"	Rare or unusual button example; may garner extra points in competition
DF—Decorative Finish	Material Supplements or Embellishments; in the button world, a DF includes a matte surface; in enameling, we use the word "finish" for the surface. In this book, I've used the word "topcoat," as using "finish" would be confusing to collectors.	A surface treatment or coating applied to button; not to be confused with OME
Émaux Peints	Limoges	A major construction type, meaning basically, "Painted enamels"
Encrustation	Beaded Enamel; Cabochonné; Moriage; Fauré method	A buildup of enamel
Gilded	When applied to enamel, the particular material used is called Liquid Metal; gold and silver are called Liquid Gold and Liquid Silver, respectively. If applied to materials other than enamel, it might still be called gilded—as in a gilded wood frame.	A DF of metallic paint, foil, or silver or gold leaf applied to another material
Gilt metal	Gold-plated metal	Metal completely overlaid with gold so that it is classed the same as gold as a material
Limoges-style Émaux Peints (not mentioned in the *Blue Book*)	Limoges with foil and transparent enamels	Émaux Peints enamel using foil and colorized by the use of transparent enamels
Mounting	Setting	Framework that holds a separate piece of enamel (see Plaquette below)
OME—Other Material Embellishment	Material Supplements or Embellishments	A material added to a button that is different from the base material of that button and is on the surface
Plaquette	When set in metal (a mounting), many jewelers will call this a "jewel"; however, the word "plaquette" is also used	A thin or small piece of enameled metal mounted in/on a separate mounting for support
Swirls in enamel (not used in the *Blue Book*)	Scrolling technique	A form of marbling colors together

Appendix E: Japanese Enamel Terminology

The *Blue Book* does mention some Japanese enameling techniques such as Gin-bari. This section lists the known Japanese enameling terms so the collector will have a reference. They are separated into categories, as not all words represent enameling techniques.

TERMINOLOGY

- **Bari** means cover or spread.

- **Cha** means tea.

- **Gin** means silver.

- **Gin-jippō**—or Gin Tai Jippō—an enameled piece on a silver substrate (foundation metal). Thus, any finished enamel piece on a silver *substrate* is Gin-jippō, regardless of any technique it might incorporate. This term is a *description* of the piece, not a *technique* of enameling. In English, it's like saying a silver enameled piece.
  In the button world, there are two styles of Japanese buttons with a silver substrate. One is actually Basse Taille (button 520), and one is the style called Japanese Enamel on Silver (button 521).

- **Ji-ita-jippō**—a finished object that uses an enameled piece (plaquette), made separately, added to a non-enameled metal or lacquered wooden piece.

- **Jungin** means pure silver. Silver Japanese hallmarks can be found online (https://www.925-1000.com/foreign_marks5.html), which will help date the period of any button you have.

- **Kin** means gold.

- **Seki** means stone.

- **Shippō yaki** (or just **Shippō**) is a *completed* enamel piece (as opposed to the material itself). Another form of the word "*Shippō*" is "**Jippō**," which is used as a suffix, as in "Gin-jippō." Enamelists in Japan are called "Shippō artists" (that is, those who make enamelware).

520. Antique silver Basse Taille button mounted in brass from Japan. This look is so similar to Gin-bari that it is often confused with that technique. However, when viewing in person, this style may be able to be distinguished from Gin-bari by the Basse Taille design being higher and/or having more details. Still, it is difficult for the untrained eye to tell the difference.
521. Antique Champlevé button, frequently called Japanese Enamel on Silver.

ENAMELING TECHNIQUES

- **Bokaski**—gradations in color without the use of wires. There is no term for this effect in American enameling other than just "shading."

- **Gin-bari** or Ginbari or GinBari—a foil technique, typically embossed. As mentioned earlier, "*Gin*" in Japanese means silver and "*Bari*" means cover or spread. Thus, Gin-bari can translate to silver cover/spread, which is what an embossed foil would do—it covers/spreads over the substrate (usually copper but does not have to be). This topic was discussed further on page 60. Note, though, that sometimes the Japanese use Gin-bari foil without embossing, but that is usually on larger items like when foil is used to cover the surface of a vase. It was developed to imitate inexpensive Basse Taille.

- **Moriage** (More-ee-a-gay)—a buildup of enamel to form a relief design. The use of this technique is typically on larger items than buttons. But the term has started to be used in the United States for any buildup of enamel.

- **Musen**—a wireless Cloisonné technique. This technique uses wires to guide where enamel should be wet-packed, but either the wires are removed before firing or it uses short wires that get covered by enamel or possibly the embedded wires are etched or dissolved in some way and the space filled with enamel. After the first firing, any wires removed might be replaced as a guide again, or the piece might be enameled without them. Musen-Shippō, an object using the Musen technique, was created to reproduce the fine look of paintings. See figure E.1.

Figure E.1 Musen bowl—wireless cloisonné; in the private collection of Fredric T. Schneider.

- **Shotai**—one of three types of Plique-à-jour. Shotai is created as in Cloisonné with a copper base and silver wires, but with a thick flux base and no counter enamel. When done, the copper base is etched away to leave a piece without a metal backing. The etchant used affects the copper but not the silver wires. It is doubtful that this method was ever used to create buttons. The other methods are discussed in the section on Plique-à-jour on pages 62–63.

- **Yūmusen**—a combination of Yūsen and Musen.

- **Yūsen**—the Cloisonné technique.

- **Zōgan**—the Champlevé technique.

SPECIAL ENAMELS

- **Chakin-seki**—translates to Tea Goldstone—a mixture of metal bits in enamel, usually using copper. See page 15 for more information. This material was also called Kinseki or just Chakin. Typically, a transparent brown was used, but other colors (such as amber, green, and blue) were also used. See figure E.2 for a sample.

Figure E.2 Chakin-seki Cloisonné box; in the private collection of Fredric T. Schneider; copyright Fredric T. Schneider.

Appendix F: Checklist for Collecting

When collecting enamel buttons, there are many considerations, depending on your interest. If collecting for competition, you will want to include the broadest representation of enamel techniques based on the class definitions in the *Blue Book* (BB). Thus, be sure to accumulate not only the various BB enamel classes but also other button attributes, such as shapes, pictorial, border, and back mark, to name a few.

If you are not competing, the choice is yours. For example, you might want to collect only enamel buttons that you think are gorgeous or make you happy, without consideration of whether they are all the same technique or have the same attributes. You might want all Division I buttons or only Studio Buttons. Alternately, you might want one of each type that is identifiable for a comprehensive collection of all types of enamel buttons. You might not even care whether the button you want is considered an NBS enamel button according to the *Blue Book* definition.

Included here is a checklist I prepared. The list does not imply anything about points in a competition; it's just a comprehensive list of what I've described in this book.

When you are collecting, consider keeping a computerized list with information about each button. The file should be in either a database or a spreadsheet (or possibly a table in a word processor). Fields, at minimum, should be as follows: division number, who you bought it from, how much you paid (including shipping), description, technique, and general notes for anything else you want to remember about the button. I also recommend organizing your buttons by assigning a number to each. I realize long-term collectors will not go back and do this, but if you are just starting out, or working on a group of buttons (such as enamels) you don't have a lot of, you might want to start numbering. Then take a photo of the button and start the file name of the photo with its number. For example, if you have a button numbered B00023, then its photo file name could be B00023_Enamel_BasseTaille. The reason for this approach is for file sorting—numbers, especially if you have leading zeros, will sort in order. I store mine in folders named 00001–00099, 00100–00199, etc. The following checklist includes a space to write your button number as in #_____. If you are not numbering your buttons, just ignore this space or use it to record how many of those types of buttons you have.

CRITERIA CHECKLIST

- ☐ **TECHNIQUES/CONSTRUCTIONS**
    - ☐ Basse Taille, #_____
        - ☐ Basse Taille sur Fond Reservé, #_____
        - ☐ Guilloché, #_____
            - ☐ Brocade engine pattern, #_____
            - ☐ Line engine pattern, #_____
            - ☐ Rose engine pattern, #_____
        - ☐ Japanese Silver Basse Taille, #_____
        - ☐ Motiwala Brothers Liquid Enamels, #_____
    - ☐ Champlevé, #_____
        - ☐ Deccan, #_____
        - ☐ Jaipur, #_____
        - ☐ Japanese Enamel on Silver, #_____
        - ☐ Kashmir, #_____
        - ☐ Multan, #_____
        - ☐ Taille d'Epargne, #_____
    - ☐ Cloisonné, #_____
        - ☐ Chinese 1, #_____
        - ☐ Chinese 2 with twisted wires, #_____
        - ☐ Japanese with 2 size wires, #_____
    - ☐ Crackle Enamel, #_____
    - ☐ Émaux Peints
        - ☐ Canton, #_____
        - ☐ Grisaille, #_____
        - ☐ Limoges-style, #_____
        - ☐ Monochrome, #_____
        - ☐ Pâte, #_____
        - ☐ Persian/Iranian, #_____
        - ☐ Polychrome, #_____
        - ☐ Russian, #_____
    - ☐ Enamel Buildup, #_____
        - ☐ Battersea-style, #_____
        - ☐ Encrustations, #_____
        - ☐ Fauré, #_____
        - ☐ Moriage, #_____
    - ☐ Eutectic Effect, #_____
    - ☐ Gin-bari, #_____
        - ☐ High Relief, #_____
        - ☐ Low Relief, #_____
            - ☐ with Cloisonné, #_____
    - ☐ Graphite Pencil, #_____
    - ☐ High-Fire Techniques, #_____
        - ☐ Scrolling, #_____
        - ☐ Webbing Design, #_____
        - ☐ Other, #_____
    - ☐ Plique-à-jour
        - ☐ Filigree, #_____
            - ☐ Buildup, #_____
            - ☐ Flat, #_____
        - ☐ Non-filigree, #_____
            - ☐ Buildup, #_____
            - ☐ Flat, #_____
    - ☐ Pull-through, #_____
    - ☐ Reticulated Foils, #_____
    - ☐ Ronde Bosse, #_____
    - ☐ Separation Enamel, #_____
    - ☐ Sgraffito, #_____
    - ☐ Stenciling, #_____
    - ☐ Transfer/Decal, #_____

☐ TOPCOATS

☐ Glossy, flash fire, #_____   ☐ Matte, #_____

☐ Glossy, hand polished, #_____ ☐ Sugar Fire, #_____

☐ EMBELLISHMENTS

☐ Embellishment on the metal portion of the border, #_____

- ☐ Cut Steel, #_____
- ☐ Paste, #_____
- ☐ Other, #_____

☐ Dichroic Extract Powders, #_____

☐ Gemstones, #_____
Types _____

☐ Glass, #_____
- ☐ Balls, #_____
- ☐ Beads, #_____
- ☐ Faux Opals, #_____
- ☐ Goldstone, #_____
- ☐ Lampwork, #_____
- ☐ Lumps, #_____
  - ☐ Enamel, #_____
  - ☐ Glass, #_____
- ☐ Molded Glass, #_____
- ☐ MUD, #_____
- ☐ Murrini or Millefiori, #_____
- ☐ Paste/Rhinestones, #_____
- ☐ Threads, #_____

☐ Glow-in-the-Dark Material, #_____

☐ Metal, #_____
- ☐ Balls, #_____
- ☐ Filings and Drill Curlicues, #_____
- ☐ Foil/Leaf, #_____
  - ☐ Foil Shapes, #_____
  - ☐ Leaf, #_____
  - ☐ Paillons, #_____
  - ☐ Pierreries, #_____
- ☐ Liquid Metal, #_____
- ☐ Mesh, #_____
- ☐ Metal Clay Overlay Silver Paste, #_____
- ☐ Metal Point, #_____
- ☐ Sheet, #_____
- ☐ Cast Metal, #_____
- ☐ Silver Deposit, #_____
- ☐ Wire, #_____
  - ☐ Plain, #_____
  - ☐ Twisted, #_____

☐ Mica, #_____

☐ Other, #_____
Include all others: _____
_____
_____

- ☐ **OTHER CHARACTERISTICS**—be sure to label these in an award
  - ☐ Eighteenth Century, #_____
  - ☐ Back mark, #_____
  - ☐ Border, #_____
    - ☐ Edge, #_____
    - ☐ Frame, #_____
    - ☐ Inner, #_____
    - ☐ Integrated, #_____
    - ☐ Interrupted, #_____
    - ☐ Outer, #_____
    - ☐ Pictorial, #_____
    - ☐ Rim, #_____
  - ☐ Coin—enameled on, #_____
  - ☐ Combined techniques, #_____
    Techniques: _____
    _____
    _____
  - ☐ Commemorative button, #_____
  - ☐ Counter enamel, #_____
  - ☐ Enamel Background, #_____
  - ☐ Mechanical/Movable, #_____
  - ☐ Metal enameled on
    - ☐ Brass, #_____
    - ☐ Copper, #_____
    - ☐ Gold, #_____
    - ☐ Silver, #_____
  - ☐ Mounted in metal, #_____
  - ☐ Openwork, #_____
  - ☐ Patterns, #_____
    Include all you have: _____
    _____
    _____
    _____
  - ☐ Pictorials
    - ☐ Animal, #_____
    - ☐ Object, #_____
    - ☐ Plant, #_____
    - ☐ Other, #_____
  - ☐ Sew-through, #_____
  - ☐ Shape, #_____
    - ☐ Contour, #_____
    - ☐ Linear, #_____
    - ☐ Realistic, #_____
  - ☐ Usage, #_____
  - ☐ Verbal, #_____

- ☐ **ART STYLES**
  - ☐ Art Deco, #_____
  - ☐ Art Nouveau, #_____
  - ☐ Arts & Crafts, #_____
  - ☐ Chinoiserie, #_____

☐ ENAMELISTS WHO MADE ENAMEL BUTTONS

- ☐ Almeyda, Diane Echnoz, #_____
- ☐ AP & Cie (Albert Parent & Company), #_____
- ☐ Carter, Helene, #_____
- ☐ Chinese Champlevé, Modern, #_____
- ☐ Chinese Cloisonné, Modern, #_____
- ☐ Chinese Plique-à-jour, Modern, #_____
- ☐ Cohen, Karen L., #_____
- ☐ David-Anderson, #_____
- ☐ Demicco, Marie, #_____
- ☐ Diem, Rose Marie, #_____
- ☐ Dingman, Sandy, #_____
- ☐ Dolbin, Vladamir, #_____
- ☐ Douglas Clock & Co., #_____
- ☐ DuBois, Nancy, #_____
- ☐ Elwyn, Marie, #_____
- ☐ Émaux Ardéchois, #_____
- ☐ Fabergé, Peter Carl, #_____
- ☐ Funnell, Joy, #_____
- ☐ Hall, Doris, #_____
- ☐ Hammer, Marius, #_____
- ☐ Haseler, William Hair, #_____
- ☐ Holmström, August Wilhelm, #_____
- ☐ Horner, Charles, #_____
- ☐ Inaba Cloisonné Company, #_____
- ☐ J. Millward Banks & Co., #_____
- ☐ James Fenton & Co., #_____
- ☐ Keim, André, #_____
- ☐ Kendall, Dorothy, #_____
- ☐ King, Jessie Marion, #_____
- ☐ Knox, Archibald, #_____
- ☐ Kokulto Co. Ltd., #_____
- ☐ Ledwin, Mona, #_____
- ☐ Levinger, Heinrich, #_____
- ☐ Liberty & Co., #_____
- ☐ Lingren, Linda, #_____
- ☐ Linley, Phil, #_____
- ☐ Litt, Chris #_____
- ☐ Lowenstein, Herman, #_____
- ☐ Motiwala Brothers, #_____
- ☐ Mower, Simon, #_____
- ☐ Nishida, Sachiko, #_____
- ☐ Noga, Carolyn, #_____
- ☐ Olsen, Ole Petter Raasch, #_____
- ☐ Ott, Glenda L., #_____
- ☐ Pearce & Sons, #_____
- ☐ Peeler (Broadhead), E. J., #_____
- ☐ Politzer, Ludwig, #_____
- ☐ Raney, Michele, #_____
- ☐ Reynolds, Linda K., #_____
- ☐ Robbins, Joy, #_____
- ☐ Smith, Ada Snow, #_____
- ☐ Spencer, Joseph H., #_____
- ☐ Tullis, Anita, #_____
- ☐ Walton, G. E., #_____
- ☐ White, Janet, #_____
- ☐ Wieler, Diana, #_____
- ☐ William Hutton & Sons, #_____
- ☐ Yanaka Red House Button Gallery, #_____

References and Bibliography

BOOKS

Albert, Lillian Smith, and Jane Ford Adams. *The Button Sampler*. New York: Gramercy, 1951.

Allio, Loïc. *A Button Odyssey*. Translated by Matthew Brown. Paris: Éditions Olisouelle, 2019.

———. *Boutons*. Paris: Éditions du Seuil, 2001.

Bates, Kenneth F. *Enameling Principles & Practice*. Cleveland and New York: World, 1951.

Berberian, Rosalie. *Creating Beauty: Jewelry and Enamels of the American Arts & Crafts Movement*. Atglen, PA: Schiffer, 2019.

Byrom, Gillie Hoyte. *The Practice of Painting in Enamel*. Norwich, Norfolk, England: Pinxit, 2018.

Campbell, Marian. *An Introduction to Medieval Enamels*. Owings Mills, MD: Stemmer House, 1983.

Chapin, Howard M. *How to Enamel*. New York: Wiley, 1911. Reprint, London: Forgotten Books, 2018.

Chu, Arthur, and Grace Chu. *Oriental Cloisonné and Other Enamels: A Guide to Collecting and Repairing*. New York: Crown, 1975.

Cohen, Karen L. *The Art of Fine Enameling*. 2nd ed. Guilford, CT: Stackpole Books, 2019.

Cunynghame, Henry H. *European Enamels*. London: Methuen, 1906.

———. *On the Theory and Practice of Art-Enamelling upon Metals*. Edinburgh: Constable, 1899. Reprint, London: Forgotten Books, 2018.

Duncan, Alastair. *The Paris Salons 1895–1914*. Vol. 5, *Objects d'Art & Metalware*. Woodbridge, Suffolk, UK: Antique Collectors Club, 1999.

Epstein, Diana. *Buttons*. New York: Walker, 1968.

Epstein, Diana, and Millicent Safro. *Buttons*. New York: Abrams, 1991.

Fisher, Alexander. *The Art of Enamelling upon Metal*. London: Offices of "The Studio," 1906.

Hughes, Elizabeth, and Marion Lester. *The Big Book of Buttons*. Sedgwick, ME: New Leaf, 1981.

Hughes, Therle, and Bernard Hughes. *English Painted Enamels*. Middlesex, England: Hamlin, 1967.

Irvine, Gregory. *Japanese Cloisonné*. London: V&A, 2009.

Jazzar, Bernard N., and Harold B. Nelson. *Little Dreams in Glass and Metal: Enameling in America 1920 to the Present*. Los Angeles: Enamel Arts Foundation, 2015.

———. *Painting with Fire*. Long Beach, CA: Long Beach Museum of Art, 2006.

Kuwayama, George. *Shippō: The Art of Enameling in Japan*. Los Angeles: Los Angeles County Museum of Art, 1987.

Leslie, Jane S. *A Reference Book on Studio Button Makers*. Wilmington, MA: Arro, 1997.

Melloy, Meagan. *Studio Buttons and the Artists Who Make Them*. 3rd ed. Privately printed, 2009.

Metropolitan Museum of Art. *Enamels of Limoges 1100–1350*. New York: MetPublications, 1996.

Millenet, Louis-Eliè. *Enamelling on Metal: A Practical Manual on Enamelling and Painting on Enamel*. Translated by H. De Koningh. London: Crosby Lockwood, 1926.

National Button Society. *Blue Book: Official NBS Classification & Competition Guidelines*. San Diego, CA: NBS, 2019–2022.

Noh Yong-suk, and Sung Da-som. *Chilbo, Korean Traditional Enameling*. Korea Craft & Design Resource Book 18. Seoul: Korea Craft & Design Foundation, 2021.

Perry, Jane. *A Collector's Guide to Peasant Silver Buttons*. Egham, UK: Lulu, 2007.

Schneider, Fredric T. *The Art of Japanese Cloisonné Enamel: History, Techniques and Artists, 1600 to the Present*. Jefferson, NC: McFarland, 2010.

Shaffer, Coral. *Shippō Yaki: Enameling in Japan*. Privately printed, 2015.

Speel, Erika. *Dictionary of Enamelling, History and Techniques*. London: Lund Humphries, 1998.

———. *Painted Enamels: An Illustrated Survey 1500–1920*. London: Lund Humphries, 2008.

Theophilus. *On Divers Arts: The Foremost Medieval Treatise on Painting, Glassmaking and Metalwork*. Translated by John G. Hawthorne and Cyril Stanley Smith. Mineola, NY: Dover, 1979.

Timblin, Helen. *Extraordinary Buttons and the Artists Who Make Them*. Eagle River, AK: Joy Journeay, 2024.

JOURNAL ARTICLES

Adams, Jane Ford. "Proposed Classification for Enamel Buttons." *National Button Bulletin*, May 1957.

Bangeman, Herman A., Jr. "Defining Limoges." *National Button Bulletin*, July 2005, 125–29.

———. "Ronde Bosse Enameling," *National Button Bulletin*, July 2004, 118–19.

———. "Silver Embellishment on Buttons." *National Button Bulletin*, October 2003, 195–99.

Barrans, Barbara. "Focus Pocus." *National Button Bulletin*, December 2011, 250.

Beck, Bruce. "Enamels of the Modern Era." *National Button Bulletin*, July 2004, 128–30.

"Brief History of Enameling." *National Button Bulletin*, May 1957.

"Briefs Liquid Enamel." *National Button Bulletin*, July 2005, 112.

Carpenter, Woodrow. "Opalescent Enamel." *Glass on Metal* 13, no. 6 (December 1994): 127.

Cohen, Karen L. "Champlevé Masquerading as Cloisonné." *Territorial News* 19, no. 2 (2021).

———. "Is It Enamel or Cold Plastic Enamel?" *National Button Bulletin*, July 2020, 115.

Cossman, Elaine. "Collecting Buttons of the Arts & Crafts Movement." *National Button Bulletin*, December 2008, 260.

———. "Gin-Bari Enamels." *Territorial News*, January 2006, 12–15.

Ellis, Tom. "Painting Enamel Materials, Part 1." *Glass on Metal* 32, no. 4 (August 2013): 85–94.

Frechette, Jamie. "Eutectic Process for Artistic Effect." *Glass on Metal* 26, no. 2 (2007): 36–40.

Helwig, Bill. "Camaïeu." *Glass on Metal* 3, no. 3 (June 1984): 34–38.

———. "Re-searching Painting Enamels, Part 1." *Glass on Metal* 4, no. 1 (February 1985). Reprint, *Glass on Metal* 21, no. 1 (Spring 2023): 11–13.

"Monochrome or Grisaille." *National Button Bulletin*, July 2005, 125.

"Motiwala: The Indian Master of Modern Buttons." *National Button Bulletin*, October 1990.

Oswald, Adrian, and Faith Russell Smith. "Discovered—a Box of Buttons." *Connoisseur* 133 (1954): 103.

"Russian Enamel Buttons." *National Button Bulletin*, December 1984, 193.

Snow, Ada (Mrs. Lawrence B.) Smith. "My Experiences as a Copper Enamelist." *Just Buttons*, February 1977, 115–22.

Speel, Erika. "English Painted Enamels, Battersea and Bilston Enamels." *Glass on Metal* 26, no. 5 (December 2007): 104–7, 112–13.

———. "English Pictorial Enamels, Part 2." *Glass on Metal* 27, no. 1 (February 2008): 12–15, 19.

———. "Enamel Portrait Miniatures—17th Century." *Glass on Metal* 6, no. 5 (October 1987): 85–88.

———. "Limoges School Pictorial Art." Pts. 1–4. *Glass on Metal* 20, no. 4; 21, no. 1; 21, no. 2; 21, no. 3 (2001–2002).

Speights, M. W. (Freddie). "18th-Century Enamel Buttons." *National Button Bulletin*, December 1999, 280.

Varah, Nancy. "Deccan Buttons." *Just Buttons*, July–August 1979.

Wilmot, Costella F. "My Visit with Motiwala Brothers." *National Button Bulletin*, November 1954.

White, Janet. "Crafty Creations: Creating Enamel Buttons with Janet White." *New York State Button Society Bulletin* 76, no. 1 (January 2022).

WEBSITES

Almagro, Mer. "Introduction to Vitreous Enamel." Enamel Workshop, 2020. https://enamelworkshop.com/introduction/.

Alvini, Joan Strott. "Glass on Gold LLC Enamel Restorations." Accessed January 19, 2024. https://www.glassongold.com.

"The Art Deco Enamels of Camille Fauré." *Canvases, Carats and Curiosities* (blog). M. S. Rau, August 5, 2021. https://rauantiques.com/blogs/canvases-carats-and-curiosities/the-art-deco-enamels-of-camille-faure.

Bernbaum, Anthony. "Origins of the Liberty Cymric Silver Range." Archibald Knox Society, 2014. https://peartreecollection.s3.eu-west-2.amazonaws.com/wp-content/uploads/2018/06/07160747/Anthony-Bernbaum-article-from-archibald-knox-soc-booklet-2014.pdf.

Bloomers and Frocks. "History of Damascene Jewelry." Accessed January 19, 2024. https://bloomersandfrocks.com/blogs/how-to-style-vintage/history-of-damascene-jewelry.

British Museum. "W H Haseler Ltd." Accessed January 19, 2024. https://www.britishmuseum.org/collection/term/BIOG80769.

Collectors Weekly. "Antique Japanese Cloisonné Brooch with Design of Traditional Instruments." Collectors Weekly Show & Tell, accessed January 19, 2024. https://www.collectorsweekly.com/stories/295850-antique-japanese-cloisonn-brooch-with?in=1018-activity.

Encyclopaedia Britannica Online. s.v. "Art Deco." Accessed January 19, 2024. https://www.britannica.com/art/Art-Deco.

———. s.v. "Birmingham Enamelware." Accessed January 19, 2024. https://www.britannica.com/art/Birmingham-enamelware.

———. s.v. "Enamelwork China." Accessed January 19, 2024. https://www.britannica.com/art/enamelwork/China.

———. s.v. "Industrial Revolution." Accessed January 19, 2024. https://www.britannica.com/event/Industrial-Revolution.

———. s.v. "Limoges Painted Enamel." Accessed January 19, 2024. https://www.britannica.com/art/Limoges-painted-enamel.

Emaux Soyer. "History." Accessed August 2021. https://www.emaux-soyer.com/en/presentation/history.html.

Fellows. "Charles Horner Jewellery." June 26, 2023. https://www.fellows.co.uk/blog/jewellery/2023/06/16/charles-horner/.

1st Dibs.com. "Liberty Archibald Knox Cymric Enamel Silver Brooch." Pinterest, accessed January 19, 2024. https://www.pinterest.com/pin/490610953133786097/.

Galler, Michelle. "Antiques Addict: Buttoned Down with Antique Buttons." Georgetowner, June 13, 2019. https://georgetowner.com/articles/2019/06/13/antiques-addict-buttoned-down-with-antique-buttons/.

Glasgow Style. "Jessie Marion King (1875–1949)." Accessed January 19, 2024. https://www.theglasgowstyle.co.uk/jessie-marion-king.

Glass Encyclopedia. s.v. "Glass Sulphides and Cameo Incrustations." Accessed January 19, 2024. https://www.glassencyclopedia.com/glasssulphides.html.

———. s.v. "Pate de Verre." Accessed January 19, 2024. https://www.glassencyclopedia.com/patedeverre.html.

———. s.v. "Silver Overlay Glass." Accessed January 19, 2024. https://www.glassencyclopedia.com/silveroverlayglass.html.

Goring, Elizabeth. "A Reflection on Studio Enamelling in Britain." British Society of Enamellers, 2011. https://www.enamellers.org/history.

Guild of Enamellers. "The Guild's History." Accessed January 19, 2024. https://guildofenamellers.org/index.php/the-guild/about-the-guild?view=article&id=19:art-guild-history&catid=86.

Hofer, Margaret K. "Clara Driscoll and the Tiffany Girls." *Behind the Scenes* (blog). New York Historical Society Museum & Library, March 27, 2015. https://behindthescenes.nyhistory.org/tiffany-girls/.

Hogarth, William, and Simon Francois Ravenet. "Marriage a la Mode: Plate 5." Art of the Print, accessed January 19, 2024. http://www.artoftheprint.com/artistpages/hogarth_william_marriagealamodecompletesetofsixplate5.htm.

Inglenookery. "Jessie M. King, Arts and Crafts Jewellery Designer." Accessed January 19, 2024. https://www.inglenookery.com/?p=1881.

Kramer, David. "Origins of the Arts & Crafts Movement in America: The Roycroft Campus." Craftsman Bungalow, accessed January 19, 2024. http://www.thecraftsmanbungalow.com/elbert-hubbard-roycroft-campus/.

Kudro, Celia. "Glossary of Engine Turning Terms." Wordpress, October 2017. https://engineturning.files.wordpress.com/2017/10/additional-information-glossary1.pdf.

Liberty Retail Ltd. "Our Heritage." Accessed January 19, 2024. https://www.libertylondon.com/us/information/our-heritage.html.

Lyon & Turnbull. "Paul Storr: The Exceptional Craftsmanship of One of Britain's Most Successful Silversmiths." Accessed January 19, 2024. https://www.lyonandturnbull.com/news/article/paul-storr/#:~:text=Paul%20Storr%20is%20deemed%20one,maintained%20to%20the%20highest%20level.

Mark Littler. "Liberty & Co.: History and Valuations." Accessed January 19, 2024. https://www.marklittler.com/liberty-co-valuations-sales-and-history/.

Mirrazavi, Firouzeh, comp. "What Is Persian Enamel (Minakari)?" Persiada, accessed January 19, 2024. https://persianhandicrafts.com/what-is-minakari.

Online Encyclopedia of Silver Marks, Hallmarks & Makers' Marks: Guide to World Hallmarks. Accessed January 19, 2024. https://www.925-1000.com/foreign_marks5.html.

Pettinger, Tejvan. "Facts about the Industrial Revolution." In *Biography Online*, February 15, 2016. Last updated February 10, 2018. https://www.biographyonline.net/facts-about-the-industrial-revolution/.

The Silver Fund. "Collecting Vintage Norwegian Enamel." January 17, 2017. https://thesilverfund.com/news/collecting-vintage-norwegian-enamel/.

Skerry, Janine. "Matthew Boulton—Manufacturer of 'What All the World Desires to Have.'" American Decorative Arts Forum, May 10, 2011. https://adafca.org/events/matthew-boulton-manufacturer-of-what-all-the-world-desires-to-have/.

Uneak Boutique. "The History of Marcasite Jewellery." Accessed January 19, 2024. https://www.uneakboutique.co.uk/pages/the-history-of-marcasite-jewellery.

Wikipedia. s.v. "Arts and Crafts Movement." Last modified December 31, 2023. https://en.wikipedia.org/wiki/Arts_and_Crafts_movement.

———. s.v. "August Wilhelm Holmström." Last modified September 26, 2022. https://en.wikipedia.org/wiki/August_Wilhelm_Holmström.

———. s.v. "Augustus Wollaston Franks." Last modified March 28, 2023. https://en.wikipedia.org/wiki/Augustus_Wollaston_Franks.

———. s.v. "Button." Last modified January 2, 2024. https://en.wikipedia.org/wiki/Button.

———. s.v. "Buttonhole." Last modified December 20, 2023. https://en.wikipedia.org/wiki/Buttonhole.

———. s.v. "Camille Fauré." Last modified March 24, 2023. https://en.wikipedia.org/wiki/Camille_Fauré.

———. s.v. "Charles Horner (Jeweller)." Last modified March 7, 2022. https://en.wikipedia.org/wiki/Charles_Horner_(jeweller).

———. s.v. "Chinoiserie." Last modified January 19, 2024. https://en.wikipedia.org/wiki/Chinoiserie.

———. s.v. "Decal." Last modified December 31, 2023. https://en.wikipedia.org/wiki/Decal.

———. s.v. "Early Netherlandish Painting." Last modified November 14, 2023. https://en.wikipedia.org/wiki/Early_Netherlandish_painting.

———. s.v. "Guilloché." Last modified October 31, 2023. https://en.wikipedia.org/wiki/Guilloché.

———. s.v. "Marcasite Jewellery." Last modified January 9, 2024. https://en.wikipedia.org/wiki/Marcasite_jewellery.

———. s.v. "Multan." Last modified January 12, 2024. https://en.wikipedia.org/wiki/Multan.

———. s.v. "Niello." Last modified August 26, 2023. https://en.wikipedia.org/wiki/Niello.

———. s.v. "Pâte-sur-pâte." Last modified May 13, 2020. https://en.wikipedia.org/wiki/Pâte-sur-pâte.

———. s.v. "Peter Carl Fabergé." Last modified January 6, 2024. https://en.wikipedia.org/wiki/Peter_Carl_Fabergé.

———. s.v. "Ronde-bosse." Last modified September 17, 2022. https://en.wikipedia.org/wiki/Ronde-bosse.

———. s.v. "Roycroft." Last modified August 12, 2023. https://en.wikipedia.org/wiki/Roycroft.

———. s.v. "Silver Overlay." Last modified August 2, 2023. https://en.wikipedia.org/wiki/Silver_overlay.

———. s.v. "Transfer Printing." Last modified January 1, 2024. https://en.wikipedia.org/wiki/Transfer_printing.

Wilcox, Mike. "Mark of the Week: Liberty & Co., Cymric Silver and Archibald Knox." WorthPoint, accessed January 19, 2024. https://www.worthpoint.com/articles/collectibles/mark-of-the-week-liberty-co-cymric-silver-and-archibald-knox.

"William Hair Haseler." *The Story of a House* (blog). Glessner House, May 5, 2014. http://glessnerhouse.blogspot.com/2014/05/william-hair-haseler-silversmith.html.

Williams, Taylor B. "A Mere Trifle: 18th Century English Enamels from circa 1750–1840." Taylor B. Williams Enamels, accessed January 19, 2024. https://www.enamels.com/Focus.htm.

Williams, Taylor B. "Eighteenth-Century English Enamels." *Antiques & Fine Art Magazine*, accessed January 19, 2024. http://www.antiquesandfineart.com/articles/article.cfm?request=158.

VIDEOS

Dickout, Sue. "Boxed Charms of Buttons." Zoom presentation, October 12, 2021.

Durell, Sylvia Liszka. "The History of Buttons: Why We Collect the Little Works of Art." Video presentation for the National Button Society, April 2021.

Thoele, Merry Jo. "Enamel Encore." Zoom presentation for the Colorado Button Connect, August 5, 2020.

World Fashion Channel. "Deboutonner la Mode Exhibition Museum les Arts Decoratifs Paris." YouTube, 2015. Video, 6:09. https://www.youtube.com/watch?v=sBflgSfukhc.

Notes

PREFACE

1. Diana Epstein, *Buttons* (New York: Walker, 1968).

1: HISTORY

1. M. W. (Freddie) Speights, "18th-Century Enamel Buttons," *National Button Bulletin*, December 1999, 280.
2. Diana Epstein, *Buttons* (New York: Walker, 1968); Diana Epstein and Millicent Safro, *Buttons* (New York: Abrams, 1991).
3. Erika Speel, *Painted Enamels: An Illustrated Survey 1500–1920* (London: Lund Humphries, 2008).
4. Alexander Fisher, *The Art of Enamelling upon Metal* (London: Offices of "The Studio," 1906).
5. Erika Speel, *Dictionary of Enamelling, History and Techniques* (London: Lund Humphries, 1998), 57.
6. *Encyclopaedia Britannica Online*, s.v., "Enamelwork China," accessed January 19, 2024, https://www.britannica.com/art/enamelwork/China.
7. *Encyclopaedia Britannica Online*, s.v., "Enamelwork China."
8. Marian Campbell, *An Introduction to Medieval Enamels* (Owings Mills, MD: Stemmer House, 1983).
9. Metropolitan Museum of Art, *Enamels of Limoges 1100–1350* (New York: MetPublications, 1996), 48.
10. Speel, *Dictionary of Enamelling*, 126.
11. Theophilus, *On Divers Arts: The Foremost Medieval Treatise on Painting, Glassmaking and Metalwork*, trans. John G. Hawthorne and Cyril Stanley Smith (Mineola, NY: Dover, 1979).
12. Theophilus, *On Divers Arts*, xxxii.
13. Metropolitan Museum of Art, *Enamels of Limoges*, 13.
14. Speel, *Dictionary of Enamelling*, 72.
15. Fisher, *Art of Enamelling*.
16. Campbell, *An Introduction to Medieval Enamels*, 43.
17. Speel, *Dictionary of Enamelling*, 108.
18. Mer Almagro, "Introduction to Vitreous Enamel," Enamel Workshop, 2020, https://enamelworkshop.com/introduction/.
19. Herman A. Bangeman Jr., "Defining Limoges," *National Button Bulletin*, July 2005, 125–29.
20. Speel, *Dictionary of Enamelling*, 119.
21. Fisher, *Art of Enamelling*, 30.
22. Bill Helwig, "Re-searching Painting Enamels, Part 1," *Glass on Metal* 4, no. 1 (February 1985); repr., *Glass on Metal* 21, no. 1 (Spring 2023): 11.
23. Erika Speel, "Limoges School Pictorial Art," pt. 4, *Glass on Metal* 21, no. 3 (June 2002): 52.
24. Henry H. Cunynghame, *European Enamels* (London: Methuen, 1906).
25. Speel, *Dictionary of Enamelling*, 50.
26. Speel, *Dictionary of Enamelling*, 90.
27. Fisher, *Art of Enamelling*, 32–38.
28. Speel, *Painted Enamels*.
29. Alastair Duncan, *The Paris Salons 1895–1914*, vol. 5, *Objects d'Art & Metalware* (Woodbridge, Suffolk, UK: Antique Collectors Club, 1999).

30. World Fashion Channel, "Deboutonner la Mode Exhibition Museum les Arts Decoratifs Paris," YouTube, 2015, https://www.youtube.com/watch?v=sBflgSfukhc.
31. Therle Hughes and Bernard Hughes, *English Painted Enamels* (Middlesex, England: Hamlin, 1967).
32. Erika Speel, "English Painted Enamels, Battersea and Bilston Enamels," *Glass on Metal* 26, no. 5 (December 2007): 104–7, 112–13.
33. Speel, *Dictionary of Enamelling*, 11.
34. Wikipedia, s.v. "Chinoiserie," last modified January 19, 2024, https://en.wikipedia.org/wiki/Chinoiserie.
35. Speel, "English Painted Enamels," 104–7, 112–13.
36. Speel, *Dictionary of Enamelling*, 117.
37. Wikipedia, s.v. "Marcasite Jewellery," last modified January 9, 2024, https://en.wikipedia.org/wiki/Marcasite_jewellery.
38. Speel, *Dictionary of Enamelling*, 32.
39. Fisher, *Art of Enamelling*.
40. Duncan, *The Paris Salons*.
41. Speel, *Dictionary of Enamelling*, 130.
42. Speel, *Dictionary of Enamelling*, 54.
43. Speel, *Painted Enamels*, 63.
44. Speel, *Painted Enamels*, 63.
45. Louis-Eliè Millenet, *Enamelling on Metal: A Practical Manual on Enamelling and Painting on Enamel*, trans. H. De Koningh (London: Crosby Lockwood, 1926).
46. Millenet, *Enamelling on Metal*, 29.
47. Speel, *Dictionary of Enamelling*, 77.
48. Speel, *Dictionary of Enamelling*, 82.
49. Noh Yong-suk and Sung Da-som, *Chilbo, Korean Traditional Enameling*, Korea Craft & Design Resource Book 18 (Seoul: Korea Craft & Design Foundation, 2021).
50. Speel, *Painted Enamels*, 77.
51. Speel, *Painted Enamels*, 116.
52. Speel, *Dictionary of Enamelling*, 92.
53. Rosalie Berberian, *Creating Beauty: Jewelry and Enamels of the American Arts & Crafts Movement* (Atglen, PA: Schiffer, 2019), 13.
54. Elaine Cossman, "Collecting Buttons of the Arts & Crafts Movement," *National Button Bulletin*, December 2008.
55. Speel, *Dictionary of Enamelling*, 85.
56. Duncan, *The Paris Salons*.
57. Speel, *Dictionary of Enamelling*, 139.
58. Barbara Barrans, e-mail to author, n.d.
59. Jane Ford Adams, "Proposed Classification for Enamel Buttons," *National Button Bulletin*, May 1957.
60. Lillian Smith Albert and Jane Ford Adams, *The Button Sampler* (New York: Gramercy, 1951), 115.
61. Speel, *Dictionary of Enamelling*, 139.
62. Ora Kuller, e-mail to author, May 2022.
63. Dianne Chmidling, e-mail to author, August 2022.

2: THE MATERIAL: ENAMEL

1. Tom Ellis, e-mail to author, May 2022.
2. Tom Ellis, "Painting Enamel Materials, Part 1," *Glass on Metal* 32, no. 4 (August 2013): 85–94.
3. Louis-Eliè Millenet, *Enamelling on Metal: A Practical Manual on Enamelling and Painting on Enamel*, trans. H. De Koningh (London: Crosby Lockwood, 1926).
4. Bernard N. Jazzar and Harold B. Nelson, *Little Dreams in Glass and Metal: Enameling in America 1920 to the Present* (Los Angeles: Enamel Arts Foundation, 2015), 11.
5. Millenet, *Enamelling on Metal*, 52.

3: BUTTONS AS ENAMELWARE

1. Barbara Barrans, e-mail to author, n.d.
2. Barbara Barrans, "Focus Pocus," *National Button Bulletin*, December 2011, 250.
3. Celia Kudro, "Glossary of Engine Turning Terms," Wordpress, October 2017, https://engineturning.files.wordpress.com/2017/10/additional-information-glossary1.pdf.
4. Tig Lichty, e-mail to author, n.d.
5. Karen L. Cohen, "Champlevé Masquerading as Cloisonné," *Territorial News* 19, no. 2 (2021).
6. Fredric T. Schneider, *The Art of Japanese Cloisonné Enamel: History, Techniques and Artists, 1600 to the Present* (Jefferson, NC: McFarland, 2010), 186.
7. Erika Speel, *Dictionary of Enamelling, History and Techniques* (London: Lund Humphries, 1998), 138.
8. Gregory Irvine, *Japanese Cloisonné* (London: V&A, 2009).

9. Schneider, *Art of Japanese Cloisonné*, 88.
10. Gregory Irvine, e-mail to author, April 2023.
11. Louis-Eliè Millenet, *Enamelling on Metal: A Practical Manual on Enamelling and Painting on Enamel*, trans. H. De Koningh (London: Crosby Lockwood, 1926), 98.
12. Bill Helwig, "Camaïeu," *Glass on Metal* 3, no. 3 (June 1984): 34–38.
13. Erika Speel, *Painted Enamels: An Illustrated Survey 1500–1920* (London: Lund Humphries, 2008), 199.
14. Millenet, *Enamelling on Metal*, 105–7.
15. Millenet, *Enamelling on Metal*, 110.
16. Erika Speel, "Enamel Portrait Miniatures—17th Century," *Glass on Metal* 6, no. 5 (October 1987): 85–88.
17. Speel, *Dictionary of Enamelling*, 10.
18. Howard M. Chapin, *How to Enamel* (New York: Wiley, 1911; repr., London: Forgotten Books, 2018), xii.
19. Speel, *Dictionary of Enamelling*, 49.
20. Therle Hughes and Bernard Hughes, *English Painted Enamels* (Middlesex, England: Hamlin, 1967), 129.
21. Jamie Frechette, "Eutectic Process for Artistic Effect," *Glass on Metal* 26, no. 2 (2007): 36–40.
22. Schneider, *Art of Japanese Cloisonné*, 176.
23. Speel, *Dictionary of Enamelling*, 119.
24. Millenet, *Enamelling on Metal*, 64.
25. Herman Bangeman, "Ronde Bosse Enameling," *National Button Bulletin*, July 2004, 118–19.
26. Erika Speel, "English Pictorial Enamels, Part 2," *Glass on Metal* 27, no. 1 (February 2008): 12–15, 19.
27. Hughes and Hughes, *English Painted Enamels*.
28. Millenet, *Enamelling on Metal*, 107.
29. Millenet, *Enamelling on Metal*, 80.
30. Millenet, *Enamelling on Metal*, 89.
31. Tom Ellis, e-mail to author, n.d.
32. Henry H. Cunynghame, *On the Theory and Practice of Art-Enamelling upon Metals* (Edinburgh: Constable, 1899; repr., London: Forgotten Books, 2018), 93.
33. Chapin, *How to Enamel*, 45.
34. Millenet, *Enamelling on Metal*, 76.
35. Speel, *Dictionary of Enamelling*, 94.
36. Herman Bangeman, "Silver Embellishment on Buttons," *National Button Bulletin*, October 2003, 195–99.
37. Bangeman, "Silver Embellishment on Buttons."

4: ENAMEL BUTTON ARTISTS, PRODUCERS, AND PURVEYORS

1. Jane S. Leslie, *A Reference Book on Studio Button Makers* (Wilmington, MA: Arro, 1997); Meagan Melloy, *Studio Buttons and the Artists Who Make Them*, 3rd ed. (privately printed, 2009); Helen Timblin, *Extraordinary Buttons and the Artists Who Make Them* (Eagle River, AK: Joy Journeay, 2024).
2. Bruce Beck, "Enamels of the Modern Era," *National Button Bulletin*, July 2004, 128–30.
3. Loïc Allio, *Boutons* (Paris: Éditions du Seuil, 2001); Loïc Allio, *A Button Odyssey*, trans. Matthew Brown (Paris: Éditions Olisouelle, 2019).
4. Allio, *A Button Odyssey*, 171.
5. Alastair Duncan, *The Paris Salons 1895–1914*, vol. 5, *Objects d'Art & Metalware* (Woodbridge, Suffolk, UK: Antique Collectors Club, 1999).
6. Leslie, *A Reference Book on Studio Button Makers*, 50.
7. Mike Wilcox, "Mark of the Week: Liberty & Co., Cymric Silver and Archibald Knox," WorthPoint, accessed January 19, 2024, https://www.worthpoint.com/articles/collectibles/mark-of-the-week-liberty-co-cymric-silver-and-archibald-knox.
8. Elaine Cossman, "Collecting Buttons of the Arts & Crafts Movement," *National Button Bulletin*, December 2008, 260.
9. Erika Speel, *Dictionary of Enamelling, History and Techniques* (London: Lund Humphries, 1998), 88.
10. Speel, *Dictionary of Enamelling*, 88.
11. Costella F. Wilmot, "My Visit with Motiwala Brothers," *National Button Bulletin*, November 1954, 434; and "Motiwala: The Indian Master of Modern Buttons," *National Button Bulletin*, October 1990, 163.
12. Ada Snow Smith, "My Experiences as a Copper Enamelist," *Just Buttons*, February 1977, 115–22.
13. Carole Koontz, "Skating in St. Moritz? One Collector's Opinion on 'Skating in Central Park,'" *National Button Bulletin*, July 2017, 118–22.
14. Janet White, "Crafty Creations: Creating Enamel Buttons with Janet White," *New York State Button Society Bulletin* 76, no. 1 (January 2022).

APPENDIX A: BUTTONS WITH ENAMEL DF OR OME

1. Barbara Barrans, e-mail to author, n.d.

APPENDIX B: ENAMEL LOOK-ALIKES

1. Karen L. Cohen, "Is It Enamel or Cold Plastic Enamel?," *National Button Bulletin*, July 2020, 115.

2. Elizabeth Hughes and Marion Lester, *The Big Book of Buttons* (Sedgwick, ME: New Leaf, 1981).

APPENDIX C: ENAMEL RESTORATION

1. Arthur Chu and Grace Chu, *Oriental Cloisonné and Other Enamels: A Guide to Collecting and Repairing* (New York: Crown, 1975).

Acknowledgments

Many people have contributed to this book with photos, information, and conversations. I would like to acknowledge and thank the following people. I am sorry if I left someone out, but thank you all!

Foremost is Barbara Barrans. Without her help, this would have been a different book. Her attention to detail and willingness to share her thoughts, opinions, and photos were invaluable. Her crash course in button classification was detailed and extremely helpful! She did quite a bit of work writing the captions to most of the photos, and I am grateful for her time and expertise. She was also my copyeditor and did a superb job. Thank you, Barbara!

I'd like to thank my enamel editor, Tom Ellis, for all our discussions and his insights into what's happening with craze lines in enamel buttons. A special thanks to my publishing staff for making this third book of mine as wonderful as the second: Candi Derr, for having faith in me and getting me the same team as before; Patricia Stevenson, for managing the production so well; Tessa Sweigert, for her wonderful book layout; Caroline Stover, for her terrific graphics work; and Emily Vollmer, for her marketing materials.

In addition, I'd like to give big kudos to Bruce Beck, who was always willing to share his vast collection of beautiful enamels (both buttons and objets d'art) and discuss them with me. His experience in owning/selling/buying enamel buttons was very helpful. Herman Bangeman was also very helpful, discussing not just buttons but also methodology. Renée Comeau was equally helpful, discussing her beautiful buttons, sharing all her photos, and aiding in research. Erika Speel was invaluable with historical references and our discussions via e-mail. Mika Jarmusz translated Japanese/English in e-mails and also during Zoom talks with two experts in Japan, Miyako Nanri (an enamelist) and Hiromasa Kobayashi (director of Shippo Art Village in Japan), both of whom I would also like to thank for their help in understanding Japanese enameling terms and techniques. Tom and Kumi Dreves provided insight into Japanese terminology and enamel button making today and historically, and they were my translators for contacts with Sachiko Nishida, a contemporary Japanese enamelist. I'd also like to thank the three who submitted artwork using buttons, as I feel this contribution added to modern history: Ora Kuller, Jean Mandeberg, and Dianne Chmidling.

Many thanks go to Al Schultz, who helped in getting me printable copies of *NBB* and *Just Buttons* articles; Judy Stopke, who helped with the cover; Barbara Weeks, who sent samples of certain buttons so I could study them in person; Merry Jo Thoele, for turn-of-the-century information; Elaine Williamson, for all her information and photos; George Gauthier, for his understanding of copper alloys like brass and other scientific information; Barbara Fox, for her advice; Sue Moncrieff, for her advice and information on Motiwala buttons; Jane Perry, for her understanding of peasant buttons and those who made enamel buttons; Gregory Irvine, retired curator of Japanese Arts of the Victoria and Albert Museum in England, for his help with Japanese enamel terminology and styles; Fredric Schneider, author of a scholarly text on Japanese enamels and owner of a 900-piece collection, for his insights into Japanese enamels and a personal tour of his collection; Coral Shaffer, enamelist, who studied in Japan at the Inaba Cloisonné Factory and discussed her experiences with me; Pam Luke, for her advice on buttons and writing; Dasom Sung, assistant curator, Korean Arts, at the Victoria and Albert Museum in England, for help with information on Korean enameling; Janine Skerry, retired curator of ceramics and metals at the Colonial Williamsburg Foundation, for her insights and leads about Birmingham; Annie Fraizer and Sheila Brudno, for all the questions they answered; Mary Libby (Bib) Neiman, for her help on modern Chinese Plique-à-jour buttons; Kathy Hoppe, for her help on modern Chinese Cloisonné and Champlevé buttons; Donna Buchwald, for all our discussions on enameling; Marilyn Tendrich, for our discussions on Grisaille; Linda Kaye-Moses and J. B. Ebert, for help with the index; William Hentges, for his advice; Ora Kuller, for her cartoons; and Anne Gaylor, for help with graphics.

Last but not least, I'd like to acknowledge all of the modern enamelists who provided biographical information and photos of their work, as well as those who submitted photos to help make this book so lively with examples and color: Diane Almeyda, Herman Bangeman, Barbara Barrans, Judi Baxter, Bruce Beck, Gilbèrte Biggie, Birmingham Museums Trust (on behalf of Birmingham City Council), Inge Borland, Elvira Luetke Bowers, Nancy Boyer, Lynn Breutzmann, William Brinker, Harriett Brittenham, Sheila Brudno, the Button Queen, Yessy Byl, Carpenter Enamel Center, Helene Carter, Dianne Chmidling, Cleveland Museum of Art, L. Renée Comeau, Elaine Cossman, Cheryl Anne Day-Swallow for Joseph H. Spencer, Nancy De DuBois, Loek Degenkamp, Marie Demicco, Sue Dickout, Sandy Dingman, Kumi Dreves, Pam East, JB Ebert, Marie Elwyn, Brenda Erickson, Lillian Fitzpatrick, Sonia Force, Diane Ford, Annie Frazier, Joy Funnell, Sallie Gibson, R. Keith Golden, Micheline Gravel, Maude Hartman, Carol Hilberg, Kathy Hoppe, Mika Jarmusz, Lynn Keller, Simone Kincaid, Freda Knight, Ora K. Kuller, Joy LeCount, Donna Ledoux, Mona Ledwin, Tig Lichty, Linda Lingren, Lion and Unicorn Auctions, Lewis Lombardi, Pam Luke, Jean Mandeberg, Vicky Mayhall of Flying Button Ranch, Nancy Moyer, Mary Libby Neiman, Glenda L. Ott, Tatiana Owen, Jane Perry, Karen J. Perry, Michele Raney, Linda K. Reynolds, Helen Richwine, Fredric T. Schneider, Donna Shirley, Peg Swassing-Meredith, Merry Jo Thoele, Nancy Varah, Don Viehman, Barbara Weeks, Barbara Wells, Ronnie Wexler, Janet White, Diana Wieler, Elaine Williamson, Louella Yeargain, and Weiling Yin.

About the Author

Karen L. Cohen was a high school math teacher before earning her master's degree in computer science. She spent most of her computer career at AT&T Bell Labs, where she was at the forefront of data communication network development and was awarded a patent on one of her inventions in 1985. It was at Bell Labs that she learned technical writing.

In the mid-1970s, Cohen started working in metals and enameling because she had loved them as a teen at summer camp. In 2002, she published her first book on enameling. In the same year, she started the enameling program at a summer art camp for kids where she later taught for 15 years and eventually coordinated their three jewelry studios—enameling, metals, and beading. In 2019, she published her completely rewritten second book on enameling, *The Art of Fine Enameling* (2nd ed.), which was double the length of the first edition.

Today Cohen is retired from computing, but she still teaches enameling and beading at various venues to both adults and children. She is a Studio Button artist but also continues to create dolls, wall pieces, jewelry, and more. In writing this book, Cohen extensively researched buttons, Japanese enameling, and old enameling techniques and is amazed at what she was able to uncover about the connections to buttons currently available for collectors.

About the Editor

Barbara Barrans began collecting buttons in the late 1980s after attending her first California state button show. Her passion for the hobby and involvement in the National Button Society (NBS) progressed from there. In 2004, she became the assistant chairperson to Joan Lindsay on the Classification Committee. She and Joan spent the year jointly reorganizing/rewriting the NBS Classification *Blue Book* into a completely new format, which was published in 2005 and continues to be in use. Early in that same year, Lucille Weingarten had asked her to assume the authorship of the "Q and A" column that appeared in the *National Button Bulletin*. This, along with other articles focused on button classification, was a regular feature in the publication. She retired from the Classification Committee after serving as chairperson for 13 years.

Index

Albert Parent & Company, 86 (images, *14, 82*)
Almeyda, Diane, Echnoz, 13, 21, 22, 63, 87 (images, *21, 35, 58, 63, 64, 74, 76, 85, 87*)
Andō Cloisonné Co., 15, 16
Andō Jubei, 15
AP&Cie. *See* Albert Parent & Company
Ardant, Maurice, 16
Art Deco, 13, 16, 18, 20, 59 (images, *17, 20*)
Art Moderne. *See* Art Deco
Art Nouveau, 13, 15, 18–19, 20, 75, 93, 95, 96, 97, 106 (images, *1, 18, 38, 53, 56, 80, 82*)
Arts & Crafts Movement, 16–17, 20, 22, 97; school of, 19, 21 (images, *17, 63, 93, 95*)
Austro-Hungarian jewels, 8, 65 (images, *8, 108*)

back marks, 20
backgrounds. *See* enamel, background buttons
Bangeman, Herman, Jr., 5, 65, 80
Baranov, Evgeny, 7
Barrans, Barbara, 19, 40, 41, 109
Basse Taille, 4, 5, 7, 13, 15, 17, 30, 32, 34, 42–45, 54, 60, 89, 90, 93, 98, 99, 111, 116, 117; Basse Taille Sur Fond Reservé, 43, 103; design styles of, 43–45 (images, *2, 4, 13, 17, 23, 28, 32–35, 38, 41–45, 47, 54, 59, 60, 73, 78–79, 82–85, 88, 90, 93, 96–100, 103, 108–9, 116*)
Bates, Kenneth, 21
Battersea: Enamel Factory, 8–9, 66; -style, 9, 14, 59, 66, 67, 75, 115; terminology, 8 (images, *9, 59, 78*)
"Battersea-Style Designs" (ETT), 59
Batto, Ev: images, *111*
BB. *See* National Button Society, *Blue Book*
Beaded Enamel. *See* Encrustations
Bilston, 7, 8, 9, 59
Birmingham, vii, 7, 9, 10, 13, 21, 49, 59, 80, 86 (images, *10, 17, 42, 96, 97*)
Blanc de Limoges. *See* Grisaille White

Blue Book. See National Button Society, *Blue Book*
borders, types of, 81–82
Boulton, Matthew, vii, 10
Bowers, Elvira Luetke: images, *105*
brass. *See* metals for enameling
Break-through. *See* Pull-through
Brinker, William: images, *44*
Broadhead, E. J. *See* Peeler, E. J.
brocade machine/engine, 44 (images, *44, 50, 89*)
Byrom, Gillie Hoyte, 7, 21

Camaïeu, 14, 56 (images, *56*). *See also* Grisaille
Camarsac, Lafon de, 12
Cameron, Beatrice, 17
Canton enamel, 8, 42, 54 (images, *8, 54, 85*)
Carter, Helene, 87 (images, *61, 66, 87*)
cast metal, 79; casting Champlevé, 10, 48
Champlevé, 1, 3, 4, 5, 10, 13, 15, 16, 38, 45–49, 51, 68, 69; Basse Taille Sur Font Reservé, 43; Chinese modern, 88; design styles of, 47–49; framed, 46; masquerading as Cloisonné, 46; pierced and soldered, 45; versus Silver Deposit, 80, 81 (images, *vii, 1, 10, 12, 15, 17–18, 20, 23, 27, 34–35, 37–38, 42, 45–49, 51, 53, 58, 69, 73, 81–85, 88, 90, 93–99*)
Chakin-seki. See glass embellishments, Goldstone
checklist, 119–22
chemistry of enamel, 36–38; counter, 5, 12, 16, 36, 39, 45, 50, 54, 74, 115; firescale, 37–38, 56; hard, 37, 53, 59, 62, 64, 65; medium, 37, 53; soft, 37, 61, 62, 64, 65, 74 (images, *36, 37, 53, 54, 65, 72, 99, 104*)
Chinoiserie, 10 (images, *10*)
chipping blue. *See* sand eye
Chmidling, Dianne, 26
Chu, Arthur and Grace, 114
Classification Blue Book. See National Button Society, *Blue Book*

Cloisonné, 3, 4, 15–16, 21, 28, 42, 49–52, 68, 69, 72, 81, 83, 88, 117; compared to Champlevé, 46–47; design styles of, 51–52; steps of, 50; terminology, 51 (images, *3, 15, 17, 21, 25, 27–28, 31, 33, 35, 46–47, 49, 51–52, 54, 58, 68, 72, 77–78, 81–83, 85, 88–89, 94, 103, 106, 117*)

Cobden-Sanderson, T. J., 17

Cohen, Karen L., vii, 89 (images, *20–21, 28–29, 31–33, 35, 37, 43, 46, 49–50, 52, 54, 59–62, 64–67, 69–79, 85, 89, 134*)

Cold Plastic Enamel (CPE), 27, 110–11 (images, *110–11*)

combined techniques, 83 (images, *83*)

copper. *See* metals for enameling

counter enamel (or enameling). *See* chemistry of enamel

court jewels. *See* Austro-Hungarian jewels

CPE. *See* Cold Plastic Enamel

Crackle Enamel, 31, 52, 64 (images, *52*)

crowning, 14, 68

Cunynghame, Henry H., 6, 8, 72

Cymric, 18, 93, 95, 97 (images, *95, 97*)

Dalpayrat, Louis, 16

David-Anderson, 86 (images, *11*)

decals. *See* transfers/decals

Deccan, 47, 100 (images, *4, 15, 47*)

Decorative Finishes (DF), 19–20, 40, 68, 70, 110, 115 (images, *109, 111*)

Demicco, Marie, 90 (images, *90*)

depletion gild, 39

DF. *See* Decorative Finishes

diaper pattern/design, 15, 115 (images, *15*)

Diem, Rose Marie, 86 (images, *21*)

Dingman, Sandy, 90 (images, *90*)

Dolbin, Vladamir, 86 (images, *58*)

Douglas Clock & Co., 86 (images, *14*)

Driscoll, Clare, 18–19

DuBois, Nancy, 91 (images, *91*)

Dufaux, Charles-Louis, 14; company, 16, 57

Dufaux, Marc-Louis, 14

"Early Style" (of enamel painting), 6

Ebert, JB, 61

Edict of Nates, 7, 92

"Effect of Firing Enamel" (ETT), 30

Ellis, Tim, 74

Ellis, Tom, 22, 30, 71, 74

Elwyn, Marie, 92 (images, *92*)

Émaux Ardéchois, 92 (images, *72, 92*)

Émaux Peints, ix, 1, 16, 31, 42, 53–58, 67, 68, 69, 83, 115; design styles of, 54–58; development of, 5, 7; terminology, 5; why it cracks, 33 (images, *viii–ix, 1–2, 5, 7–11, 13–14, 16–18, 22, 24–28, 31–36, 38, 43, 47, 53–59, 65–67, 69–70, 72, 75, 77–78, 80–85, 87, 89, 94, 96, 98, 100, 102, 104–6, 108*). *See also* Camaïeu; Grisaille; Limoges, -style; Pâte; transfers/decals

embellishments, 70–81; Dichroic Extract Powders, 70; gemstones, 70; glass, 71–75; glow-in-the-dark, 76; metal, 76–81; mica, 81; not on enamel, 70. *See also* foil; lampwork embellishments; leaf; liquid metal; Metal Clay Overlay Silver Paste; metal embellishments; mica; Silver Deposit

E.M. Paris: images, 57

enamel, 27–39; background buttons, 41, 83, 108; firing temperatures, 28–29; forms of enamel, 30–33; look-a-likes, 110–13; manufacturers, 22; restoration, 114; types of colors, 33–35 (images, *31*). *See also* Battersea, -style; chemistry of enamel; enamel buildup; Encrustations; Moriage

enamel buildup, 54, 55, 56, 58–59. *See also* Encrustations; Fauré, Camille; Grisaille

"Enameling in Relief" (ETT), 65

"Enameling Modern Plique-à-jour" (ETT), 64

"Enameling over a Patterned Substrate" (ETT), 54

Enamel Tech Talk (ETT). *See specific ETT entries*

Encrustations, viii, 27, 37, 58, 62, 64, 70, 71; Battersea-style, 59 (images, *viii, 10, 27, 35, 49, 53, 58, 72, 78, 81, 87*)

engine turning, 11, 34, 42; similar methods, 43. *See also* Guilloché

"Engine-Turning Machines for Guilloché" (ETT), 44

English Painted Enamels, 8, 9, 59, 67

enlevage à l'aiguille, 6, 16, 59, 65

Eutectic Effect, 60 (images, *60*)

Fabergé: House of, 16, 21, 65, 92; Peter Carl, 7, 43, 65, 92

Fauré, Camille, 20, 59

Filigree, 3, 4, 41 (images, *37, 63, 74, 76, 87*). *See also* Plique-à-jour, design styles

"Fine Style" (of enamel painting), 6

firescale. *See* chemistry of enamel

Fisher, Alexander, 1, 4, 13, 14, 21

flash fire topcoat. *See* topcoats

flower wafers. *See* glass embellishments, murrini

fluxing, 14, 68

foil, 5, 6, 7, 16, 33, 34, 45, 56, 64, 66, 76–77, 78, 79, 115, 117; application, 77; under glass, 111; versus leaf, 77; use in Plique-à-jour, 62, 63; use in steps of Cloisonné, 50 (images, *7, 14, 21, 43, 46, 49, 54, 56, 61, 64, 66, 75–76, 83, 85, 89, 90, 93, 106, 111, 114*). *See also* Gin-bari; Paillons; Pierreries; Reticulated Foils

"Foil Application" (ETT), 77

Ford, Diane, 114

Funnell, Joy, 86 (images, *38*)

Geneva, 7, 13, 14, 16, 53, 56, 86. See also Dufaux, Charles-Louis; Dufaux, Marc-Louis; Millenet, Louis-Elié
gilded. See liquid metal
Gin-bari, 15, 45, 60–61, 77, 83, 93, 106, 117; design styles, 60; steps of, 61 (images, 60, 71, 83, 85)
Gin-jippō, 43, 48, 116 (images, 43, 45, 48, 116)
glass embellishments: balls, 71; Faux Opals, viii, 35, 38, 72, 73; Goldstone, 15, 72, 117; lumps, 61, 71–72, 73, 99; molded, 37, 75; murrini (and millefiori), 61, 73–74; paste, 75; seed beads, 71–72; threads, 61, 75 (images, vii, 2, 15, 21, 28, 34–35, 37, 58, 61, 66, 69, 71–75, 84, 89–90, 92, 99, 104–5, 117)
Glass on Metal (magazine), 23, 60
glossy topcoat. See topcoats
glow-in-the-dark materials, 76 (images, 76)
gold. See metals for enameling
GOM. See Glass on Metal
Graphite Pencil, 61, 66 (images, 61, 85)
Grisaille (En Grisaille), 4, 5, 6, 14, 16, 31, 32, 54–56, 57, 68; differences from Monochrome, 55; other names for, 56; terminology, 55 (images, 46, 53, 55–56). See also Camaïeu
Grisaille White, 6, 16, 31, 55
Guild and School of Handicraft, 17 (images, 17)
Guilloché, 11, 14, 16, 34, 42, 43, 44, 53, 54 (images, 6, 9, 11–14, 21, 35, 43, 54, 72, 78, 83, 89, 93, 96). See also engine turning

Hall, Doris, 21 (images, 21)
Hammer, Marius, 86 (images, 4)
hand polish topcoat. See topcoats
hard enamel. See chemistry of enamel
Harrell, Jan Arthur, 66
Haseler, William Hair, 93, 97 (images, 93)
Hattori Tadasaburō, 16
Helwig, William (Bill), 22, 42, 56, 64
Hentges, William, 113
high-fire techniques, 61–62; Scrolling, 28, 36, 61, 110; Webbing Design, 62 (images, 28, 61, 62, 66, 73, 85, 87, 99, 104, 111)
Hollander, Lori, 21
Holmström, August Wilhelm, 93 (images, 93)
Hoppe, Kathy, 88 (images, 88)
Horner, Charles, 13, 93 (images, 93)
"How Crackle Enamel Works" (ETT), 52
Hungarian jewels. See Austro-Hungarian jewels

Inaba Cloisonné Company, 15, 23, 94, 132 (images, 15, 23, 51, 94)
India, 15. See also Deccan; Jaipur; Kashmir

Jaipur, 15, 47 (images, 47)
James Fenton & Co., 17, 86 (images, 17)
Japan/Japanese, 15–16, 52; Basse Taille, 43; enamel on silver, 48; enamel terminology, 116–17; Golden Age of Enameling, 15, 94 (images, 15, 43, 45, 48, 52, 94)
Jippō. See Shippō
J. Millward Banks & Co., 86 (images, 42)
Just Buttons (magazine), 1, 104

Kaji Tsunekichi, 15
Karlson, Karl, 17
Kasamaki, Ken, 95. See also Kokuto Co. Ltd.
Kashmir, 48 (images, 48)
Kawade Shibatarō, 16
Keim, André, 94 (images, 33, 54, 94)
Kendall, Dorothy, 94 (images, 94)
Kim, Arthur, 94
King, Jessie Marion, 17, 19, 95, 97 (images, 95)
Knox, Archibald, 13, 18, 95, 97 (images, 95)
Kokuto Co. Ltd., 95, 107 (images, 110)
Korea, 16, 52
Kulicke, Fredicka, 21
Kuller, Ora, 25; cartoons, 107, 113 (images, 24, 25)

Lalique, Rene, 14, 18, 20
lampwork embellishments, 37, 71, 72, 73 (images, 72, 92)
Lanza, Judith C., 89 (images, 32)
leaf, 66, 76–78, 79 (images, 77). See also metal embellishments
"Leaf Application" (ETT), 78
Ledwin, Mona, 96 (images, 67, 96)
Levinger, Heinrich, 14, 96 (images, 43, 96)
Liberty & Co., 13, 17–18, 93, 95, 97 (images, 18, 95, 97)
Lichty, Tig, 44 (images, 43, 44, 89)
Limoges: city of, 4, 5, 6; Limoges School Revival, 5, 14, 16, 56; painting, 3, 6, 7, 59, 65; precursor of, 4; -style, ix, 5, 7, 16, 34, 42, 54, 56, 68, 77, 78, 115 (images, 6, 16, 32, 34–35, 53–54, 56). See also Émaux Peints
Limosin, Leonard, 5, 6
Lindsay, Joan, 19, 135
Lingren, Linda, 98 (images, 77, 98)
Linley, Phil, 98 (images, 98)
"Liquid Gold Application Today and Yesteryear" (ETT), 79
liquid metal, 5, 6, 78; application of Liquid Gold, 59, 79; Battersea-style, 59 (images, 2, 9, 11, 18, 32, 54–56, 59, 77–79, 94)
Litt, Chris, 86 (images, 49, 76)
Lowenstein, Herman, vi, 13, 73, 99 (images, 34, 61, 66, 73, 74, 79, 85, 99)
luster. See mica

Mandeberg, Jean, 23 (images, *23*)
marcasite, 12–13 (images, *13, 83*)
Marquis, Eugene, 14
"Matte Enamels" (ETT), 69
matte topcoat. *See* topcoats
mechanical bond, 15, 38
mechanical/movable, 84 (images, *52, 66, 72–73, 76, 84, 102, 105*)
medium enamel. *See* chemistry of enamel
Metal Clay Overlay Silver Paste, 79, 80
"Metal Embellishment Application" (ETT), 79
metal embellishments, 76–81. *See also* foil; leaf; Paillons; Pierreries
metal oxide, 6, 30–31, 32, 34, 80; copper oxide, 37
metals for enameling, 38–39; metal clay, 38, 63, 79 (images, *38, 96*)
metal under glass. *See* foil, under glass
mica, 63; embellishment, 74, 81 (images, *20, 74, 77, 81*)
millefiori. *See* glass embellishments, murrini
Millenet, Louis-Elié, 14–15, 38, 53, 57, 63, 76
minakari, 15, 58
"Minute Style" (of enamel painting), 6
"Modern Style." *See* Art Nouveau
"Modern Transfers" (ETT), 67
Monochrome. *See* Émaux Peints
Moriage, 16, 59, 117 (images, *59*)
Motiwala Brothers, 12, 31, 66, 100; Liquid Enamel, 23, 45 (images, *23, 34, 45, 100*)
mounted in/on metal, 84
movable. *See* mechanical/movable
Mower, Simon, 101 (images, *101*)
Mucha, Alphonse, 18; *See also* Art Nouveau
MUD, 59, 75 (images, *75*)
Multan, Pakistan, 47, 48–49 (images, *48–49*)
Musen, 117 (images, *117*)

Namikawa Sōsuke, 15
National Button Society (NBS), viii, ix, 1, 19–20, 36, 40–41, 47–48, 56, 81, 83–84, 86, 93, 97–99; *Blue Book*, viii, ix, 19–20, 40, 56, 83; bulletins, 1, 19
National Palace Museum of Korea, 16
NBB. *See* National Button Society, bulletins
NBS. *See* National Button Society
NBS Blue Book. *See* National Button Society, *Blue Book*
Neiman, Mary Libby, 88 (images, *88*)
Niello, 4, 108, 112 (images, *112*)
Nishida, Sachiko, 95, 101, 107 (images, *101*)
Noga, Carolyn, 102 (images, *102*)
non-filigree, 41, 63 (images, *63*)
Nousailher family, 16

Official Classification Competition Guidelines. *See* National Button Society, *Blue Book*
Olsen, Ole Petter Raasch, 86 (images, *11*)
OME. *See* Other Material Embellishments

Onglaze enamel painting, 6, 7, 8, 13, 14, 16, 31, 53
opalescent enamel, 33, 34, 35, 42, 45, 50, 53, 54, 62, 64, 72, 93 (images, *32, 35, 58, 72, 87*)
opaque enamel, 4, 13, 30, 31, 33, 35, 36, 37, 42, 45, 50, 53, 54, 58, 62, 64, 65, 70, 73, 75 (images, *33, 35, 43, 47, 54, 62*)
openwork enamel button, 4, 41, 84 (images, *vii, 1, 10–11, 45, 52, 58, 62, 64, 73, 82, 84, 85, 100*)
Orange Peel: images, *29*
"Order of Fusing in Embellishments" (ETT), 74
"Original Transfers" (ETT), 67
Other Material Embellishments (OME), 19–20, 40, 70, 108. *See also* embellishments
Ott, Glenda, 102 (images, *102*)
Overglazes. *See* Painting Materials
oxide. *See* metal oxide

Paillons, 4, 12, 59, 76; terminology, 78 (images, *viii–ix, 2, 11–12, 28, 31, 35, 43, 49, 54, 59, 62, 70, 77, 78, 83, 85, 89*). *See also* foil; Pierreries
Painting Materials, 7, 12, 14, 31–33, 53, 55, 56, 66, 67, 68, 69, 70; Overglaze, 31–32; Underglaze, 31–32 (images, *7, 32–33, 54, 61, 74, 98*). *See also* Émaux Peints; Onglaze enamel painting; Pâte
Pâte (enamel), ix, 13, 14, 35, 53, 56, 57–58, 69 (images, *13–14, 57*)
Pâte de Verre, 57, 75 (images, *75*)
Pâte sur Pâte, 57 (images, *112*)
Patterson, Gertrude Howell, 19
Pearce & Sons, 86 (images, *17*)
Peeler, E. J. (Edwina), 102 (images, *102*)
Pénicaud, Leonard (Nardon), 5, 6
Pertapghar [faux] enamels, 112 (images, *112*)
Peter the Great, 16
Petitot, Jean, 7
pictorials, 84
pierce (jewelry technique), 41, 45, 63
pierced. *See* openwork enamel button
"Pierced and Soldered Champlevé" (ETT), 45
Pierreries, 4, 6, 12, 59 (images, *ix, 11–12, 28, 59, 85*). *See also* foil; Paillons
plaquette, 40, 84, 112 (images, *5, 37, 58, 84, 87, 98, 102, 108–9*)
Plique-à-jour, 3, 4, 5, 16, 17, 18, 21, 23, 35, 41, 62–64, 78, 96, 107; design styles, 63; Shotai, 51, 117 (images, *21, 35, 58, 62–63, 74, 76, 85, 87–89, 91, 101–2, 109, 114*)
pointillé/Pointillism, 7, 16, 58
Politzer, Ludwig, 86 (images, *85*)
Polychrome. *See* Émaux Peints
porcelain, 5, 16, 22, 32, 57, 67, 79, 80, 112–13 (images, *112*)
"Pre-doming Millefiori" (ETT), 74
Pull-through, 37, 62, 64 (images, *37, 64*)

Rae, Merry-Lee, 59
Raney, Michele, 43, 103 (images, *4, 43, 103*)
repair, enamel. *See* enamel, restoration
resin. *See* Cold Plastic Enamel
Reticulated Foils, 64 (images, *64*)
Reymond, Pierre, 5, 6
Reynolds, Linda K., 103 (images, *72, 81, 103*)
Robbins, Joy, 86 (images, *66*)
roll printing, 42, 61 (images, *21*)
Ronde Bosse (or En Ronde Bosse), 3, 14, 17, 64–65 (images, *64–65*)
rose engine. *See* Guilloché
Roycroft (community), 17
Russia, 16, 21, 58, 62, 92, 93 (images, *16, 58, 93*)

Sadler and Green, 9
Safro, Millicent, 1
Samson et Cie, 14
sand eye, 3 (images, *3*)
Schneider, Fredric T., 48, 52, 117
School of Handicraft. *See* Guild and School of Handicraft
Scovill Manufacturing Company, 86 (images, *66*)
Scrolling. *See* high-fire techniques
seed beads. *See* glass embellishments, seed beads
Separation Enamel, 65 (images, *65, 73*)
sew-through, 85
Sgraffito, 6, 58, 65–66, 78 (images, *31, 53, 58, 64, 65–66, 70, 77, 87, 90*)
shapes (button characteristic), 85
Shippō, 116, 117
silver. *See* metals for enameling
Silver Deposit, 41, 79, 80–81 (images, *80*)
"Silver Deposit Process" (ETT), 80
Silver Overlay. *See* Silver Deposit
Silver Resist. *See* Silver Deposit
Smith, Ada Snow, 61, 66, 104 (images, *104*)
soft enamel. *See* chemistry of enamel
Sookmyung Women's University Museum, 16
Spencer, Joseph, H., 28, 104 (images, *104*)
stenciling, 66 (images, *66, 72, 79, 90, 103, 105*)
"Steps of Cloisonné" (ETT), 50
"Steps of Gin-bari" (ETT), 61
straight-line engine. *See* Guilloché
Strass, Georges Frederic, 11 (images, *11, 12*)
Strasser, Joseph, 11
stringers. *See* glass embellishments, threads
Sugar Fire topcoat. *See* topcoats
Suyeoka, George, 88

Taille d'Epargne. *See* Champlevé
Takahara Komajiō, 52
Tea Goldstone. *See* glass embellishments, Goldstone
Theophilus, 3–4
Thompson Enamel, 22, 81
threads. *See* glass embellishments
Timofeev, Valeri, 21, 87
topcoats, 33, 41, 53, 56, 57, 68–70, 78, 79, 115; flash fire, 32, 50, 68, 69; glossy, 29, 32, 68–69; hand polish, 57, 64, 68–69, 76; matte, 32, 33, 63, 68, 69; Sugar Fire, 29, 69–70 (images, *28, 32–33, 47, 62, 68–69, 70, 75, 81, 89, 94, 96*)
Toutin, Jean I., 7
transfers/decals, 8–9, 12, 66–67, 100 (images, *9, 12, 29, 62, 65–67, 70, 73, 76, 79, 85, 89, 96, 98, 100, 105, 111*)
transparent enamel, 4, 5, 6, 7, 15, 16, 18, 28, 31, 32, 33–34, 35, 39, 42, 43, 45, 53, 55, 56, 58, 60, 64, 65, 70, 72, 78, 99; on copper, 37 (images, *4, 32–33, 35, 47, 54, 62, 70, 87*). *See also* Basse Taille; Gin-bari; Limoges; Plique-à-jour
travail à l'aiguille. *See* enlevage à l'aiguille
Tullis, Anita, 86 (images, *76*)

Underglazes. *See* Painting Materials

verbal, 85 (images, *10, 26, 49, 51, 58, 67, 73, 85, 94*)
Viehman, Don: images, *68*
vitreous enamel, viii, ix, 3, 5, 23, 27, 41, 110

Wagener, Gottfried, 15
Walton, G. E., 86 (images, *34*)
warping, metal, 39
Webbing Design. *See* high-fire techniques
Weingarten, Lucille, 135
White, Janet, 84, 105 (images, *34, 52, 66, 72, 73, 75, 76, 79, 84, 105*)
"Why Some Enamels Crack" (ETT), 33
Wieler, Diana, 21, 26, 54, 106 (images, *22, 26, 35, 106*)
William Hutton and Sons, 17, 86 (images, *17*)
Winter, Edward, 21

Yanaka Red House Button Gallery, 95, 101, 106–7 (images, *106*)